The Dramatic Clash Between the Culture of Life and Culture of Death

Its Relevance to the African Context

J. Tab Charoa

The publisher wishes to acknowledge and thank Dr. Douglas H. Johnson for his invaluable help and support for Africa World Books and its mission of preserving and promoting African cultural and literary traditions and history. Dr. Johnson and fellow historians have been instrumental in ensuring that African people remain connected to their past and their identity. Africa World Books is proud to carry on this mission.

Copyright © 2023 J. Tab Charoa

All rights reserved. It is illegal to reproduce, duplicate or transmit any part of this book in either electronic means or printed format. Recording of this publication is strictly prohibited. No part of this publication may be reproduced, stored in a retrieval system, or transmitted, in any form, or by any means, electronic, mechanical, photocopying, recording or otherwise, without the prior permission of the publishers.

ISBN: 9780645972368

This book is sold subject to the conditions that it shall not, by way of trade or otherwise, be lent, re-sold, hired out or otherwise circulated without the publisher's prior consent in any form of binding or cover other than in which it is published and without a similar condition including the condition being imposed on the subsequent purchaser.

Cover design, typesetting and layout: Africa World Books
Unit 3, 57 Frobisher St, Osborne Park, WA 6017
P.O. Box 1106 Osborne Park, WA 6916

Dedication

The Book entitled 'The Dramatic Clash between the Culture of Life and Culture of Death: Its Relevance to the African Context' is dedicated to St. John Paul II who used the phrase "*culture of life and culture of death*" while speaking to journalists at Stapleton International Airport near Denver Colorado in America in 1993. The phrase culture of life and culture of death is stipulated and articulated in his Encyclical Letter *"Evangelium Vitae"* the Gospel of Life. In his words, John Paul II states…: we are facing an enormous and dramatic clash between good and evil, death and life, the culture of death and the culture of life" (*Evangelium* Vitae no 28). The Gospel of Life which the culture of life" means the resurrection or victory over death won by Christ.

Contents

Acknowledgement   xiii
Overview   xvii
Foreword   xxvii
Preface   xxxi

Chapter 1: Biblical Origin of Culture of Death

Introduction	1
1. The Concept of Serpent in the Ancient Near East	1
1.1 Metaphors of Sin and the Verdicts	3
1.1 Verdict Against the Serpent (Lucifer)	5
1.1.1 Warning Against the Return of Unclean Spirit	8
1.2 Verdicts Against the Woman	9
1.2.1 The Impact of Eve's Charges on Other Women	12
1.3 The Third Verdict Upon the Man	15
1.3.1 The Impact of Man's Verdicts on the Earth (Soil)	18
1.3.2 The Impact of Lucifer on Our Life	19
1.4 Lack of Repentance as the Culture of Death	22
1.5 Confrontation Between Jesus and Lucifer	24
1.6 Jealousy and Envy as Culture of Death	28
1.7 The Dramatic Clash Between Michael and Dragon	30

1.8 Jesus' Teaching Authority over the Demons ... 31
Conclusion ... 32

Chapter 2: Philosophical Theories and World Wars on Culture of Death

Introduction ... 33
2. The Tension Between the Soul and Body ... 33
2.1 Aristotelian Theory of Culture of Death ... 35
2.2 Thomas Hobbes on Natural Theory of Violence ... 35
2.3 Recap of World I ... 37
2.4 Recap of World War II ... 38
2.5 Recap of Cold War ... 42
2.6 Terrorist Attack on September 11, 2001 ... 43
Conclusion ... 45

Chapter 3: Sociological Interpretation of the Culture of Death

Introduction ... 46
3. Conceptual Analysis of Culture of Violence ... 46
3.1 Definition of Violence ... 48
3.2 Social Tangibility of Violence ... 50
3.3 Seven Theories of Violence ... 51
3.3.1 Relative Deprivation ... 51
3.3.2 Biological Interpretation of Instinctive Violence ... 53
3.3.3 Egoistic Theory of Culture of Violence ... 54
3.3.4 Calculative Rational Theory of Culture of Violence ... 55
3.3.5 Frustration Reduction Theory of Culture of Violence ... 56
3.3.6 Cultural Conditioning Theory of Culture of Violence ... 57
3.3.7 Violence for Social Change ... 58
Conclusion ... 58

Chapter 4: Sin as Culture of Death

Introduction	59
4. General Concept of Sin	59
4.1 The Nature and Features of Sin	63
4.2 Definition of Sin	65
4.4 Two Kinds of Sin	67
4.5 Three Elements of Mortal Sin	69
4.5.1 Matter	69
4.5.2 Awareness	70
4.5.3 Consent	70
4.6 Seven Capital Sins	71
4.7 Causes of Sin	72
4.7.1 Internal Causes	72
4.7.2 External (Remote Causes)	72
4.8 Criteria for Judging Sin by Moralists	73
Conclusion	73

Chapter 5: Freedom as a Culture of Life and Culture of Death

Introduction	74
5. General Concept of Human Freedom	74
5.1 Freedom as Personal Responsibility	75
5.2 Education to Freedom	77
5.3 Limits of Human Freedom	77
5.4 Grace as Culture of Life	81
Conclusion	84

Chapter 6: Principles of Active Nonviolence

Introduction	85
6. Jesus' Precepts and Other Principles of Non-Violence	86
6.1 Jesus' Precepts of Culture of Life	87
6.1 Style and Literary Characters of Jesus' Precepts	88
6.2 Correct Interpretation of Christ's Precepts	90

6.3 The Church's Magisterium on Two Ways — 93
6.4 American Politicians on Culture of Life in 2000 — 96
6.5 Veritable Structure of Sin as Culture of Death — 98
6.6 Techniques of Artificial Reproduction — 101
6.7 Legal Systems and Theories of Culture of Death — 103
6.8 Dr King's Triple Evils of Culture of Death — 104
6.8.1 First Triple Evil of Poverty — 104
6.8.2 The Second Triple Evil of Racism — 105
6.8.3 The Third Triple Evil of Materialism — 106
6.9 Six Principles of Culture of Nonviolence — 107
6.9.1 Dr. King's Seven Techniques for Social Change — 108
6.10 Mahatma Gandhi on Principles of Nonviolence — 109
Conclusion — 111

Chapter 7: African Contribution to Culture of Life and Culture of Death

Introduction — 112
7. Moral Evil as a Culture of Death — 112
7.1 Main Form of Powers — 114
 7.1.1 Traditional Powers — 115
7.1.1.1 The Papal Power (Leadership) — 115
7.1.2 Kingly Power — 116
7.2 Two Types of Powers — 118
7.2.1 Naked Power — 118
7.2.2 Revolutionary Power — 120
7.3 Rwanda Genocide — 120
7.4 Colonial Period — 123
7.5 The Dilemma of Post-Colonial Period — 125
Conclusion — 126

Chapter 8: The Covid-19 Pandemic

Introduction	127
8. Pre-Epidemic and Covid-19 Pandemic	128
8.2 The Blame Game Between America and China	132
8.3 Covid-19 Pandemic as a Transferal Disease	135
8.4 Covid-19 Pandemic Symptoms and Its Ethics	138
8.5 The World Responses to Covid-19 Pandemic	141
8.5.1 Public Health Guidelines for the U.S. Citizens	142
8.5.2 Ugandan Presidential Guidelines for Covid-19 Pandemic	143
8.5.3 South Sudan Precipitation on Covid-19 Pandemic	144
8.5.3.1 Presidential Guidelines for the South Sudan	146
8.6 Covid-19 Pandemic: A Disease for Everybody	147
8.7 Humanity in Solidarity with Each Other	148
8.8 The Deaths of COVID-19 and Recent Events in the Globe	152
Conclusion	152

Chapter 9: The Mythological Confusions of Covid-19 Pandemic

Introduction	154
9. The Role of Myths About Covid-19 Pandemic	154
9.1 Myths Versus Realities	156
9.2 Quiz-Myths According to W.H.O on Covid-19 Pandemic	158
9.3 Other False Myths for COVID-19 Pandemic	159
Conclusion	160

Chapter 10: Evaluation and Conditions for the Reopening

Introduction	161
10. World Leaders' Management on Covid-19 Pandemic?	161
10.1 The Impacts of the COVID-19 Pandemic on the World	163
10.2 Guidelines and Criteria for the Reopening	164
10.3 Vaccine and Antibodies	165

10.3.1 Earlier Positive Updates on Vaccines	167
10.3.2 Scientific Achievements of Vaccines	168
10.4 New Variants of Delta & Omicron of Covid-19 Pandemic	169
10.5 Campaign for the Third Booster Shot.	172
10.6 Conspiracy Theories Concerning Vaccines	173
10.7 The Inconclusive Origin of Covid-19 Pandemic	175
10.8 When will the Covid-19 Pandemic End?	176
10.9 My Testimony on the Day of My Vaccination	177
Conclusion	180

Chapter 11: Theological Reflections

Introduction	182
11. The Purpose of Theological Reflections	183
11.1 The Centrality of Christ in Creation	184
11.2 Human Progress in the Course of History	185
11.3 Biblical Origin of Original Sin	187
11.3.1 Sacred Scripture on the Contagious Diseases	191
11.4 Holy Scripture on Physical and Moral Evil	193
11.5 Principle of Preferential Option for the Vulnerable	196
11.6 Eschatology and COVID-19 Pandemic	197
11.7 The Last Things about the Future of God's People	199
11.7.1 The Pilgrim Church (People of God)	200
11.7.2 The Second Coming of Christ (Parousia)	204
11.7.3 The Faith in the Second Coming of Christ	205
11.7.4 The Time of the Second Coming of Christ	206
11.7.5 The Concept of Anti-Christ (Serpent)	208
11.7.6 The Sacred Scripture on the Signs of Anti-Christ	210
11.8 The Signs of Anti-Christ in the Course of History	211
11.10 Signs of Antic-Christ in Slavery and in Racism	214
11.11 Signs of Anti-Christ in Human Trafficking	216
St. Bakhita	218

11.12 Death and Resurrection	221
11.13 The Significance of the Problem of Resurrection	222
11.14 The Sacred Scriptures on Resurrection	223
11.15 The Church's Magisterium on Liturgy and Resurrection	226
11.16 Theological Problems about the Resurrection	227
11.17 The Judgment of the World	229
11.17.1 The Nature of the Final Judgment	231
Conclusion	234

Chapter 12: Recommendation

Introduction	235
12. Ethics of Power	236
12.1 Dialogue and Negotiation as Culture of Life	236
12.2 South Sudan Four Days Reports on National Dialogue	238
12.2.1 Summary of the Proceedings Issues in the Debate	239
12.2.2 The Second Day Key Emerging Points	239
12.2.3 The Third Day Key Emerging Points	240
12.2.4 Fourth Day Key Emerging Points	241
12.3 Identification of Stakeholders and Criteria for Selection	242
12.3.1 Stakeholders in the Country	243
12.4 The Benefits of Dialogue and Negotiation	244
12.5 The Sudan Catholic Bishops' Conference on Dialogue	245
12.5.1 Favourable and Unfavourable Conditions for Dialogue	246
12.5.2 Fruitful Dialogue	247
12.5.3 Readiness to Unlearn and Demands for Openness	248
12.5.4 Mutual Respect of Differences in Dialogue	249
12.5.5 Severe Judgment upon Ourselves and Our Opponents	250
12.5.6 Dialogue for an Action and Its Difficulties	252
12.6 For Geologists	254
12.7 For Meteorologists	255

12.8 For Physicians and Nurses	256
12.9 Presuppositions of Ethics for Everyone	259
12.10 The Loser or Winner Between the Two Cultures	262
Conclusion	266
Bibliography	269
Index	

Acknowledgement

Writing a book is not an individual achievement, but it involves everyone because it is to preserve reality and for public consumption. Therefore, in the acknowledgement, it is not always a surprise to mention and acknowledge those who gave their time tirelessly to contribute to the success of the book.

I would to express my gratitude to His Eminence Stephen Cardinal Ameyu Martin Muall of the Archbishop of the Metropolitan of the Archdiocese of Juba for accepting to write an imprimatur for the book for the third time. May God bless him as lead the flock of the Christ to the Promised Land. In addition, I would like to thank Msgr. Lonut Paul Strejac, the Secretary of Nunciatur to South Sudan for consulting the competent offices of the Secretariat of State Vatican Rome, to allow me to put the picture of the late Pope John Paul II, on the page cover of my book. May God bless him and his work in South Sudan.

My humble gratitude goes to Rev. Prof. Guido Oliana, who also for the second time has accepted to write a forward for my book. I am aware and I know that writing a foreword of a book. It is tedious work and not an easy task because the foreword of a book, presents the summary of the book. Rev, Prof. Guido Oliana recently wrote a very excellent foreword for my book entitled 'Ecology: The Key Catholic

Principle of Stewardship of Creation and its Relevance to the African Context.' I appreciate his readiness and positive response to write again, the foreword of my book. May God bless, protect, and grant him good health so he may continue to offer assistance to those who may approach him for academic help.

Also, I would like to express my thanks to Rev. Fr. John Wajaras, the Vice-Rector of St. Paul's Major Seminary *Theologicum*, Brother Tadeo Tumwesigire and Brother John Bosco Kiragu AJ, for their tireless efforts of suggestions of some ideas and comments this book. May God give them more patience and good health to continue helping others.

I would like to express my gratitude in a special way to dear Rev. Sr Anne Kiragu, a sister from the Congregation of Daughters of St. Paul for her humble and tireless commitment to proofread my manuscript. After I received back my manuscript from her, was satisfied because I discovered that she read my work page by page and word by word. Because of her excellent contributions of the rest, therefore, I declare this book entitled 'The Dramatic Clash between the Culture of Life and Culture of Death Its Relevance to the African Context' to be for public consumption and I hope, it will be useful for the those who will use it. May God bless and protect her always and the rest.

Furthermore, I would like to express my sincere gratitude to Rev. Prof. Guido Oliana, who accepted to write a foreword for my book, specifically chapter eleven on theological reflections on Covd-19 pandemic. I should also acknowledge that this is not the first time for him to write a foreword of my book, but even the third time. I appreciate and thank him for his commitment by giving up his private time, in order, to offer this tedious academic service. May Almighty God continue to give him good health and protection to serve Him more in His vineyard specifically in the area of intellectual service.

My humble gratitude, however, goes to Dr. John Thaloka Tur Chop, a graduate of the University of Bahri, Khartoum Sudan. Dr. John is a general practitioner to specialize in tropical medicine. He agreed to proofread the first three chapters of this book based on the fact that they are in his area as a physician. His critiques and suggestions have stamped the scientific knowledge needed about the COVID-19 pandemic in this particular study. May God grant him protection and good health.

Furthermore, I would also like to express my heartfelt thanks to Rev. Fr. John Andrea who has agreed to proofread the manuscript before it could reach its final stage of publication. I appreciate and acknowledge his readiness and willingness. May God grant him patience and endurance to serve Him more in St. Paul's Major Seminary *Philosophicum* and *Theologicum*.

My gratitude goes to Mr. Samuel Reihok for agreeing to proofread my manuscript before its publication. May God bless him and grant him wisdom. Also, I would like to extend my gratitude to all those who helped me in one way or another be it encouragement, advice and other necessary support. May almighty God bless them all.

Finally, my gratitude goes to God the Father, God the Son and God the Holy Spirit for having protected me throughout this time of the COVID-19 pandemic. Once more, I thank God for giving me patience, and encouragement instead of panicking but with the strength to face the Covid-19 Pandemic with hope in God the Father, God the Son and God the Holy Spirit. May his Holy Name be blessed forever.

Overview

By Rev. Prof Guido Oliana

The book begins with the biblical considerations on basic texts, in particular on Genesis 3 and the so-called 'original sin' with emphasis on Satan as Lucifer, the cause of all our existential trouble, in particular of the culture of death.' No demand for an exegetical investigation is made. The style is almost catechetical and rather popular in its approach. The chapter reviews also some historical philosophies and instances of the "culture of death" and presents three tragic events exemplifying such history: the First World War, the Second World War, and September 11, 2001 (chapter I). The discourse moves to a more complex conceptual analysis of seven theories of the culture of violence (chapter II). The concept of sin and its manifestations as the real matrix of the "culture of death" are then considered. Dogmatic insights on the matter would further enlighten the problem (chapter III). The difference between the culture of life and the culture of death is then discussed. Freedom is stressed as needing to be enlightened and empowered by the divine gift of grace as to be directed towards a "culture of life." This freedom should be translated into a rigorous personal and collective responsibility towards the respect of the human person created in the image and like of God (chapter IV).

The Dramatic Clash Between the Culture of Life and Culture of Death

The principles of 'culture of life' are highlighted as embodied in three exemplary figures (Jesus, Martin Luther King, Jr., and Mahatma Gandhi) to move, thereafter, to the particular contribution of St. John Paul II in his Encyclical letter "*Evangelium Vitae" (1995)*. The relevance of the tropic in our African context is then stressed. The genocide in Rwanda is presented as the epitome of the "culture of death" in Africa. Hints at the same culture of violence during the colonial and post-colonial periods are equally considered. Our South Sudanese present situation of civil war is also an expression of the same "culture of death" (chapter VI). Ethical recommendations for world political leaders conclude the book. Dialogue, which respects and interacts creatively with the differences of the partners, avoiding any form of temporary interested superficial compromise, is presented as the best political way forward to guarantee peace and justice as the foundation stone of the "culture of Life"(chapter VII).

On the whole, the book is informative and useful for an initial reflection on the subject that should lead to further deepening. In this letter perspective, I would like to add four basic considerations: (a) "The Gospel of life" becoming "culture of death," B) The "curse of sin" and in particular "original sin" as the matrix of the "culture of death," c) The Paschal mystery and the theory of the "escape goat" of Renè Girard as the redeeming way of the "culture of death," d) Dialogue as a political way forward to overcome the culture of death.

The Gospel of Life and the Culture of Life *Evangelium Vitae* of St. John Paul II is based on the dynamic process of translating the "Gospel of Life" into a "culture of life." A deep understanding of the terms "Gospel and culture" is essential to appreciate the importance of the Encyclical.

"Gospel" means the announcement of the good news of salvation that brings transforming joy, enthusiasm, and strength to live its message thanks to the empowerment of divine grace. "The Gospel of life is at the heart of Jesus' message. Lovingly received day after day by the church, it is to be preached with dauntless fidelity as 'good news' to the people of every age and culture' (EV 1). The Gospel of life, therefore, is a treasure of immense value that needs to be shared with the whole of humanity and creation. "The Gospel of life includes everything that human experience and reason tell us about the value of human life, accepting it, purifying it, exalting it and bringing it to fulfilment"(EV 30).

"Culture" refers to all possible dynamic ways that make Christian values appreciated and digested, inspiring and empowering, accepted and wholeheartedly lived in the transformative process of one's cultural way of life. Fr. Pedro Arrupe, former Superior General of the Jesuits, defines Inculturation as "the incarnation of Christian life and the Christian message in a particular cultural context, in such a way that this experience not only finds expression through elements proper to the culture in question (this alone would be no more than a superficial adaptation) but becomes a principle that animates, directs and unities the culture, transforming it and remaking it to bring about a 'new creation'[1] Paul VI echoes the same perspective when in its encyclical *"Evangeli Nuntiadi"* says that evangelizing people and culture is not announcing the Gospel "in a purely decorative way as if it were by applying a thin veneer, but in a vital way, in-depth, and right to their every root"(n.20).

This is to be applied also to the Inculturation of the "marvellous newness" (EV 80) of the Gospel of life" to create "a new culture of human life" (cf. EV 78-101). This means for the church "to preach the Gospel of Life, to celebrate it in the Liturgy and our whole existence, and to serve it with the various programs and structure which support and promote life" (EL 79). The programs, among others, include catechesis, various forms of preaching, personal dialogue and all

---

1   Quoted in A. SHORTER, Toward a Theology of Inculturation, Maryknoll, NY: Orbis Books, p. 1988, 19922, 11

educational activity (EV 82); daily prayer, a celebration of the liturgical year and the sacraments (EL 84); service of charity (EV 87); counselling and health centres (EV 88); legislative measures (EV 90); forming consciences in family life and ecclesial communities (EV 95-96); formation of intellectuals and media (EV 98).

The Inculturation of the "Gospel of life" forms a "people of life" who rejoice "in being able to share its commitment with so many others." In this way, there is a felt wish that "the people for life" constantly grow in number" and a new culture of love and solidarity develop for the true good of the whole of human society" (EV 101). This is just by human means. Only the cross of Jesus becomes "the sure hope of finding freedom and redemption" (EV 50).

"Original sin" as the matrix of the culture of death" The source of life is the Gospel of Jesus culminated on the cross as the supreme manifestation of life in accepting self-sacrifice to gratuitously give life to others. On the contrary, sin is the matrix of death in oneself and others.

The problem of evil has been a crucial issue for philosophers and theologians of all ages. St. Augustine first thought that Manicharism could give a theoretical solution to the problem of evil by postulating two metaphysical principles: a good principle (like God) as the source of good and light and an evil principle (like Satan) as the source of evil and darkness. Dissatisfied, After eight years of adherence to the movement, through the neo-platonic view of evil as "deprivation of good," avoiding, however, the identification of evil with the matter, Augustine approached the Christian way in the conviction that no being is evil but becomes evil through our guilt, namely through our bad use of freedom. St. Thomas too sees evil in the good.

The author states that Tatha Willy defines original sin as "sustained unauthenticity" which is experienced empirically. "It is the root of what frustrates human development and the possibilities for fulfilment in both the personal and social spheres. It is the source of domination systems, the violence that supports them, and the massive dehumanization they engender. It is the cause of major or minor ways in which we sabotage our relationships and fail those who would love us without reserve. It is the reason for God's searching us out in redemptive love. Sustained unauthenticity is that which the indwelling presence of the divine compassion transforms in us and through us, the social structures and history we create."[2]

Whatever interpretation we may give to "original sin" that fact is that evil, causing the "culture of death." This is due to a lack of perception of the beautiful, the good, and the true and the incapacity of choosing them, due to our personal and collective spiritual myopia and vulnerability and thus to our being conditioned by the selfish environment in which we live.

The Paschal mystery and the theory of the "escape goat" of Renè Girard are the redeeming way of the culture of death. As seen above, *Evangelium Vitae* underlines the cross of Jesus as being "the sure hope of finding freedom and redemption" (EV 50). We may pose a question: how can the cross of Jesus, which is the supreme expression of the culture of death." Become instead the source of the Christian "culture of life"?

Before the "culture of death," which is so pervasive in our world, we may cry out with St. Paul: "Who will deliver me from this mortal body? Thanks be God through Jesus Christ our Lord! (Rom 7:24-25). Jesus is the "scapegoat" for our human and spiritual problems. Jesus' death is the supreme manifestation of someone who did not look for an "escape goat" outside of himself to solve the problems of the human predicament but accepted to become "victim of expiation" on behalf of all. "The Son of Man did not come to be served, but to serve and to give his life as a ransom for many (Mk 10:45). How can we participate in his atoning action?[3]

---

2   TATHA WILEY, Original Sin: Origins, Developments, Contemporary Meanings, New York/Mahwah: Paulist Press 2002, 208. The volume is useful for a discussion on the various interpretations of original sin from St. Augustine to our present times.

3   For this paragraph, I have quoted ad litteram a passage from my book: G.

Jesus died, taking on himself our rejection of God and our spirit of rivalry and revenge. By accepting to die innocently, Jesus broke the chain of hatred and violence, which are expressions of the witchcraft mentality," the illusory attempt to detect the enemy or the "scapegoat" to eliminate. By accepting in freedom and in love to absorb evil in him as a victim, as a "scapegoat" for all human problems, as a sacrifice of expiation and reconciliation, he broke this fatal destructive chain. Prophet Isaiah foresaw Jesus' atoning destiny: my servant, the just one, shall justify the many, their iniquity he shall bear" (Is 53:11). Jesus Christ could be called our "lightening conductor," the absorber of all negativities in us. Jesus' death exorcised the powers of the evil expressed in human scapegoating. Jesus' atonement is summarized by the sentence Jesus uttered before dying: "Father, forgive them, they do not know what they do' (Lk 23:34). Jesus dies with an attitude of love and confident self-surrender, notwithstanding the anguish of death: Father, into your hands I commend my spirit" (Lk 23:46). In this way, Jesus' selfless love on the cross became the final solution to our human predicament.[4]

Dialogue as a political way forward to overcome the culture of death: the term "dialogue" comes from two Greek words (dia=through; logos=speech, reason) implies a dialectical interaction between two parties, whereby the differences of the dialoguing partners are not eliminated, but shared, compared, and discussed, to reach a common

---

OLIANA, the Joyful Power of the Gospel. A Spirituality for the New Evangelization, Nairobi: Paulines Publications Africa, 2014, repr. 2015, 91

4   For this paragraph, I have quoted ad litteram a passage from my book G. OLIANA, The joyful Power of the Gospel, 93. In these passages, I have tried to apply in my own way the thought of Renè Girard, who is "the world's premier thinker about the role of violence in cultural origin and about the biblical illumination of these origins and our present human condition", among other books, cf. R. GIRARD, I See Satan Fall Like Lightening, Maryknol, NY: Orbis Books 2001. The above quotation is by JAMES J. WILLIAMS, "Foreword," in ibid, ix. See in particular Part three of the book: The Victory of the Cross, in Ibid, 101-106

understanding, agreement and cooperation about life values. It is a process that needs time. It might be laborious and painstaking. Hence dialogue is not the imposition of one's position on the partner, nor away of one party to win over the opponent. Dialogue is thus an enriching and transforming experience. In a political realm, the National Dialogue does not consist of convincing the so-called opponent (or rebels) in conflict with the government establishment to give up their position and come at times underpayment or special favours the side of the government. The values and the views have to be considered. Ways must be found to reach a wish understanding and an effective agreement consisting of a peaceful and creative collaboration for the common good of the citizens. A mere discussion that leads to a simple power and wealth sharing is not dialogue.

Some time ago, an African politician told a European diplomat: "Here in Africa the Western understanding of democracy does not work. Here we African politicians have our way of solving problems, if necessary also by waging war against our opponents and militarily defeating them"[5] Violence will never bring to any solution. Not even the simple absence of war brings peace which expresses the "culture of life." Peace is not simply the absence of war but a constructive way of intelligent and creative collaboration where any form of antagonism and violence is eliminated. Albert Einstein used to say "Peace is not merely the absence of war but the presence of justice, of law, of order, in short, of government."[6] Jane Addams,[7] echoed by Martin Luther

---

5   Report to me personally by the diplomat himself

6   Quoted in https://www.goodreads.com/guotes/729410-peace-is-not-merely-the-abscence-of-war-but-the

7   Jane Addams (1860-1935) is known as the "mother" of social work. She was a pioneer American settlement activist/reformer, social worker, public philosopher, sociologist, public administrator, protestor, author, and leader in women's suffrage and world peace. In 1931, she became the first American woman to be awarded the Nobel peace Prize (cf. https://en.wikedia.org/wiki/Jane_Addams).

King Jr., stated: "True peace is not merely the absence of tension: it is the presence of Justice."

Vatican II's *Gaudium et Spes*, no.78 echoed this statement by developing a real deterrent of the "culture of death." "Peace is not merely the absence of war; nor can it be reduced solemnly to the maintenance of a balance of power between enemies; nor is it brought about by dictatorship. Instead, it is rightly and appropriately called an enterprise of justice. Peace results from that order structured into human society by its divine Founder, and actualized by men as they thirst after ever greater justice. The common good of humanity finds its ultimate meaning in the changing as time goes on; peace is never attained once and for all but must be built up ceaselessly. Moreover, since the human will is unsteady and wounded by sin, the achievement of peace requires a constant mastering of passions and the vigilance of lawful authority."

I reiterate what said was above. Fr. Tab's book is informative. It is useful for an initial reflection on them. It is a stimulus for further explorations in particular from the biblical and theological systematic.

Fr. James Tab has committed himself to include in his book the Covid-19 pandemic which has affected the whole world. This predicament makes all human beings feel vulnerable in the same way. Hence, there is an urgent need to cooperate at the planetary level in the solution of the problem, especially by the prompt production and equal distribution of vaccines. This is an impelling necessity not only motivated by humanitarian or Christian reasons but also dictated by the urgency for the physical survival of the human species.

Against this universal tragedy, the word of Pope Francis, encouraging the development of a culture of solidarity and fraternity, is a providential reminder to translate existentially the Christian call to be good Samaritans to each other.

While Pope Francis was writing his Encyclical letter "*Fratelli Tutti on Fraternity and Social Friendship*" (3rd *October 2020*), the Covid-19 pandemic broke out. Hence, he felt even more motivated to address his message of solidarity and fraternity. "As I was writing this letter, the Covid-19 pandemic unexpectedly erupted, exposing our false securities. Aside from the different ways that various countries responded to the crisis, their inability to work together became quite evident. For all our hyper-connectivity, we witnessed a fragmentation that made it more difficult to resolve problems that affect us all. Anyone who thinks that the only lesson to be learned was the need to improve what we were already doing, or to refine existing systems and regulations, is denying reality" (n. 7).

In his letter, the Pope first analyses the "Dark Clouds over a Close World" (Chapter 1). He then presents the Parable of the Good Samaritan as an inspiring way to transform the world (Chapter 2). He further highlights the need for "Envisaging and Engendering an Open World" sensitive to the universal social crisis (Chapter 3) and invites to foster "A Heart Open to the Whole World" (chapter 4). He suggests a "Better Kind of Politics" (Chapter 5) and calls for "Dialogue and Friendship in Society" (Chapter 6). He furthermore proposes "Paths of Renewed Encounter" among people (Chapter 7) and, finally, calls all world religions to be "at Service of Fraternity in our World" (Chapter 8).

The Pope offers a message of hope amid these dark clouds in which humanity finds itself at present and highlights the seeds of goodness that are already present in humanity which need to be supported and developed. He appreciates the spirit of solidarity and charity shown by many people in facing the medical and social problems caused by the pandemic. "Despite these dark clouds, which may not be ignored, I would like in the following pages to take up and discuss many new paths of hope. For God continues to sow abundant seeds of goodness in our human family. The recent pandemic enabled us to recognize and appreciate once more all those around us who, in fear, responded by putting their lives on the line. We began to realize that our lives are interwoven with and sustained by ordinary people valiantly shaping the decisive events of our shared history: doctors, nurses, pharmacists, storekeepers and supermarket workers, cleaning personnel, caretakers, transport workers, men and women working to provide essential services and public safety, volunteers, priests and religious (n. 54).

His Holiness Pope Francis stresses that hope should illumine and empower people. Hope is "a bold virtue" because it helps to transcend personal interests and favour a world of truth, goodness and beauty, justice and love. Quoting his message given in Havana (Cuba) on 20th September 2020, Pope Francis invites a renewed attitude of hope. "I invite everyone to renewed hope, for hope 'speaks to us of something deeply rooted in every human heart, independently of our circumstances and historical conditioning. Hope speaks to us of a thirst, an aspiration, a longing for a life of fulfilment, a desire to achieve great things, things that fill our hearts and lift our spirit to lofty realities like truth, goodness and beauty, justice and love… Hope is bold; it can look beyond personal convenience, the petty securities and compensations which limit our horizon, and it can open us up to grand ideals that make life more beautiful and worthwhile. Let us continue, then, to advance along the paths of hope" (n. 55).

The timely book of Fr. James Tab Charoa sensitises the readers to the physical and moral gravity of the COVID-19 pandemic. In the conclusion, he also offers a theological reflection that intends to help us see and live this tragic situation in the light of faith. In this dramatic situation, we are called to reflect on the meaning of life as a gift of God and on the honour we give to God when we put ourselves at the service of the life of our needy brothers and sisters in the spirit of Christ. As stated by the theologian Michael Schmaus, quoted by the author, "This means that the life of every man and the significance of every action and every institution is appraised according to the service it has rendered to fellow human beings."

Foreword

By Dr. John Thaloka Tur Chop

I consider it a privilege to be asked by Rev. Fr. James Tab to write a foreword for his book on the COVID-19 pandemic which is entitled; *The Dramatic Clash Between Humanity & Covid-Pandemic Its Theological Reflections e*specially, the first three chapters on Covid-19 pandemic. This is due to my experience as a general practitioner to specialize in internal medicine. Let it not be a surprise for the readers of this book to see that there are two forewords in one book. This is due to respect for the special field of educational learning. The author asked both of us, Dr John Thaloka Tur Chop, a graduate of the University of Bahri, Khartoum Sudan and Rev. Prof. Guido Oliana, who is both a dogmatist Liturgist and a doctorate holder about that respect.

Fr. Tab has written several books mostly in his field of moral theology and ethics. His forthcoming books are 1. *Socrates' Concept of Justice as Voluntary Belief & love for Truth in Plato's Dialogue.* 2. *The Nuạr Origin, Culture & Moral Evaluation,* by Rafiki Printing and Publishing. 3. *The Day When the Bridegroom was Taken Away The Call for Catholics to Reflect on Advent and Lenten Seasons* by Paulines Publications Africa, Nairobi.

Fr. James Tab's book consists of four chapters plus the appendix which is the supplementary readings on human vulnerability. This reminds us of human attack by the invisible enemy Covid-19 pandemic that has turned the whole globe into a battlefield. The author has followed critically the scientific information of the COVID-19 pandemic from its first initial stage in China's Wuhan province. In response to the COVID-19 pandemic, the invisible enemy, Fr. Tab has documented the declaration of guidelines for the COVID-19 pandemic from the Task Force Committees in three countries that is South Sudan, Uganda and the United States of America.

I would like to mention in a special way that the field in which the author has engaged is not his specialization. He is not a physician; however, the painful experience of the Covid-19 pandemic might have compelled him to jump into the territory of the medical field. Fr. Tab concurs with the former Prime Minister of the United Kingdom, Churchill who once said, and 'Specialization does not mean knowing everything about nothing.' That is, one cannot say 'I know everything in the field of my specialization and know nothing about other areas of life. The author is to be appreciated for taking bold and tough documentation of the COVID-19 pandemic.

As I read throughout the first three chapters of his book which focus on the Covid-19 pandemic, I can rightly agree that the information he documented about the Covid-19 pandemic is scientifically correct. Most information he documented is from the World Health Organisation, and Task Force Committees of some countries such as the U.S.A., South Sudan and Uganda which the author took as examples. He added one chapter on myth because of the confusion it plays in the minds of many people during this era of the COVID-19 pandemic. As a moralist, the author was very keen to document the 'rigid principles' of the Covid-19 pandemic in detail. He has dedicated his time to following critically and attentively the progress of the COVID-19 pandemic from the onset in Wuhan Province, China in 2019.

Furthermore, according to my opinion, the author was motivated to document information about the Covid-19 pandemic based on the general threat and fear it has brought to human lives. I assume the author made a decision not to be passive during the COVID-19 pandemic as other people chose to be the spectators of the drama and scenarios of the COVID-19 pandemic. He decided to move from the level of being a listener to information about the COVID-19 pandemic to the level of being an active participant by writing about it. Therefore, below is the general description of the Covid-19 pandemic that might have prompted the author to document it.

The COVID-19 pandemic is one of the emergent public health problems in the 21st century. It has taken and threatened the lives of human populations across the globe. Although the COVID-19 pandemic is not new in human medicine, the novel COVID-19 pandemic became strange which is difficult to handle scientifically and scared every individual whether elderly or young. It has exhibited radical hostility to every person, even it has infected some heads of State. With the COVID-19 pandemic, everyone is on the frontline, however, medical physicians and nurses have taken the lead in the fight against it. The risk groups are elderly people with pre-existing chronic illnesses, such as diabetes mellitus; heart disease; asthma and most immunocompromised ailments; plus, people with high and low blood pressure.

So far, there is no definitive treatment, but the communities of scientific research for the drug of cure and the everlasting human Covid-19 pandemic vaccine are still searching. Some countries have made scientific progress in areas of vaccine such as the United States of America where Pfizer and Modena vaccines have been discovered with high levels of efficacy. For example, the American Company Pfizer announced that early data show covid-19 vaccine is 95% effective and another American Company Modena, early data show covid-19 vaccine to be 94 % effective. Johnsons & Johnsons and AstraZeneca vaccines have caused blood clotting to some few people, out of millions. Some countries suspended the use of those two vaccines and some countries still use them. There are other vaccines as well that are effective.

Preface

The title of the book is 'The Dramatic Clash between the Culture of Life and Culture of Death Its relevance to the African context' never came out of the blue. but as a result of a course I took in the Department of Moral Theology at the Catholic University of Eastern Africa when I did my licentiate degree in moral theology as from 2014-2016. The phrase "culture of life and culture of death" which we shall use throughout the book, entails two important things. First, the phrase culture of life and culture of death is used throughout the book to promote the doctrine of John Paul II who used the phrase 'culture of life and culture of death' while speaking to journalists at Stapleton International Airport near Denver Colorado in America in 1993. Second, according to the phrase culture of life and culture of death is equal to nonviolence and violence. Pope John Paul II, used the phrases culture of life and culture of death about two moral problems that is, abortion, and euthanasia. He also used the phrase culture of life and the culture of death in the Encyclical letter *'Evangelium Vitae'* the Gospel of life.

The phrase culture of life and culture of death has its historical background from the time of the apostolic period. In chapter five of the book Beyond Holy Scripture, a possible source for this philosophy is the *Didache*, described as "a first-century Christian document" which exposes the doctrine of two ways: the way of life and the way of death. This culture of life and culture of death is part of the Magisterium of the Catholic Church and many people popes often cite it as part of the doctrine of the Catholic Church which defined human life.

Pope John Paul II in April 1995 returned to the theme through the encyclical *Evangeliu Vitae*ae (Gospel of Life). The phrases culture of life and the culture of death are also used in theological discourse in moral theology from the Catholic perspective. The phrase culture of life is based on theological truth which asserts that human life at all stages from the moment of conception through natural death is sacred. Therefore, it is opposed to the culture of death such as abortion, euthanasia, embryonic stem cells, contraception, capital punishment, unjust war, sadistic humiliation, narcissism, and excessive selfishness.

I use the phrases culture of life and the culture of death throughout this book, to send a message across, about the doctrine of Pope John Paul II. This doctrine can influence everyone and everyone must promote the culture of life rather than promoting the culture of death. I would like to encourage every person to renounce the culture of death (violence) and to embrace the culture of life nonviolence. I am sure, the meaning of original sin in the sacred Scripture will be, and that the tricks of Lucifer (Satan) are carefully handled so obedience, loyalty, faithfulness, and respect for the first commandment are to be observed.

Furthermore, this book entitled, The Dramatic Clash between culture of Life and Culture of Death, Its Relevance to the African Context was written based on the fact that nature is a 'school of learning' specifically during the Covid-19 pandemic. Therefore, I concur with B. Bujo when he says, "If long and wide human experience is any kind of teacher, then, it is possible that much more could be learned…"[8] On his

---

8   Běnězet Bujo, The Ethical Dimension of Community, The African Model

part, the former Prime Minister of the United Kingdom, Churchill once said, 'Specialization does not mean knowing everything about nothing.' That is, one cannot say 'I know everything in the field of my specialization and know nothing about other areas of life. Life experience presents us with some tough lessons which should offer us an opportunity to learn otherwise, ignorance about them will be suicidal. Holiness Pope Francis on his part warns that 'fragmentation of knowledge is a sin' and ought to be avoided at all costs. Furthermore, there is a common belief which says that 'when we touch one thread, we automatically touch every thread.' Therefore, in this book, readers are exposed to various forms of "Antic-Christ" in with the COVID-19 pandemic.

In this period of predicament, I chose to write my reflections on Advent, Christmas, and Lenten Seasons plus the COVID-19 pandemic. I was convinced that I needed to write about these events. I thought it was not wise to focus my reflection only on Advent, Christmas, and Lenten Seasons but also on the catastrophic event of the COVID-19 pandemic. I was aware that it was the COVID-19 pandemic which had led to the suspension of social and spiritual activities. Although, I knew that everybody was panicking including myself, nevertheless, I believed and upheld that God can bring good out of evil, and we too, human beings can bring good out of evil.

When I was writing this book, I was aware of many challenges that I was going to face such as lack of lecture room. However, when the whole world became the epicenter of the COVID-19 pandemic, in terms of contamination and broadcasting, I decided to choose between being a passive listener or an active listener, between learning and not learning, and between choosing to remain ignorant or to know more about Convid-19 pandemic. I was convinced that the differences among those choices are great. His Holiness Pope Francis on the same line, said

---

and the Life Dialogue Between North and South, Nairobi, Paulines Publications Africa, p. 1997, pp.106-107.

you are calling on us to seize this time of trial as a time of choosing. It is not the time of your judgment, but of our judgment: a time to choose what matters and what passes away, a time to separate what is necessary from what is not.

In addition, among the challenges I faced was the lack of material relevant to the Covid-19 pandemic. Worse still was that I had no access to the internet at the time. Nevertheless, I dedicated myself to following the daily news updates on the CNN TV channel and wrote down all the relevant information related to the COVID-19 pandemic that I needed for the accomplishment of this book since COVID-19 was dominating every headline in CNN as it did to other channels. I was convinced that not being a scientist, does not mean that one should not research on correct information that is concerned with issues with regards to life.

Using the CNN channel to get some information about the Covid-19 pandemic, was a blessing for me. It offers me an occasion to learn a lot about the coronavirus pandemic specifically from worldwide top scientists, nurses, politicians, and those who were affected by the COVID-19 pandemic and those who lost their dear ones. Therefore, in my attempt to follow earnestly COVID-19 pandemic daily updates, and activities, I can guarantee my readers that the information I have documented is relevant and scientifically correct. My engagement in learning from the COVID-19 pandemic has offered me an opportunity to be a self-learner, other than waiting for others to educate me on the COVID-19 pandemic. Therefore, in life, we must move from verbal narrative to written narrative to preserve reality for ourselves and others. Consequently, this book serves as a testimony on the Covid-19 pandemic and its theological reflections which consider the Covid-19 pandemic as one of the signs of anti-Christ.

Therefore, I deem it necessary to conclude this preface by concurring with the words of the great master of thought and spirituality, St. Bonaventure who invites the reader to recognize the inadequacy of "reading without repentance, knowledge without devotion, research without impulse of wonder, prudence without the ability to surrender to joy, action divorced from religion, learning sundered from love, intelligence without humility, study not sustained by divine grace, thought without the wisdom inspired by God." [9]

---

[9] Cf. John Paul II, Encyclical Letter Fides et Ratio, Nairobi, Paulines Publications Africa, 1998, No. 105.

Chapter One:
Biblical Origin of Culture of Death

Introduction

Chapter one presents the biblical narratives on the Serpent's trick, the verdict upon the serpent, the verdict upon the woman and the verdict upon the man. It also presents the impacts of Lucifer on our lives. It further presents the lack of repentance as the culture of death, the confrontation between Jesus and Lucifer, and jealousy and envy as the culture of death. It also presents the war which broke out between Michael and the angel battling against the dragon, the New Testament warning against the culture of death.

1. The Concept of Serpent in the Ancient Near East

Since we are dealing with concepts of culture of life and culture of death, we must make ourselves familiar with the term 'serpent.' According to L. McKenzie, there are at least 33 species of the serpent in Palestine, several venomous, and allusions to the serpent are common in the bible. 1. As a symbolic figure, the serpent is an important figure in the religions of the ancient Near East the Old Testament and the New

Testament. "The serpent is a demonic figure in many regions of the world, and it is such in the mythology of Mesopotamia, Persia, Egypt, Greece, and Rome."[10] L. McKenzie states that as a demonic figure, it may be beneficent or maleficent. The serpent is a divine or demonic symbol on Mesopotamian boundary stones and is included among the gods who are invoked to bring imprecations on the trespasser of the boundary. Its symbolism as a divine figure or a divine emblem is obscure, however, its association with the deities of fertility is ever assured. According to L. McKenzie, as a symbol of fertility, the serpent becomes a figure of life and health as in the modern caduceus, the emblem of medicine, which is derived from the emblem of the Greek healing god Asclepius (Salvation).

But the serpent is also a cosmic figure, identified with a monster of chaos conquered by the creative deity. It is the very emblem of the power of evil and darkness. This serpentine character of the monster of chaos is explicit in the mythological text of Ugarit. Some argue that the symbolism of the serpent is not therefore uniform and must be identified by the context in which the symbol appears. The symbolism of the ancient Near East must be recalled in explaining the symbolic value of the serpent in the bible. As a celestial demonic figure, the emissary of Yahweh, the serpent is noticed under SHERAPH. The serpent as a cosmic figure appears in some OT allusions: Yahweh smites the fleeing serpent, the twisted serpent, and the dragon in the sea (Jb 26:13; Is 27:1). The adversary of the creative deity appears in the mythological texts of Ugarit described in the identical words used in Is 27:1. Am 9:3 alludes to the serpent on the floor of the sea, the cosmic serpent. More obscure and much more discussed in the symbolism of the serpent in Gn 3. The identification of the serpent with Satan occurs only in late Jewish literature, from there it passed to the New Testament (WS 2:24,

---

10   John L. McKenzie, *Dictionary of the Bible*, New York, Simon & Schuster, 1995, P.789.

2 Co 11:3). The Serpent here is just one of God's creatures but hostile to him and humans.

Our urge to understand the concept of the culture of death about 'violence' requires that we should know the root meaning of the word violence. Etymologically, the term violence is from the Latin *violenia* which denotes force. It is described as a great force, excessive force, or constraint. The two first words are taken from the viewpoint of the agent's activity, while the second implies a norm; the third is from the passive principle which is the activity of the agent. St. Thomas Aquinas concurs with Aristotle in the third meaning that is a constraint in the stricter sense, stating that ... "violence of which the principle is extrinsic, the thing suffering the violence contributing nothing."[11]

1.1 Metaphors of Sin and the Verdicts

Although we shall discuss sin thoroughly in chapter four, however, there is a need to treat it in this chapter due to its relevance to it. The term 'sin' in the Hebrew language has no equivalent. Hebrew uses other words rather than sin. Etymologically, in Greek, the hamartia verb means "to miss the mark." This signifies not merely an intellectual error in judgments but a failure to attain a goal. Adam and Eve had a miss calculation reason and they failed to attain a goal. Their disobedience signifies rebellion against God. Rebellion can be an agreement between nations and people. Sin is also described as disloyalty to either part of the agreement. The failure of an inferior to fulfil his obligations (Gn 31:36; 42:22) or of the host to fulfil his duty of hospitality (Gn 20:9). Based on these and other passages J. Pedersen "remarks that the kernel of sin is a breach of covenant."[12] However, the same writer also observes, considering the basic meaning of "miss the mark," failure

---

11   *Webster's New Encyclopedic Dictionary*, Cologne, Könemann, 1993, p.690.

12   John L. McKenzie, *Dictionary of the Bible*, p. 817.

to achieve an objective, that sin is a non-action; this consideration of sin as a failure is seen in other worlds also. The term 'iniquity means deviation which includes the element's failure and distortion. Iniquity means that reality has become what ought not to exist. These metaphors the culture of death attempt to express the damage of sin to the sinner; his guilt is not only a liability before Yahweh, but also a corruption of the person. Therefore, Adam and Eve after sinning, found themselves in those metaphors of culture of death.

According to L. McKenzie, the serpent of Gn 3 is represented as a serpent (outside of his loquacity), but the curse of the serpent (Gn 3: 14ff) reduces him to his natural serpentine character, and it is conceivable this is intended to be another version of the victory of Yahweh over the cosmic serpent. In the messianic age the serpent becomes harmless (Is 11:8). The promise of protection in Ps 91:13 includes the power to tread upon serpents.

Based on those above-mentioned metaphors of sin and the role of the serpent to perpetuate chaos, Christians believe that violence as a culture of death has come to this world through original sin committed by our first parents, Adam and Eve. The first parents had brought the culture of death to all human races by ignoring the warning from God. The Holy Scriptures asserts that "The Lord God gave the man this order: You are free to eat from any trees of the garden except the tree of knowledge of good and evil. From that tree you shall not eat; when you eat from it you shall die (Gen 1:16-17). From this Biblical citation, it is clear that mankind's freedom was limited. When Adam and Evil violated this limit by disobeying God's command, they lost their status from paradise. Thus, the doctrine of the "tree of life" (tree of knowledge of good and evil) represents the culture of life while any attempt by a rational being to possess the 'knowledge of good and evil, and to try to become independent from God, is an attempt to possess the culture of death. The doctrine of the knowledge of good and evil is preserved by God. Human history so far has proved to be subject to error, specifically in decision-making on real issues of life. This happened to St. Paul, and it had become a constant contradiction in his life. Paul calls it "weakness." This is evidenced in his words to the Romans, "What I do, I do not understand. For I do what I want, but I do what I hate" (Roma 7:15).

As a consequence of their disobedience and disloyalty to God's command, God pronounced his judgment upon each. Then, "the Lord God said to the sake: Because you have done this, cursed are you among all the animals, tame, or wild; on your belly, you shall crawl, and dust you shall eat all the day of your life, I will put enmity between you and the woman, and between your offspring and hers; they shall strike at your head, while you strike at their heel" (Gen 3"14-15). Such ruin of the relationship between God and his perfect creature Adam and Eve was brought by Lucifer whose duty is to ruin the harmony and happiness between the couple. A famous well-known British poet Shakespeare presented a certain character of confusion, disharmony, and ruination of relationships between people by the name '*Lago*.' In this specific reference, "Lago reveals in the idea that he would work for the ruination of the perfect happiness of Othello and Desdemona,"[13] which was also the work of Lucifer to ruin the perfect relationship between God and our first parents.

1.1 Verdict Against the Serpent (Lucifer)

We did mention earlier for good reason that the serpent is also a cosmic figure, identified with a monster of chaos conquered by the creative deity. The serpent is the very emblem of the power of evil and darkness. However, we have pointed out earlier that the serpent is also a cosmic figure, identified with a monster of chaos conquered by the

---

13   Cf. K. N. Khandelwal, *Shakespeare's Othello*, Narain, Educational Publishers, Agra-3, Revision Edition, p.73.,

creative deity. The God with creative power and who is the creative deity, condemned the serpent because the serpent has brought chaos to destroy the harmonious relationship between God and his creatures. The hostile creature against God and humans was first judged because he deceived and intoxicated the minds of our first parents. God knows the mind of the serpent and therefore, he never dared to ask for any justified reasons as to why he did it. He pronounced the word 'curse' against the serpent without hesitation. The word curse means wishing evil things to happen against someone. Its worse meaning is to pray always for bad things to happen to someone whom you intently dislike. In the Sacred Scripture, the serpent is presented as an excellent deceiver and the most cunny trickery among other creatures in the Garden of Eden. However, when God pronounced judgment against him, he could not open his mouth to utter any reason for justification. The Serpent remained silent as a sign of admitting his dirty game.

God cursed the serpent among all animals both tame and wild. He pronounced multiple charges against the serpent which represents the worst condemnation of its kind. Those multiple charges such as 'to walk on its belly, to crawl and to eat dust all the days of his life. This worse condemnation demonstrates the culture of death for the serpent. However, we need not explain this condemnation yet, we must read them between the lines to get their meanings. Today, we see a serpent walking on its belly and crawling on the ground which seems to become the serpent (snake).

This strong condemnation pronounced by God against the serpent was based on the strong weight of the role which the serpent had played by deceiving Adam and Eve to become like God. The Sacred Scripture states "But the serpent said to the woman: "You certainly will not die! God knows well that when you eat of it your eyes will be opened and you will be like God, who knows well good and evils" (Gen 3:4-5). This seems to be the most deceptive motivation provided by Lucifer to our first parents Adam and Eve. Merriam-Webster's Collegiate Dictionary describes the word "Lucifer" as the morning star, a fallen rebel archangel, the Devil.[14] The cosmic figure (serpent) who possesses both the power of evil and darkness and who executes chaos, such activities of Lucifer are demonstrated in his continuous accusations against Job.

The activities of the serpent have been demonstrated more clearly in the false accusation by Judas the Iscariot against Jesus his Lord. The Gospel of St. Mark puts it "Then while he was still speaking, Judas the Iscariot, one of the Twelve arrived, accompanied by a crowd with swords and clubs who had come from the chief priests, the scribes and the elders. His betrayer had arranged a signal with them saying, "The man I shall kiss is the one; arrest him and lead him away securely" (Mk 14:43-44). Judas the Iscariot (Lucifer) is the par excellence of the culture of death. St John's Gospel puts the incarnation of the Devil (Lucifer) in the heart of Judas the Iscariot clearly as he states "So he dipped the morsel and (took it and) handed it to Judas, son of Simon the Iscariot. After he took the morsel, Santa entered him. That means the culture of death entered him, and consequently, Judas the Iscariot chose darkness rather than light, evil rather than good and chaos rather than harmony.

No wonder, Lucifer (the Devil) might have brought with it "seven evil spirits" more than itself and entered Judas the Iscariot. Jesus knew what was in the heart and the mind of Judas the betrayer and he said to him, "What you are going to do, do it quickly" (Jn 13:26-27). When the Lucifer (Devil) enters into the human heart, the result is the absolute rejection and refusal of recognition of what is good in all its forms. This is a serious sin against the Holy Spirit. There is a distinction between hating a person and acknowledging his good works. Jesus in his teaching has made this distinction very clear by stating "If I do not perform my Father's works, do not believe me; but if I perform them, even if you do not believe me, believe the works, so that you may realize

---

14 *Merriam Webster's Collegiate Dictionary,* Eleventh Edition, Massachusetts, Merriam-Webster, incorporated, 2003, p.739.

(and understand) that the Father is in me and I am in the Father" (Jn 10:37-38).

1.1.1 Warning Against the Return of Unclean Spirit

According to St. Mathew's Gospel, "When an unclean spirit goes out of a person, it roams through arid regions searching for rest but finds none. Then it says, "I will return to my home from which I came. But upon returning, it finds it empty, swept clean, and put in order. Then it brings back with itself seven other spirits more evil than itself, and they move in and dwell there, and the last condition of that person is worse than the first. Thus it will be with this evil generation. Therefore, the role of Lucifer is very complex when it incarnates itself in a human form; its culture is one of trick and deception which are the cultures of death. The role of Lucifer (the Devil) is to mislead others from the right path to the wrong one, from righteousness to wickedness, from obedience to disobedience, from observation of moral norms to abrogation of them, from believing to disbelieving, from humility to pride, and from absolute truth to falsehood. These are the activities of Lucifer the initiator of the culture of death and evil generation according to St. Mathew's Gospel.

Jesus in his moral teaching has issued a serious warning to such kind of behaviour. "Whoever causes one of these little ones who believe (in me) to sin, it would be better for him if a great millstone were put around his neck and he were thrown into the sea" (Mk 9:42). Jesus also expresses this when he said, "For the Son of Man indeed goes, as it is written of him, but woe to that man by whom the Son of Man is betrayed. It would be better for that man if he had never been born" (Mk 14:21). Judas the Iscariot cursed himself to death by committing suicide after betraying the Lord as the Gospel of St. Mathew asserts "Then Judas, his betrayer, seeing that Jesus had been condemned, deeply regretted what he had done, he returned the thirty pieces of silver to the chief priests and elders, saying, I have sinned in betraying innocent blood. ... Flinging the money into the temple, he departed and went off and hanged himself" (Mt 27:3-5). He was deeply regretted for betraying his Lord after it was too late.

The consequence of listening to Lucifer is leading to the termination of one's own life by committing suicide like Judas Iscariot who was not alone in this business of suicide. Perhaps, many people might have committed suicide after they discovered that they were guilty of what they had done to innocent blood. Just observe what is taking place in our contemporary society, there are many attempted suicides and those who have committed suicides. This is the culture of death which needs to be confronted with the doctrine of the culture of life of John Paul II. Suicide has become more subtle in our contemporary society because of avoiding its real name. Contemporary physicians call it *"euthanasia"* while St. John Paul II calls it the culture of death. Whether suicide is done by a person to terminate his/her life or is done by facilitating it with euthanasia, it will always remain violence against the culture of life. For example, it is like inflicting violence upon oneself which is against the culture of life.

1.2 Verdicts Against the Woman

In dealing with a verdict against the woman, we ought to have a comprehensive understanding of women in the ancient Near East religions. In the ancient world, woman was depressed, and less human than the male. According to L. McKenzie, her rights in law, marriage, and the family, and civil society were inferior to the rights of the man. Thus, this double standard of morality existed, and restraint was imposed only upon the woman. In this double standard of morality, woman was reconsidered as the creature of man's pleasure and as the drudge who performed lowly domestic duties while she bore man's children.

It is asserted that a woman, who could give the man his supreme animal pleasure, was worshipped as a goddess precisely in her sexual character, as a goddess Ishater, Astarte, or other such deities found in most ancient Near East religions. To Hebrew, this view of woman was a perversion of the position assigned to a woman by God in creation, depressing her on the one hand, from her place as a helper fit for a man (Gn 2:20) and elevating her on the other hand to a deity. This perversion of the position of the female sex found expression in the cult of the goddess of fertility. She was recognized as the source of life; and her union with the male deity, celebrated in the annual myth-ritual cycle of fertility, was the sign and symbol of the renewal of life. According to L. McKenzie, "the worshippers entered into communion with the deities of fertility by themselves participating in the rites through intercourse with priestesses who represented the goddess of fertility."[15] Thus the worshippers became like gods (Gn 3:5, 22).

The Hebrews rejected this belief; according to them, sex was instituted in the animal world and man by God's creative act. The distinction of sex implied a relation between man and woman which did not correspond to the historical position of woman known to the Hebrews.

However, we are told in the story of Gn 3, that man was strangely inactive; the dialogue takes place between the serpent and the woman, who plays the leading role in tempting the man. After they ate the fruit of the tree of knowledge of good and evil, the Sacred Scripture "states that..."the eyes of both...were opened, and they knew that they were naked; so they sewed fig leaves together and made loincloths for themselves"(Gen 3:7). "When they heard the sound of the Lord God walking about in the garden at the breezy time of the day, the man and his wife hid themselves from the Lord among the trees of the garden being shamed and felt guilty because they were enticed by the hostile creature. Caution ought to be made that the snake should not be identified with Satan yet. It is just one of God's creatures but hostile

---

15   John L. McKenzie, *Dictionary of the Bible,* p.272.

to him and human beings. Furthermore, It is stated that the tempter is in the guise of a snake, because of the latter's cunning in popular belief (cf. MK 10:16). The phrase which said "they hid themselves" demonstrates the sense of shame which was the loss of harmonious relationship between them and God.

"The Lord God then asked the woman: What is this you have done? The woman answered instinctively with a justifiable reason without any "remorse" by stating that "The snake tricked me" so I ate it (Gen 3:13). What is this trick that the serpent used to convince the woman? It is this, but the snake said to the woman: "You certainly will not die! God knows well that, when you eat of it your eyes will be opened and you will be like gods, who know good and evil" (Gen 3:4-5). The tricks which the serpent used to entice the woman are the opposites of what God had said to Adam and evil. The three reasons used by the serpent to entice the women are as follows: 1. You will not die! 2. God knows well that when you eat of it your eyes will be opened. 3. You will be like the gods, who know good and evil. Based on this deception of chaos, God passes verdicts to the woman, he says, "I will intensify your toil in childbearing; in pain, you shall bring forth children. Yet your urge shall be for your husband, and he shall rule over you" (Gen 3:16). Thus, these three multiple charges were pronounced by God against the woman.

However, to read those multiple tricks and their verdicts literally, will not help and to dismiss their applications to our practical life will lead to contradiction. Every human person wishes to live for eternity, which is the plan of God and not of Lucifer. Your eyes will be opened! Were Adam and Eve created blind? This is just a "sweet trick" which was presented to our first parents by the serpent. You will be like gods (not God) who know good and evil. The atheists have arrived at this level. They measure what is good and what is evil based on their judgment not referring to God. Just observe our contemporary society and whether people have become like gods. In our normal life, how do we participate in an evil act? T. Aquinas has identified eight ways of cooperating in an evil act to the detriment of justice. 1. "To counsel someone to carry out an evil.[16]" 2. To participate by commanding him. 3. To give okay that is consent. 4. By flattering. 5. By receiving. 6. By partaking. 7. By not preventing when possible. 8. by not denouncing the evildoers.

The answer given by the woman to God that the snake tricked me, indicates that she has learned from the serpent not to be sincere and not to admit her participation in disobeying the Lord. She had developed a culture of lies which is the culture of death. She has adapted the attitude of rationalization. She did not dare to ask for God's mercy which is the culture of divine life. A. Cencini states "The first possible form of evident distortion when confronted by sin is that of being prompt by the pretence of eradicating it from one's life."[17] Furthermore, A. Cencini argues that we are speaking of an implicit claim never admitted even to oneself, which is rooted in a need, felt by everyone, even though it is never mentioned: the need for omnipotence. When we deny our sins, we become liars as K. Khandelwal asserts "There are millions now alive, who sleep every night in beds not their own, and yet they will swear them to be their beds."[18]

1.2.1 The Impact of Eve's Charges on Other Women

The first trick which says you will not die, on the contrary, has brought more suffering to the women as God said to Eve, "I will intensify your toil in childbearing; in pain, you shall bring forth children." Just let us observe what is taking place before, during, and after the delivery of any woman. Although nobody knows about the exact second, minute, hour, and day in which the *fetus'* life begins in the womb of her mother,

---

16   Cf. Paul Glenn, *A Tour of the Summa of St. Thomas Aquinas*, (Qq. 57-80), Bangalore, Theological Publications in India, 2007, p.233.

17   Amedeo Cencini, *To Live Reconciled, Psychological Aspects*, Bologna, St. Paul Publication, 1988, p. 18.

18   K. N. Khandelwal, *Shakespeare's Othello*, p. 111

however, the doctrine of the Catholic Church asserts that life begins from the first moment of conception as sacred to natural death. The words of God remain true, that is the intensification of toil in childbearing, and in pain, you shall bring forth children among women remain authentic. Yet, no woman is ready to give up marriage because of those difficulties. For example, at nine months into the pregnancy, still every woman wants to get married and bear children. Naturally, any child is supposed to come to life through sexual intercourse, second, pregnancy, and third, delivery after nine months as we have mentioned earlier. In these steps, we can have a clue about the intensification of childbearing; in pain, you shall bring forth children. These are biological truths.

For instance, initially, and during the pregnancy, our observation tells us that each woman has a unique experience during pregnancy. In my Dialogue with several women, some expressed that during the first month of pregnancy, they constantly experience vomiting, spitting, and selection of some food, while others said that they hate either their husbands or other particular people. Still, some said, they like to eat mud which resembles the condemnation of the snake to eat dust. If there is a miscarriage, some can die too. Without a doubt, some die during the delivery. For example, the late Madam Estella Juan, the wife of ex-seminarian James Lodu died during the delivery in 2017, late Madam Josephine Woro, wife of Mr. Joseph Kenyi, died during the delivery and the late Madam Suzan Poni, wife of Mr. Michael Inyani also died during the delivery. These are related to physical, biological, and psychological truths and they are undeniable facts. Is this pronounced judgment a reality?

We may be tempted to conclude that the judgment upon the woman through intensification in childbearing; in pain, you shall bring forth children, includes both the culture of violence and death. With these sufferings and violence, which have resulted in the death of many women, no woman will give up even those who are not yet married are already to be married and to beget children. Why do women always take such bold determination? The answer was given by God Himself when He said, yet your urge shall be for your husband, and he shall rule over you. But are men aware of the sacrifices that women are making by risking their own lives by giving birth to children? Can we take everything as normal if delivery occurs? Pope John Paul II states that part of this daily heroism is also the silent but effective and eloquent witness of all those" brave mothers who devote themselves to their own family without reserve, who suffer in giving birth to their children and who are ready to make any effort, to face any sacrifice, to pass on to them the best of themselves.

All humans believe there is violence during pregnancy and during delivery which can sometimes lead to death. Women are caught up in this mystery of ambivalence, during delivery, they experience serious pain, but after successful delivery, they experience everlasting joy by bringing new life to the world. We must also know that delivery is the mixture of the culture of life and the culture of death (nonviolence and violence) while pain is inevitable in this specific occasion of delivery for any woman.

The charges against women have nothing to do with adultery as some people assume. From the way God pronounced verdicts against the woman, they directly violate the first commandment which says "You shall have no other gods before me" and not the six commandments which say, "You shall not commit adultery. Mind you, there was no other man with a wife in the Garden of Eden and there was no other woman with a husband except Adam and Eve. 1. God knows well that when you eat of it your eyes will be opened. 2. You will be like gods, who know good and evil. Original sin is the worse sine because of the rejection of the commandment of love which says "Love the Lord your God with your heart, with all your soul and with all your strength." Original sin has nothing to do with eating an apple as some people presume. Mind you, we are still eating apples to this day.

The conclusion about the suffering inflicted upon the woman

during the delivery, should not lead us to frustration even though many women are losing their own lives. God through the woman has made this promise "I will put enmity between you and the woman, and the between your offspring and hers. They will strike at your head, while you strike at their heel" (Gen 3:5). In our daily life, our enmity with snake is evident. For example, when we see the tail of a snake, we instinctively run away before seeing its head or even when moving on a road and see a rod that looks like a snake, we instantly jump for our life.

Thanks God through this woman who was "Eve" which in Hebrew "Hawwa" which is translated simply as "living "or according to The reek version, the woman's name is the source of life in the human family. With that promise, God demonstrates that the culture of death, mortality) will be substituted with the culture of life (immortality) through the birth of His Son from the woman, named the Blessed Virgin Mary Mother of God.

1.3 The Third Verdict Upon the Man

The dilemma of the fall of man or what is traditionally called 'original sin' according to modern scholars prefer to treat the account as a story through which Hebrews enunciated their belief that man fell from his primitive harmonious relationship with God. L. McKenzie argues that the story was constructed by elements drawn from the beliefs and traditions of the ancient Near Eastern world. But it was governed by the unique Hebrew conception of God which made it impossible for them to accept the beliefs about the origin of man found in ancient Near Eastern myths. It is further asserted, that the condition of man and his relations with God could not be explained by the assumption created evil, or that man as he existed could be in harmonious relations with God who imposed His moral will on the will. However, the present condition of man can be due only to his failure to meet the standards which God has set for him.

L. McKenzie states that the question of the reality of the fall of man, which is theologically connected with the reality of redemption is distinct from the question of the historical character Gn 2-3. If man had not fallen, man needed no redemption nor was he redeemed by the death of Jesus Christ. It is argued this theological certainty, however, does not repose on a "history" of the fall of man understood in the sense in which we employ the word, but on the biblical awareness of the reality and universality of the hostility which man exhibits to God, which is responsible for his estrangement from God. Therefore, from this estrangement, only God can deliver him. Hence the Yahwist account describes the fall of man in terms of his own time and his civilization as identical with the cult of fertility, which he represents as the radical rebellion which alienates man from God and takes away the dominion over nature which God conferred upon man in creation. According to L. McKenzie, "This does not mean that the writer intended to affirm that the original fall was historically the adoption of the fertility cult, but rather that in the fertility cult there appeared the rebellion which originally sundered man from God and made the achievement of happiness impossible for him. Therefore, it is a result of man's rebellion against God that he is doomed to death."[19]

Therefore, due to the hostility, rebellion, and estrangement which man exhibited towards God, the sacred Scripture is very systematic in presenting those verdicts on man according to its gravity. God addresses Adam and Eve as man and woman. "The Lord God then called to the man and asked him. Where are you? He answered, I heard you in the garden; but I was afraid because I was naked, so, I hid." Then God asked: Who told you were naked? Have you eaten of the tree of which I had forbidden you to eat? The man instinctively replied with no 'hesitation and remorse' "The woman whom you put here with me, she gave me fruit from the tree, so I ate it (Gen 3:9-12).

---

19   John L. McKenzie, *Dictionary of the Bible*, P.273.

Consequently, God says "To the man he said: Because you listened to your wife and ate from the tree about which I commanded you, you shall not eat from it, cursed is the ground because of you! In toil you shall eat its yield all the days of your life" (Gen 3:17). It is unfortunate to hear Adam speaking as if it was the first time for him to stay with Eve, and as if, Eve was imposed on him by God. The same expressed his satisfaction after seeing Eve being offered to him by God as completing his nature. The Sacred Scripture asserts "So the Lord cast a deep sleep on the man, and while he was asleep, he took out one of his ribs and closed up it's placed with flesh. God then built the rib that he had taken from the man into a woman. When he brought her to the man, the man said: "This one, at last, is bone of my bones, flesh of my flesh" (Gen 2:21-23).

Here, we ought to learn something from Adam our grandfather. 1. Rationalization (defend mechanism). 2. Deserting our dear one in times of difficulty such as avoiding our guilt. Imagine, when God passed the verdict to Eve, we presumed that Adam was listening. The verdicts passed to Eve by God were heavy; however, Adam himself should feel happy, especially in the last two verdicts passed against the woman which say, 1. Yet, your urge shall be for your husband. 2. He shall rule over you. Another verdict says, 'I will intensify your toil in childbearing, in pain you shall bring forth children. With this verdict, was Adam expecting God to pass more verdicts to the woman based on his justification? The Sacred Scripture confirms that Adam replied to God saying, 'The woman whom you put here with me she gave me fruit from the tree, so I ate it.

In our normal life, when we discover that we have done something wrong that lowers our self-esteem, we try our level best to project it to someone else who can become a scapegoat for our fault. This is a typical rationalisation of defense mechanism as psychologists termed it. According to A. Cencini, "The first, most typical of projection is that of attributing unconsciously to another definite person the very sentiments, intentions, attitudes, that are linked with one's immaturity."[20] He argues that it is as if the other becomes an easy screen and a convenient container into which to pour one's integrated into his identity. Although Adam claims that his eyes are opened and that he already become like gods, who know good and evil, his rationalization and defence mechanism did not prevent God from passing a verdict on him. In this way, Lucifer's reasoning, pretending to become wise, smart, and clever in a satanic manner, does not help. Just observe what is taking place in our contemporary society, how many women with children deserted by their husbands in times of difficulty such as financial crises in the family, and betrayal in marital fidelity, just to mention a few. It is better to read that drama in the book of Genesis and apply it to our concrete life; otherwise, we shall miss their serious lessons.

1.3.1 The Impact of Man's Verdicts on the Earth (Soil)

The verdict which says cursed is the ground because of you! In toil, you shall eat its yield all the days of your life, which involves many factors. Traditionally, man was believed to be the provider of his family. Ancient antiquity asserts that man goes hunting to feed his family and cultivate to feed his family and all the tough work is done by man to get his daily bread for his family. For a long time, the verdict seemed true. But in our contemporary society, if we are not careful, more verdicts are given to women by men besides the natural ones passed by God to the first woman. Every man should rule his family by love specifically his wife.

Curse is the ground because of you, involves not only hard work done by man but that nature itself is affected by the sin caused by man and his wife. Yes, there is a guarantee for toiling, but sometimes, there is no product. For example, there a droughts, earthquakes, floods, and different diseases which affect all living organisms and mankind

---

20   Amedeo Cencini, *To Live Reconciled, Psychological Aspects*, p.28

continues to inflict violence on planet Earth. What happened in Haiti during the earthquakes in 2010 could raise a lot of questions about the "curse is on the ground." "Haiti earthquakes of 2010, large-scale earthquakes that occurred January 12, 2010, on the West Indian island of Hispaniola, comprising the countries of Haiti and the Dominican Republic."[21] The same websites argue that the most severely affected was Haiti, occupying the western third of the island. Exact death toil proved elusive in the ensuing Chaos. The official Haitian government count was over 300, 000, but other estimates were considerably smaller. Hundreds of thousands of survivors were displaced. Fire sometimes out of negligence claims a lot of lives and electric fires also claim a lot of lives.

From the time of floods during Noah's time, nature has presented itself as the culture of death (violence) against living organisms. The Sacred Scripture asserts that "Everything on dry land with breath of life in its nostrils died. The Lord wiped out every being on earth: human beings and animals, the crawling things and the birds of the air; all were wiped out from the earth. Only Noah and those with him in the arks were left" (Gen 7:22-23). Can we understand this lesson literally? Can we learn something from it? When we hear of tornados, hurricanes, volcanoes, floods, droughts, and various diseases which claim a lot of lives, should we not admit that nature also is inflicting violence on us including different living organisms here on planet Earth? We need to widen our ways of understanding violence; we need to have a holistic approach to violence, and not limit ourselves to human discretion.

1.3.2 The Impact of Lucifer on Our Life

Among all other organisms, humans from the time of birth seem to imitate the serpent. If we observe closely, a human baby always walks

---

21   www.britannica.com/even/Haiti-earthquake-of-2010, retrieved as from 19/07/2019.

on its belly by crawling on the ground. The consumption of mud by a child walking on its belly by crawling on the ground is evident. We who are grown up look at them with pity, and through our help, children can walk upright. We have noticed that sometimes, children are not innocent. On the one hand, the synoptic Gospels present children as models for learning because children do not keep grudges, they can forget the hurt easily, but when we observe children. Sometimes, we are amazed by their persistent stubbornness in discharging violence through crying. Sometimes, they do this with no justified reason. Sometimes, children are ready to grasp everything. For instance, during breastfeeding, they bite the mother's breasts. Sometimes, the mother may lose her temper to slap the child. This I observed and witnessed silently several times. For example, fighting over food is normal for them, and sometimes, they demand something beyond their parent's capacity. Each of us can wonder, why so much violence exists from childhood. The Church calls it the original sin committed by our first parents Adam and Eve. After the sin of Adam and Eve, the serpent seems very incarnate in us and we seem liable to listen to its tricks in various ways.

If the activity of violence which is the characteristic of the culture of death is manifested in children, how worst is it for an adult? If Lucifer (Satan) entered into Judas's mind and heart, Judas the Iscariot was very close to our Lord Jesus Christ, how sure are we whether Lucifer (Devil) has also entered into our minds and hearts or not? Is there anyone who has accused anybody or spoken badly against another person? Can there be any person who has never violated the dignity of the human person? Is there anybody who has never committed injustice of reviling; injustice of backbiting; injustice of whispering injustice of derision; injustice of cursing; and injustice of cheating? Or is there any person who has never participated in the six known cases of abuse against the dignity of the person such as rejecting, psychological and emotional abuses; the injustice of ignoring the human person; the injustice of terrorizing the human person; the injustice of isolating children; the injustice of corrupting children; the injustice of exploiting children; the injustice of sexual abuse; and injustice of gossip? If Lucifer has never invited you to participate in those above-mentioned issues, you must be the most blessed person among all humans.

'If you have never committed any sin at all in your life please, 'stone this woman who was caught in the very act of committing adultery.' This seems to be Christ's X-ray to judge each of us before God. Those various issues mentioned, are the activities of the culture of death as opposed to the culture of life. Such violation of divine warming by Adam and Eve according to belief in the doctrine of the church has great repercussions on the progeny of all humans. It is called "Original sin." Just let us observe what is happening in every human structure, and every system, there is always a Lucifer, the initiator of violence, the initiator of the culture of death, and the constant accuser in the law court. Remember the accusations against Job by Lucifer and the accusations against Jesus by Judas the Iscariot, the par excellent incarnated Lucifer.

The impact of Lucifer in our lives at personal relationships is that it negatively influences our relationships with others. When people discover that you are an accuser and that the accusations have become part of your life, then everybody will be reserved. Your interaction with people will be dealt with care and everyone will try his/her level best to avoid you. People will treat you with suspicion and everybody in your presence will calculate his/her word. When you realize that everyone has known you as an accuser, people will become afraid of you, you will suspect that everyone is against you. People will isolate you and you will be looked at like a tomb and worse, they will treat you like a serpent (Lucifer). You will walk with your belly and crawl on the ground which means; your freedom of movement will be limited and will be restricted by relating with others. People will not trust you they will have lost confidence in you. This can lead to depression and if not handled well, suicide can be possible like Judas the Iscariot. Therefore, it would be unfortunate for any Christian who tries to explain violence which is the culture of death without relating it to Lucifer while we can sometimes, take responsibility for the sins we committed.

The implication of the warning which says, you may eat from any tree of the garden except the tree of knowledge of good and evil to our practical life requires the deepest attention. God has set from the onset that our human freedom to choose between good and evil is limited. It is a capacity reserved to God as we did mention earlier. But we need to ask ourselves essential questions. How often did we categorically refuse warning even with issues related to our health? For example, there are issues such as HIV/AIDS, corruption, the danger of becoming an alcoholic, the danger of becoming a smoker, and the danger of involving oneself in criminal acts. Jesus would warn us if we are not ready to repent we shall even die like Adam and Eve.

1.4 Lack of Repentance as the Culture of Death

The warning of Jesus for each of us is very practical in the call to repentance. Jesus urges each of us to repentance as the Gospel of Luke states, "At that time some people who were present there told him about the Galileans whose blood Pilate had mingled with the blood of their sacrifices. He said to them in reply, "Do you think that because these Galileans suffered in this way they were greater sinners than all other Galileans? By no means! But I tell you, if you do not repent, you will all perish as they did. Or those eighteen people who were killed when the tower at Siloam fell on them do you think they were guiltier than everyone else who lived in Jerusalem? By no means! But I tell you, if you do not repent you will all perish as they did" (Lk 13:15).

The above-mentioned passage from the gospel of St. Luke reminds us of true repentance from our hearts before it is too late. R. Brown argues that "In his counsel that disciples learn from the unexpected death of others that they should repent and be ready for judgment."[22] He further E. states that Jesus shows no sign of hatred or vengeance when told of Pilate's cruelty to his compatriots. He is for the culture of life rather than the culture of death. Hatred and vengeance are the culture of death and should find no place, neither in Jesus' moral teaching nor in his disciples' way of life.

The Gospel of St. John presents a call to repentance to the unnamed woman who was caught in the very act of committing adultery. "Then the scribes and the Pharisees had brought a woman who was caught in the very act of committing adultery and made her stand in the middle. They said to him, "Teacher, this woman was caught in the very act of committing adultery. Now in the Law, Moses commanded us to stone sa uch woman. So what do you say? They said this to test him, so they could have charges to bring against him. Jesus bent down and on the ground to them, "Let the one among you who is without sin be the first to throw a stone on her. A gain he bent down and wrote on the ground. And in response, they went away one by one, beginning with elders. So she was left alone with the woman before him. Then Jesus straightened up and said to her, "Woman, where are they? Has no one condemned you? She replied, No one, sir." Then Jesus said, "Neither do I condemn you. Go…from now on do not sin anymore," (Jn 8:3-11).

In the summary of Jesus' mission, the Gospel of St. Mark states "Jesus came to Galilee proclaiming the gospel of Good News: this is the time of fulfilment. The kingdom of God is at hand. Repent, and believe in the gospel" (Mk 1:14-15).

The scribes and the Pharisees on one occasion asked for a sign but Jesus replied, "An evil and unfaithful generation seeks for a sign, but no sign will be given them except the sign of Jonah the prophet. Just as Jonah was in the belly of the whale three days and three nights, so

---

22 Raymond E. Brown. (ed), *The New Jerome Biblical Commentary*, London, Prentice-Hall, Inc., 1990, p. 705.

will the Son of man be in the heart of the earth three days and three nights"(Mk 12:38-40). Jesus realized that the request made by the Scribes and the Pharisees for a sign contained the toxin of the Lucifer. The scribes and the Pharisees, ask Jesus for a sign just for entertainment and to tease him. Jesus concludes with their lack of faith saying, "At the judgment day, the men of Nineveh will arise with this generation and condemn it, because they repented at the preaching of Jonah, and there is something greater than Jonah here. At the judgment day, the queen of the South will arise with this generation and condemn it, because she came from the ends of the earth to hear the Wisdom of Solomon, and there is something greater than Solomon here"(Mk 12:42). King Solomon who humbly asked for the tree of knowledge of good and evil, and for good reason, it was granted to him as it is stated, "So give men the wisdom I need to rule your people with justice and know the difference between good and evil, otherwise, how would I ever be able to rule this great people of yours" (Kg 3:9).

1.5 Confrontation Between Jesus and Lucifer

Lucifer, the hostile creature won the game by enticing our first parents Adam and Eve; however, that was not the end of the game. St. Mathew's Gospel presents three "enticements" presented by Lucifer to Jesus. The temptations happened immediately after the baptism of Jesus in which the Spirit led him into the desert to be tempted by the Lucifer the mastermind of the culture of death. In the deserts, the Sacred Scripture asserts that Jesus fasted for forty days and forty nights which he became hungry. Lucifer, the liar, approached Jesus humbly as if it were out of concern saying: 1. If you are the son of God command these stones become loaves of bread." He said in reply, "It is written: 'One does not live by bread alone, but by every word that comes forth from the mouth of God" (Mt 4:3-4). If we analyze this temptation, on the one hand, it is a mixture of subtle recognition of Jesus as the son of God which indicates the unique filial relationship between Jesus and his heavenly father and on the other hand, the request to order the stones to become loaves of bread, presents the enticement of Lucifer to ask Jesus to perform a miracle in his name.

In response to the miracle demanded by Lucifer to turn the stones into loaves, Jesus showed his trust in God, unlike the people of Israel who grumbled in the desert about manna. In a time of shortage of food, a faithful wife and her children still have hope in the living word of God. They can choose to remain Christians while bearing the absence of material needs for a while. They can still hope that things will improve through the help of God. But how many in our contemporary society remain faithful to their faith when material needs seem scarce and unavailable? Giving in to the material needs ordered by the Lucifer will eventually lead to the culture of death.

2. "Then the devil took him to the holy city, and made him stand on the parapet of the temple, and said to him, "If you are the Son of God, throw yourself down; for it is written: He will command his angels concerning, and with their hands, they will support, lest you dash your foot against a stone. Jesus answered him, "Again it is written, "You shall not put the Lord your God, to the test" (Mt 4:5-7). Lucifer uses the same title for Jesus saying, "If you are the Son of God and he uses it in the second temptation. Lucifer uses the same word it is written, in the first temptation and also in the second temptation, he uses our ignorance of the bible to entice us. Jesus response remains the same by manifesting his obedience to God and he quotes the first commandment to make the Lucifer aware that violation of the commandment of God is the culture of death. It is said that the parapet indicates the highest point, the principle. Its description entails something which projected out sideways like a wing. It is stated that it simply refers not to the top of the temple proper, but probably to the south-east corner of the outer court. It is further stated that there is possibly a messianic element in this temptation, i.e. that Jesus is at the top of the temple.

Rabbinic source records: "When the King Messiah reveals himself he will come and stand on the roof of the temple (Ps 91:11-12).

3. "The devil took him up to a very high mountain, and showed him all the kingdoms of the world in their magnificence, and he said to him "All these I shall give you if you prostrate yourself and worship me." Jesus said to him, get away, Satan! "The Lord, your God, shall you worship and him alone you shall serve" (Mt 4:8-10). Jesus lost his temper and called the tempter by his name, the Satan not more serpent." This evil request from Lucifer to Jesus is a direct disobedience to the first commandment of the Lord. In contrast with the first Adam, Jesus was loyal to his Father. Jesus' response to Satan was referring to the first commandment in which he says, the Lord your God, shall you worship and him alone shall you serve. He said, Get away, Satan! Here, Satan is the reminder of the need for constant alertness and paying attention to God.

E. Brown argues that there was no doubt about the historicity of the event of the temptation of Jesus and the disciple knew it. But essentially, the experience of Jesus about the temptation was very personal and inner, and the disciples did not know what had gone on in Jesus' consciousness. According to E. Brown, the Qumran version in Mathew and Luke thus presents a Midrash narrative or interpretation of the event in such a way as to make it pastorally possible for believers."[23] He confirms this is done by connecting the 40-day fast with Moses and Elijah in the desert and with the great temptation or trial of God's patience by the people in the exodus who rebelled against the divine nourishment (manna). The people worshiped the golden calf which they have made for themselves.

According to E. Brown, "All of Jesus' answers to the tempter are quotations from Dt 6-8. The individual tempter in Matthew are not as bizarre as they appear at first glance; they are all based on various

---

23   Raymond E Brown, (ed.), *The New Jerome Biblical Commentary*, p.638.

ways of sinning against the great commandment to Love God, "With all your heart, and with all your soul, and with all your might (Dt 6:5) as the command was understood by early rabbis: "heart" refers to the two affective impulses or drives, good and evil; "Soul" means life even martyrdom: "might mean wealth, property, and other external possession."[24]

The theme of the love of God in the narrative brings about the unity between Jesus and His Heavenly Father. Lucifer uses the word "Son of God" for Jesus as the representative of Israel. *Stones*: E. Brown argues that turning stones into bread would involve the sin of rebellion against divine obedience. By bread alone which was the reply of Jesus to Lucifer, came from (Dt 8:3) which requires the word of God in the entire context in (Dt 6-8) to get its significance. However, the word of God is the chief nourishment.

Lucifer presents to Jesus with unnecessary demand to risk his life as E. Brown puts it 'a mockery of martyrdom and the future passion'. Jesus simply replies "not to tempt the Lord" which has its biblical basis in two sources (DT 6:16 and 1 Cor. 10:9). The assertion according to E. Brown is that one must serve the Lord with one's life but not slightly. Lucifer refers to the material world to himself saying to Jesus as E. Brown states "All the kingdoms of the world and their glory: Glory is the biblical term for out or manifest splendor or wealth, fullness of being."[25] His enticement refers to choosing power and wealth to the love of God apprehended as unfaithfulness to the covenant with him. Jesus answered, him only shall you serve. According to E. Brown, Jesus took this quotation from the book of (DT 6:13) which summarizes the great Old Testament message of ethical monotheism.

According to E. Brown, the temptation of Jesus has a universal significance: 1. Jesus stands for Israel because he is the beginning of

---

24   Ibid.
25   Ibid.

the new people of God, the founder of the new humanity: 2. The basic temptation is not to love with a unified heart, at the risk of life, at the cost of wealth. Jesus has shown himself to be the perfect lover of God (Hb 4: 15). Only through the perfect love of God culture of life can flourish in our lives. This perfect love of God requires ethics over things and the superiority of spirit over matter."[26] For example, if we observe, our contemporary society, we may not be surprised to see that many people have other gods to worship. For example money, power, alcohol, women, thievery, digital technology, and, just to give a few examples.

1.6 Jealousy and Envy as Culture of Death

Christians do believe that the culture of death was first initiated by Cain. This belief is based on the Sacred Scripture which states that "Over time Cain brought offering to the Lord from the fruit of the ground, while Abel, for his part, brought the fatty portion of the firstlings of his flock. The Lord looked with favour on Abel and his offertory, but on Cain and his offering, he did not look with favour. So Cain was very angry and dejected. Then the Lord said to Cain: Why are you angry? Why are you dejected? If you act rightly, you will be accepted; but if not, sin lies in wait at the door: its urge is for you, yet you can rule it" (Gen 4:3-7).

The Holy Scripture asserts "Let us go out in the field." When they were in the field, Cain attacked his brother Abel and killed him. Then the Lord asked Cain, where is your brother Abel? He answered, "I do not know, am I, my brother's keeper?" God then said: what have you done? Your brother's blood cries out to me from the ground! (Gen 4:8-10). We need to know what prompted this violence of the culture of death initiated by Cain. The Holy Scripture is very clear by using

---

26   John Paul II *Encyclical letter, Redemptor Hominis,* The Redeemer of man, no. 16

specific terms that relate to our own life. What made Cain not to be happy was the response of God to his offertory. God did not favor his offering but favoured one of his biological brothers Abel. When God favoured the offering of Abel, Cain was angry and dejected. God asked two questions with a warning. 1. Why you are angry? 2. Why are you dejected? 3. If you act rightly, you will accept but if not, sin lies in wait at the door; its urge is for you, yet you can rule over it. Therefore the three essential elements in the mind of Cain were Anger, dejection, and sin. Cain has fueled their mind with violence prompted by jealousy and envy to initiate the culture of death through anger and dejection.

Cain was accepting a reward of favours, he was expecting a word of congratulation and appreciation from God. But on the contrary, all these blessings went to his brother Abel. He has disappointed and chose anger, dejection, jealousy and envy which are the culture of death. According to Merriam-Webster's Collegiate Dictionary, the word jealous is described as 1. Intolerant of rivalry or unfaithfulness. 2. Disposed to suspect rivalry or unfaithfulness. 3. Hostile toward a rival or one believed to enjoy an advantage. 3. vigilant in guarding a possession."[27] The same Dictionary describes envy as 1. A "painful or resentful awareness of an advantage enjoyed enjoying another with a desire to possess the same advantage." Because of jealousy and envy, the Sacred Scriptures also state that Midianite traders who passed by pulled Joseph up out of the cistern. They sold Joseph for twenty pieces of silver to the Ishmaelite, who took him to Egypt" (Gen 37:28) though there was a divine plan behind this evil act.

Unfortunately, that advantage and privilege will never be enough for everybody in our contemporary society and even God distributes his graces as He wishes. The Sacred Scripture has recorded the history of the culture of death between Cain and Abel and between Joseph

---

27   *Merriam Webster's Collegiate Dictionary,* Tenth Edition, Massachusetts, Merriam-Webster, Incorporated, 2000, p.626

and his brothers to present to each of us a lesson to learn. In the darkest part of our lives, behind the curtain, numerous issues of each case are prompted by jealousy and envy. Just let us observe to see what is happening between many brothers and sisters in areas of inheritance or when parents show favouritism among their children. In appointment to various offices or the areas of opportunity for further studies, what mood do we see among those who consider themselves less fortunate?

1.7 The Dramatic Clash Between Michael and Dragon

The book of Revelation dramatically presents the fight between good and evil or light and darkness. Unfortunately, the author of the book of Revelation presents a dramatic fight in heaven between Michael and his angels against rebellious angels led by the dragon (Lucifer), the "Ring Leader" of rebellious angels. The author says, "Then war broke out in heaven: Michael and his angels battled against the dragon. The dragon and its angels fought back, but they did not prevail and there was no longer any place for them in heaven. The huge dragon, the ancient serpent, who is called 'Satan', who deceived the whole world, was thrown onto the earth with its angels (Rev 12:7-10).

The author has presented this symbolic and stylistic drama to signify hostilities against the church of Christ. Satan in this account, signifies the accuser in court. Lucifer continues inflicting violence, deceiving people and misleading them away from God's plan. The activity of the Dragon (Lucifer) is demonstrated in the book of Job chapter 1: 1-22; 2:1-7. Prophet Isaiah presents them as fallen angels. How you have fallen from heavens, O morning Star, son of the dawn! How you have been down to the earth, you who conquered nations! (Is 14:12)

Lucifer constantly accuses Job of God and persuades God to put Job to the test. Can we dismiss the fact; let us just look around at our societies, how many people suffering from false accusations by Lucifer? Even some innocent people were put to death. Therefore, the culture of death in the bible through false accusation is very relevant to our situation today.

1.8 Jesus' Teaching Authority over the Demons

In the New Testament, the origin of the culture of death can be deduced from the teaching of Jesus Christ himself. "Jesus said in reply, "O faithless and perverse generation, how long will I be with you and endure you? (Lk 9:41). He testified with many other arguments and was exhorting them, "Save yourselves from this corrupt generation" (Acts 2:40). Jesus was very clear on specific words such as O faithless, perverse generation, and warning his disciples to be careful in dealing with corrupt generations of their time. What do we expect from faithless, perverse, and corrupt generations of our world today? We should not be taken by surprise to see violence all around us because of lack of faith, and perverse and corrupt generations.

In the pastoral ministry of Jesus, we could see him healing many people from unclean spirits, and the demons tormenting them. In the Gospel of St. Matthew for instance, we have a testimony of Jesus' healing the Gadarene Demoniac. St. Matthew asserts that "When he came to the other side, to the territory of the Gadarenes, two demoniacs who were coming from the tombs met him. They were so savage that no one could travel by that road. They cried out, "What have you to do with us, Son of God? Have you come to torment us before the appointed time?"(Mt 8:28-29). The same violence of the demoniac was presented by St. Mark's Gospel (Mk 5:1-10).

Our contemporary psychiatric hospitals are full of different people who are affected by various psychiatric disorders. You can imagine the magnitude of violence in those psychiatric hospitals and the patience of the nurses taking care of them. Some can shout at you for no reason or even slap you if you come closer to them. Violence in this circumstance is evident. Therefore, it was part of Jesus' ministry to face demons.

Jesus explains implicitly the activity of Lucifer in the allegory of the sowing seeds. The disciples could not understand the parable because of its complexity. Jesus offers an opportunity to expound to them the mystery of the parable. He explains, "The seed is the word of God. Those on the path are the ones who have heard but the devil comes and takes away the word from their heart that they may not believe and be saved…" (Lk 8: 11-15). We have many devils in our contemporary society today. Those who mislead, those who deceive, those who give wrong advice, those who act contrary to social norms, and wish no one to live a good moral life. Those who become an obstacle to faith such as atheists. No wonder, some continuously destroy the reputation of others to frustrate them.

Teaching with Authority (Luke 4:31-32) When Jesus did teach in the synagogue, however, he startled people: "They were amazed at his teaching because his message had authority" (4:32). "Jesus came to them and said, 'All authority in heaven and on earth has been given to me. Therefore go and make disciples of all nations, baptizing them in the name of the Father and of the Son and the Holy Spirit, and teaching them to obey everything I have commanded you" (Mt 28:18–20).

Conclusion

Chapter one has presented the biblical narratives on serpents' trick, the verdict upon the serpent, the verdict upon the woman, and the verdict upon the man. It also illustrated the impacts of Lucifer on our lives. The chapter also highlights the lack of repentance as the culture of death and it demonstrates the confrontation between Jesus and Lucifer. Besides, it also highlighted that jealousy and envy are cultures of death. It also indicated the war which broke out between Michael and his angel battled against the dragon, and the New Testament warning against the culture of death.

Chapter Two: Philosophical Theories and World Wars on Culture of Death

Introduction

Chapter two presents the Philosophical theories and world-historical records on the culture of death, the Aristotelian theory on the culture of death and the natural theory of culture of death according to T. Hobbes. The chapter also revisits the recap of historical keynotes on the culture of death which consists of: World War I, 1914-1918, World War II, 1945-1963, Cold War, and finally, it presents the terrorists' attacks on World Trade Center on September 11, 2001.

2. The Tension Between the Soul and Body

Among various Greek philosophers, beliefs and discussions between the soul and the body are very famous in philosophic history. For example, Anaxagoras declared that the moving cause of things to be soul, while Pythagoras proclaimed that molecules were in the air, others, what moved them to be soul. Democritus stated that the soul is a sort of fire or a hot substance... Plato in the *Timaeus* fashions the soul out of his elements; for like, holds, is known by like and the moon, sun, the plants and the world in heavens, and are in perpetual movement."[28]

According to R. McKeon, the knowledge of the soul admittedly contributes greatly to the advance of truth, and above all, to our understanding of nature. The soul is in some sense, the principle of animal life. Yet, the paradox is that the soul is considered imprisoned in the body and that it needs liberation from the body. This has created tension that amounted to violence between the two existing principles. The soul must be embodied in a material such as described by the other. Some philosophers associate the soul with "harmony" and the body with "contrary" and the question is how can something "harmonious" exist with something "contrary?" we need not dismiss the fact, let us observe how our bodily needs in their various forms contradict our soul (spiritual) needs, in their various forms. The tension between the two principles can lead to violence and sometimes, it does.

Ancient Greek philosophers are making a point that we must recognize and take care of it. When bodily needs overshadow our soul needs, we become inhuman and insensitive to the needs of others. Acknowledge that there is a natural conflict of interest between the body and soul as two natural principles. This philosophical traditional theory of violence needs serious observation. The doctrine of believing in the liberation of the soul from the body by Greek philosophers was demonstrated when they deserted St. Paul "When they heard about the resurrection of the death, some began to scoff, but others said, "We shall like to hear you on this some other time" (Acts 17:32).

---

[28]   Richard McKeon, *Introduction to Aristotle,* New York, Random House, Inc, 1947, p.153-154

2.1 Aristotelian Theory of Culture of Death

J. Tab concurs with Aristotle by stating that the just, therefore, involves at least two terms. 1. for the persons for whom it is just. 2. The things in which it is manifested, the objects that are distributed are the same equality which will exist between the persons and between the things concerned; for as the latter things concerned are related, so are the former. Therefore, both J. Tab and Aristotle argue…" that if the former and later things are not equal, they will not have what is equal, and "this is the origin of quarrels and complaints." When either equal have and are awarded with unequal shares."[29]

If we observe, what is taking place in our well-organized societies, with all its laws in their various forms, yet; sometimes, we witness immense violence in our midst based on unequal distribution of resources for various needs among citizens. Such unequal distribution of natural resources sometimes prompts armed rebellion against the governments. For example, sometimes, the word "marginalization" is used to fuel up the minds of everyone to fight against the systems. Therefore, Aristotle is making a serious point on quarrels or violence based on having awarded people unequally when they do not deserve so. This can result in a culture of death and, often it does.

2.2 Thomas Hobbes on Natural Theory of Violence

Among the outstanding figures in the natural theory of violence is a well-known British philosopher by the name of T. Hobbes. According to P. Copleston, "T. Hobbles, author of one of the most celebrated political treatises in European literature, was born at Westport near

---

29   Cf. J. Tab Charoa, *Beyond the Four Classic Cardinal Virtues: The Basic Principle of Social Justice and Their Relevance to Our Contemporary Society*, Juba: Universal Printers Company Limited, 2018, p.8

Malmesbury in 1588."[30] His natural theory of violence is articulated and stipulated as F. Copleston concurs with him, "So that like man, we find three principal causes of quarrel. First, competition, secondly, diffidence (that is, mistrust), thirdly; glory."[31]

T. Hobbes asserts that the natural state of war, therefore, is the state of affairs in which the individual is dependent for his security on his strength and his wits. "In such condition there is no place for industry; because the fruit thereof is uncertain and consequently, no culture of the earth; no navigation, nor use of the commodities that may be imported by sea; no commodious building; no investments of moving and removing such things required much force; no knowledge of the face of the earth; no account of time; no art; no letters; no society; and which is worst of all, continual fear and danger violence; and the life of man, solitary, poor, nasty, brutish and short."[32]

F. Copleston and T. Hobbes highlight that the natural state of war is a deduction from the consideration of man and his passion, no one can dismiss this natural theory of violence, we need to look at the validity of the conclusion, try to observe what is happening in all human well-organized societies. F. Copleston asserts that everyone carries arms when he takes a journey, bars his door at night; he locks up his valuables.

T. Hobbes argues that this shows clearly how each of us thinks of our fellow humans. Well well-organized society may be there, guided

---

30   Fredrick Copleston, *A History of philosophy*, New York, Doubleday, 1959, p.1. His father was a clergyman. In 1608, when Hobbes went down from oxford, he entered the service of the Cavendish family and spent the years 1608-10 traveling in France and Italy as tutor to the son of Lord Cavendish future and of Devonshire. …he occupied himself with literary pursuits and translated *Thucydides* into English, the translation being published in 1628. He had relations with France Bacon (d. 1626) and with Lord Herbert of Cherbourg; but he had not yet given himself to philosophy.

31   Ibid

32   Fredrick Copleston, *A History of Philosophy*, New York, Doubleday, 1959, p.1

by precepts, injunctions, natural and positive laws, church law and conscience. Yet, the tendency to cling to violence is highly leading in some individuals.

2.3 Recap of World I

T. Hobbes's natural theory of the state of war is a deduction from consideration of name and his passion. From the time of the original sin which has affected every creature and cosmic system, from Cain's culture of death and various natural catastrophes as we have noticed, the propensity for the culture of death seems unfortunately progressing in human history. Thus, such unfortunate situations of natural catastrophe and human violence such as competitive military capabilities have resulted in high death toll records on high. Therefore, the doctrine of T. Hobbes says that "like man, we find three principal causes of quarrel. First, competition; secondly, diffidence (that is, mistrust); thirdly, glory." These three principal causes of quarrel are the "main sources" of both World War I and World War II. However, there were also other four main causes of World War I: these include; militarism, alliances, imperialism, and nationalism. World War I resulted directly from these four main causes, but also, it was triggered by the assassination of the Austrian Archduke Franz Ferdinand and his wife by Serbian nationalists in Sarajevo, Bosnia in 1914.

Between 1914 and 1918, it has been recorded that over 30 nations declared World War I. The majority joined the side of the Allies, which included Serbia, Russia, France, Britain and Unit States. They were opposed by Germany, Austria-Hungary, Bulgaria and the Ottoman Empire, who together formed the Central Power."[33] The website argues that the small conflict in Southeast Europe became a war between

---

33   www.iwm.org.uk/history/5-things-you-need-to-known-about-the-first... retrieved as from 24/07/2018.

European empires. "Britain and its Empire's entry into the war made this a truly global conflict fought on a geographical scale never seen before."[34] The website further asserts that the fighting escalated not only on the Western front but also in Eastern and Southeast Europe, Africa and the Middle East. World War I forced its campaigners of the culture of death to formulate slogans such as; "it is For Better to Face the Bullets than to die at our homes." It lacks an ethical and moral approach, it was a war of production, it was a war of innovation and a war of destruction.

Regarding this culture of death during World War I, the website cited before claims that … "an estimated 16 million soldiers and civilians dead and countless others physically and psychologically Wounded."[35] It has been asserted that the war also forever changed the world's social and political landscape. It has brought changes in attitudes toward gender and class and it has led to the collapse of the Russian, Austro-Hungarian, and Ottoman empires. The victorious European Allies defeated the central powers. It has brought with it the creation of a new language, for example, Remembrance Sunday and the two-minute silence at 11 a.m. each 11 November. This can be seen in cities, towns, schools, places of worship and workplaces, Did humans learn from World War I and understand that the culture of death which claimed the lives of 16 million soldiers and civilians dead bad? Why World War II?

2.4 Recap of World War II

The hunger for power had brought Germany into an ambitious dream under the dictatorship of Adolf Hitler. According to U. Faulkner, Germany, smarting under her World War 1 defeat, fell under the

---

34   Ibid.
35   Ibid.

influence of Adolf Hitler, who" preached the superiority of the Nordic race" glorified war, and promised Germany world conquests. Based on that ambition: in September 1939, Hitler after having over much territory with no hesitation to go to war suddenly invaded Poland. Faulkner states that within 10 months, Germany had occupied Denmark, Belgium, the Netherlands, Luxembourg and France; it began massive aerial bombings on Britain.

The escalation of World War II in 1941 started when Germany turning on its former ally, invaded Russia while Japan on her part by the middle of December of that year, attacked an American naval base in the Philippines islands and at Pearl Harbor in the Hawaiian Islands the United States was at war. In that single attack, eighty warships and about 4,500 American men smashed or disabled at Pearl Harbor. "within hours of the attack, the United States had declared war on Japan, Germany, Italy, and later, on such Axis-dominated governments such as those of Bulgaria, Hungary, Romania, Albanian Burma, Manchukuo, Nanking, Croatia, Slovakia, and Thailand"[36]

An article entitled "Article History or Second World War, WWII" by R. Smith and A. Hughes gives detailed information about an unprecedented evil act of World War II initiated by the most brutal German dictator Adolf Hiller. Some state that "By the early part of 1939, German dictator Adolf Hitler had become determined to invade and occupy Poland"[37] Meanwhile Poland had guaranteed military support from both France and British, should there be any military attack by Germany. A. Hitler undermined the military supports from France and British for Poland, but focused his attention on Russia.

According to R. Smith and A. Hughes, Germany had first to diffuse the possibility that the Soviet Union would not resist the invasion of its

---

36   Cf. Harold U. Faulkner, *"World War II"* In the Catholic Encyclopedia for School and Home, New York, McGraw-Hill Book Company, (1965), p 534-536.

37   www.britannica.com/event/world-War-II, retrieved ad from 25/07/2018

western neighbour. Some further state that secret negotiation was going on August 23-24 that had led to the signing of the Germany–soviet Nonaggression pact in Moscow. Both Germany and Russia affirmed that "in a secret protocol of this pace, Germany and the Soviet agreed that Poland should be divided between them, with the western third of the country going to Germany and the eastern two-thirds being taken over the U.S.S.RA. Hitler underestimated the military intervention by either the British or the Soviet Union. He gave the order for the invasion to start on August 25. Meanwhile, the British and Poland signed a formal treaty of mutual assistance between the two on August 25, which led to the delay of the attack. A. Hitler was determined and ignored the diplomatic efforts of Western powers to restrain him. Some state that, "Finally, at noon on August 31, 1939, A. Hitler ordered an attack. In response, Great Britain and France declared war on Germany on September 3, at 11:00 a.m. and 5:00 p.m., respectively, World War II had begun."[38]

During the years 1939-45, some say that the principal belligerents were the Axis powers Germany, Italy and Japan, while the Allies were: France, Great Britain, the United States, the Soviet Union and to a lesser extent, China. In their argument, the war was in many after an uneasy 20-year hiatus of the dispute left unsettled by World War I. According to R. Smith and A. Hughes, in the World War II, Battle of Stalingrad, (1942-1943), the advancing Germans were finally stopped by the Red Army in desperate housing-fighting. Some say that in World War II, the Allied won the victory in 1963.

H. Faulkner explains American and British advantage towards Germany and her allies by confirming that General Douglas MacArthur and Admiral Chester Nimitz directed massive land and sea forces in a gruelling but increasingly successful war against Japan in the Pacific. Other American forces fought their way through North Africa and

---

38   Ibid

Sicily, and onto the Italian Mainland. It is confirmed that on June 6, 1994, paratroopers were dropped into France by 1,000 planes and gliders, and 2,400 American and British bombers attacked installations. According to Faulkner, the attacking forces totaled 2, 876, 000 men (17 British divisions, 20 American divisions) supported by 5, 049 fighter planes, 3, 467 bombers, 1,645 light bombers, 2,316 transport aircraft, 2,591 gliders, and 4, 000 ships of all kinds.

With all those above-mentioned attacks on Germany, it took a year to push back and subdue the Germans on their soil. Some point out that the most spectacular phase of the campaign was the daring operation of the American armoured divisions. In 1944, Italy surrendered. On May 1, 1945, A. Hitler had committed suicide. The suicide Adolf Hitler committed goes with a common saying "The one who caused evil to another should also expect greater evil. The evil person according to Aristotle is the one who treats himself and others badly. Planning day and night to destroy the lives of others to become great is very risky and many dictators have ended their lives very disgracefully because of this theory. Finally, Berlin surrendered on May 2, 1945, and Germany asked for an armistice, which it signed on May 7, 1945.

H. Faulkner states that the United States was still at war with Japan despite the destruction of the Japanese air force, sinking of most of the Japanese possessions, Japan's reoccupation of the Philippines, and the capture of Japanese possessions, Japan continued to fight on. It is assets that, "The end came, however, with the dropping of the first atomic bomb, on Hiroshima, on August 4, 1945. This bomb killed 78,150 persons and injured 37, 425, another 13, 000 were missing. Three days later another atomic bomb was dropped on Nagasaki, Japan, killing 73, 884. Japan surrendered on August 14, 1945."[39]

Other detailed information about the causalities of World War II according to Smith and Hughes stated that 40,000, 000–50, 000,

---

39   Harold U. Faulkner, *"World War II"* 1964, p. 534-536

000 deaths in World War II had made it the bloodiest conflict, as well as the largest war in history. "On August 6, 1945, during World War II (1939–1945), an American B-29 bomber dropped the world's first deployed atomic bomb over the Japanese city of Hiroshima."[40] Some state that the explosion wiped out 90 per cent of the city and immediately killed 80, 000 people; Tens of thousands more lately died of radiation exposure. Furthermore, some argue that three days later, a second B-29 dropped another A-bomb on Nagasaki, killing an estimated, 8000 people. This second atomic A-bomb on Nagasaki had forced Japanese Emperor Hirohito in a radio address on August 15, citing the devastating power of "a new and most cruel bomb."[41]

2.5 Recap of Cold War

Cold War can be described as a lengthy struggle between the United States and the Soviet Union in the aftermath of the surrender of A. Hitler's Germany in 1945. According to political expert R. Aron, the "Cold War system is compared with a phrase that says "hits the nail on the head:" impossible peace, improbable war. W. Churchill defines it as "iron curtain that now divided Europe into two. The Cold War was the conflict of interest between the new world powers gradually multiplied and characterized by the climate of fear and suspicion that reigned. The Cold War was a global conflict that affected many countries, particularly the continent of Europe.

Divergent viewpoints created rifts between those who had once been allies (the United States and the Soviet Union). Europe was divided into two blocs, and it became the main theatre of the war. Western Europe was integrated and was supported by the United States whereas

---

40   www.histroy.com/topics/world-war-II/bombing-of...retrieved as form 19/08/2018

41   Ibid.

countries of Eastern Europe became satellites of the USSR. The tensions reached localized armed conflicts without actually causing a full-scale war between the two powerful nations.

In 1947, the two adversaries employed all the resources at their disposal of intimidation and subversion. Clashed in a lengthy strategic and ideological conflict punctuated by crises of varying intensity. Although the United States and the Soviet Union, did not fight directly however, they pushed the world to the brink of nuclear war on several occasions. There was an arms race. The Cold War reached its first climax with the Soviet blockade of Berlin. The explosion of the first Soviet atomic bomb in the summer of 1949 reinforced the USSR in its role as a world power.

The Soviet Union accused the United States of spearheading imperialist expansion whereas the United States was concerned with the Soviet Union ('s Communist expansion and accused Stalin of breaching the Yalta Agreement on the right of free people to self-determination. The Cold War finally, ended in 1989 with the fall of the Berlin Wall and the collapse of the communist Regimes in Eastern Europe.

2.6 Terrorist Attack on September 11, 2001

On September 11, 2001, America was attacked by terrorists using planes targeting strategic places. Some state that groups of attackers boarded four domestic aircraft at three East Coast airports, and soon after takeoff, they disabled the crews, some of whom may have been stabbed with box cutters the hijackers were secreting. It is confirmed that the hijackers then took control of the aircraft, all large and bound for the West Coast with full loads of fuel. Some further say that (1) at 8:45 am, the first plane, American Airlines flight 11, which had originally flown from Boston, was piloted into the north tower of the

World Trade Center in New York City."[42] (2) The second plane, United States Airlines Flight 175, also from Boston, struck the south tower 17 minutes later and thus, the United States was under attack.

(3) The third plane, American plane flight 77, taking off from Dulles Airport near Washington D.C., struck the southwest side of the Pentagon at 9:37 a.m., touching off a fire in the section of the structures. After these three intensified attacks by planes used by hijackers. It is confirmed that minutes later, the Federal Aviation Authority ordered a nationwide ground stop, and within the next hour (at 10:03 am) the fourth aircraft, United States Airlines Flight 93 from Newark New Jersey, crashed near Shankswville in Pennsylvania after its passenger-informed of events via cellular phone-attempted to overpower their assailants. It is asserted that:

> At 9:59 am the World Trade Center's heavily damaged south tower collapsed and the north tower fell 29 minutes later. Clouds of smoke and debris quickly filled the streets of Lower Manhatta office workers and residents ran in panic as they tried to outplace the billowing debris cloud. Several other buildings adjacent to the Twin Towers suffered damage, and several fell. Fires at the World Trade Center site smouldered for over three months.[43]
>
> Some say that after the rescue operation, nearly 3,000 people had perished: some 2,750 people in New York, at the Pentagon and 40, in Pennsylvania; all 19 terrorists also died. The total in New York City was over 400 police officers and firefighters, who had lost their lives after rushing to the scene and into the towers.

---

42   www.britannica.com/event/Semptember-11-attack, retrieved as from 25/05/2018

43   Ibid

At 8:30 pm President George Bush addressed the nation from the Oval Office in a special that laid out a key doctrine of his administration's future foreign policy: "We will make no distinction between the terrorists who committed these acts and those who harbour them." Standing on top of a wrecked fire, Bush grabbed a bullhorn to address the rescue workers working feverishly to find any survivors. When one worker said that he could not hear what the president was saying, Bush, made one of the most memorable remarks of his presidency: "I can hear you. The rest of the World hears you. The people who knocked these buildings down will hear from all of us soon."

Conclusion

Chapter two has treated briefly the philosophical theories and the World's historical records on the culture of death, the Aristotelian theory on the culture of death and the natural theory of the culture of death according to Thomas Hobbes. Finally, the chapter also has presented the recap of historical keynotes on the culture of death which consists of: World War I (1914-1918), World War II 1945-1963, Cold War and terrorists' attacks on September 11, 2001.

Chapter Three:
Sociological Interpretation
of the Culture of Death

Introduction

Chapter three presents the conceptual analysis of the culture of violence, its social tangibility, the seven theories of the cause of the culture of violence such as relative deprivation, biological interpretation of instinctive violence, egoistic theory of culture of violence, cultural conditioning theory of culture of violence and finally, violence and social change.

3. Conceptual Analysis of Culture of Violence

Violence by the description, involves physical use of force against a person or object. It is used often in terms of the physical sense however; it is also referred as to verbal abuse against persons or objects. E. Miller argues that physical injury ranges on a continuum from superficial injury to death, while verbal violence involves a violation of the character or dignity of the person. He asserts that "the analysis of violence generally is of two types: 1. Personal violence, as in the case of rape, homicide, child abuse, and wife battering. 2. Collective violence, as in the case of strikes, riots, rebellions, revolution, terrorist activities, and wars."[44] According to this analysis presented by E. Miller, violence whether at a personal level or the collective level, has a culture of death. Therefore, it is better to call it the culture of death which may unnecessarily mean physical.

"Violence is an act which can be defined either concerning the source of the violence, is an act reference to the recipient of the violence."[45] Some argue that we examine what it means to receive violence, and then we get to the core of the ethical meaning of the term. The etymological meaning of the word "violence" is from the Latin verb "to violate" or "rape." "It…means to violate the dignity or integrity of a person."[46] Therefore, the term violation can be extended to many things for example, such as violating law, property, custom, and promises. Some say that in ordinary language, violence covers all acts contrary to the law. He gives an example by saying "During the civil rights and Vietnam War protests, the news media often used the term "violence" indiscriminately to cover all acts of disruption, destruction of property, and violation of laws."[47]

It is necessary to bring in the ethical dimension of the term violence which means the violation of a person. We must distinguish three levels of violence to a person. The first level of violence is the violent act, the one in which a person's dignity or self-esteem is harmed or damaged. The second level of violent action is the one in which a person's bodily integrity is violated to cause physical harm to the person. For example; one either does damage to his body or withholds from him/her the life support systems of physical health such as withholding of nutritious

---

44   D. Earl Miller, (ed.), *"Violence"* in the Dictionary of Pastoral Care and Counseling, Nashville: Abingdon Press, (2005), p 1303-1305

45   Duane K. Friesen, *Christian Peacemaking and International Conflict: A Realist Pacifist Perspective,* Pennsylvania: Herald Press, 1971, p. 143

46   Duane K. Friesen, *Christian Peacemaking,* p. 143

47   Duane K. Friesen, *Christian Peacemaking,* p.146

food. Violence is not only the absence of an act but also when prerequisite sustenance of life is omitted etc., physical or psychological damage may either be temporary or permanent. It is believed that when the injury is permanent such that it hurts the person's life for the rest of his life, which may result in a lack of protein that may cause permanent brain damage or a blow that cripples a person for life, then the violence is ethically more violence. For example, a physical injury which may heal in a short time. This third level of violence is present when human life is taken. This is the most extreme form of violence ethically the most serious violation of a person because of its finality to human life.

Violence can be direct or indirect depending on its organization in society. Scholars use the term "structural violence" which refers to violating persons that indirectly come to people by the way a society is structured. Some say that some people use the term "structural violence" in a polemic way to argue that since there is structural violence, we are, justified in using other forms of violence. What characterizes structural violence is that it is institutionalized…"deliberated and organized and planned for and that they are used with the deliberate intent either to threaten or to do harm to persons."[48]

3.1 Definition of Violence

It has been asserted that the word "violence" involves two principles. The two principles are constraining and constrained. According to B. Schepers, the latter constrained principle of violence always requires passive relative to the agent inflicting violence either as an active or passive principle. It is asserted that if it is an active principle, he suffers violence from an extrinsic agent. It is an act contrary to his inclination or prevented from acting according to it.[49] On the one hand, inclination

---

48   Ibid. p. 143

49   M. B. Schepers, ed.), *"Violence"* in the New Catholic Encyclopedia, New

is the intrinsic source of activity of the bodies: such constrained as a principle of violence. According to this view, it demands three types of activity. The first activity is the "will" for rational life, the second activity is the sensory desire of sentient life, and the third activity, is the tendency of the form or nature with both vegetable life and the spontaneous, non-vital activities of the bodies.

But if it is a passive principle, the one which demands an eternal agent to bring in to act, it suffers violence when moved to an act, that is. As from or determination opposed to the one to which it is naturally, though passively, inclined; or when prevented from receiving from a corresponding natural agent. It's a proper act to which it has a natural passive inclination. This natural inclination bases its primary matter already disposed of for a certain act or in the secondary receptive principle of any natural substance. B. Schepers asserts that the agent or patient to which violence is done contributes nothing since there is an opposition to the intrinsic, voluntary natural, active or passive inclination. Some state that this constraining (involuntary) principle of violence, must include end. Therefore, in this sense, violence in the strict sense, cannot be understood without reference to "final causality," violent movement in the natural world is beyond understanding unless it is connected to two natural principles that imply an intrinsic principle of activity or passive relative to certain determinate ends.[50]

According to, the Webster's New Encyclopedia Dictionary, the word "violence "whether it is an active or passive principle, denotes the following meanings. 1. Using physical force so it harms a person or person's property. 2. Injury especially to something that deserves respect or reverence. 3. An intense furious, and offer destructive action or force: vehement feeling or expression. 4. Improper or damaging alteration for

---

York: McGraw-Hill Book Company, (1967), p.690

50   M. B. Schepers, (ed.), *"Violence"* in the New Catholic Encyclopedia, p. 690

instance, as of the wording or the meaning of a text.[51]

According to E. Miller, liberation theologians have broadened the definition of violence to include the violence implicit in institutional and political forms such as colonialism and sexually defined role expectations. From this perspective, violence is an act or set of rules which denies humanity and assumes an overt active expressive, as physical violence. In a very subtle manner, violence may be implicit in different forms of oppression supported by stable governments that established structures in society. Some even say that there is a belief in violence in one's view of the future and attitude toward change. In this sense, there are two different understandings of violence. 1. For the person afraid of the future and a new definition of reality, violence is everything that disturbs or threatens the world and fear has built. For example, everything that trends to usher in the new moves toward changes, everything that opposes the structures that claim to be destined for eternity is violence. 2. However, for a person free to meet the future, violence has a totality different meaning." It is whatever denies him a future, whatever aborts his project to create a new tomorrow; the power keeps his prison of the futureless structures of a futureless world."[52] Violence is that which denies people the possibility of exercising their freedom.

3.2 Social Tangibility of Violence

When we talk of a culture of violence, we must remind ourselves about the social tangibility of the culture of violence. We walk about concrete and physical culture of violence anchored here and now in our concrete and physical environment. Violence, being exercised at the personal or the collective level, touches our self and affects those who are victims of

---

51   Website's New Encyclopedic Dictionary, p. 1163

52   D. Earl Miller, (ed.), *"Violence"* in the Dictionary of Pastoral Care and Counseling, (2005), p 1303-1305

the culture of violence. In its very physical reality, the culture of violence in the social context arises, when for example, cultural normative principles are in question and the political structure is experiencing drastic rapid change. Some argue that violence, in such contexts, expresses protest, often by groups within a society whose members feel inadequate represented in the political process and who feel discriminated against economically.

Some people believe that violence predictably increases in periods of social stress or transition and declines in periods of social stability. It is said for example, that Holland and Sears have shown that lynching increased during economic depressions and declined in periods of prosperity. Some state that "viewed individually or psychologically, violence coincides with the breakdown of social norms and changes in subgroup expectations."[53] Furthermore, some argue that alienation and anomie are consistent correlates of increases in collective violence.

3.3 Seven Theories of Violence

Violence is not limited to descriptions and definitions. Its meaning goes beyond descriptions and definitions. There are articles written by different writers in various encyclopedias which contain deep exploration and excavation of theories of violence. Therefore, below are theories of violence.

3.3.1 Relative Deprivation

E. Miller in his article entitled "Violence", has identified at least seven types of theories of violence. The first theory of violence… is "relative deprivation."[54] According to Merriam, the word theory has a lot of

---

53   Ibid
54   D. Earl Miller, (ed.), *"Violence"* in the Dictionary of Pastoral Care and

descriptions. From Greek, the root meaning is *theriōa,* from *therein.*' According to Merriam, it means: 1. Analysis of a set of facts in their relation to one another. 2. Abstract though; speculation. 3. The general or abstract principles of a body of fact. 4. Believe, policy, or procedure proposed or followed as the basis of action. 5. An ideal or hypothetical set of facts, principles, or circumstances often used in the phrase in theory. 6. A plausible or scientifically acceptable general principle or body of principles offered to explain phenomena. 7. The hypothesis assumed for argument or investigation. 8. A body of theorems presenting a concise systemic view of a subject."[55]

The relative deprivation theory is perhaps the most widely held view regarding the source of violence. Theory and collective violence result from perceived discrepancy between one's expectations and the social and political restraints within which one lives (valves capabilities). Thus, this collective theory of violence results from dissatisfaction, discontent, or frustration which one considers to be unjust and inequitable in concrete circumstances. This theory of collective violence is evaluated based on the situation in which one feels deprived.

It is evaluated based on the fact that often, this deprivation is experienced when one's social group gains economic benefits while other groups seem to stagnate. The theory of relative deprivation argues that advertising often plays a considerable role in indiscriminately raising the expectations of social groups while only selected populations may have the economic ability to purchase given goods and services. It is further confirmed that according to the relative deprivation hypothesis, violence expresses frustration because of holding unchangeable expectations. It may be concluded that if people did not feel deprived, they would not be discontent.

Counseling, (2005), p 1303-1305

[55] Merriam Website's Collegiate Dictionary Eleventh Edition, p. 1296

3.3.2 Biological Interpretation of Instinctive Violence

The second interpretation explicates violence based on instinctual reactions. This theory is based on all living organisms having a natural instinctual reaction. For example, animals appear to be famous for instinctual reactions. This theory of instinctual reaction is exercised in the concrete practical situation that is, in the environment where living organisms live and control their territorial space. Some argue that threats to the personal territory which includes home or nation arouse in individuals aggressive-defensive violence. Numerous studies have been done with animals demonstrating that conditions of overcrowding generate violence, the parallel being extended to slum dwellings and affected urban environments.

According to V. Noordwijk, a relationship between organisms is found among them when they depend on the same food or resources. In such a situation, competition is the only means of survival among living organisms sharing the same territory. We do speak of competition as a limiting factor where violence can rise. Severe competition occurs, the strong competition is found between members of the same species. Such service competition requires that several types of behaviour have evolved to divide the available resources among them in the best way. For example, many animals show territorial behaviours which enable successful organisms to secure a certain area (territory) for themselves specifically for feeding or breeding. It is believed that birds mark these territories by singing; mammals often mark them by scent. An easy-to-study example of territorial behaviours is the rainbow lizard (agama) common on many buildings."[56] In this view, all these points are examples of niche differentiation, affirming that by the niche of organisms, we mean both the place where it lives and the functional role it plays

---

56   Meine Van Noordwijik, *Ecology Textbook for the Sudan*, Khartoum: Khartoum University Press, 1984, p 92

in the ecosystems, which means also the food it takes.

Some argue that living organisms can naturally avoid competition at least in four ways. 1. By developing a different hunting technique, catching different types of food; (e.g. the open-bill stork hunts for snails, while other storks hunt for fish). 2. By choosing a different micro-habit to live in and developing the appropriate adaptation; (e.g. the Nile Lechwe feeds on grass inside the swamps, while most other antelopes live outside the swamp). 3. By choosing a different time of day for activity (e.g. swallows catch flying insects during the day and the bats hunt for them at night in the same way). 4. By choosing a different season (time of year) for the main activity requiring food (e.g. reproduction) and adjusting the life cycle;(e.g. several dragonflies survive during the dry season as adults and breed just after the first rains; other species survive the dry season in the mud as larvae and breed later).

3.3.3 Egoistic Theory of Culture of Violence

The third view of the cause of the culture of violence is more on theological and philosophical premises in chapter one. In chapter one, we discussed T. Hobbes's doctrine as following the biological theory of instinctive reaction. It is believed that humankind is inherently evil and self-interested. E. Miller concurs with T. Hobbes "Except for the existence of coerces institutions such as the state, men and woman would plunder, rob, and violate each other indiscriminately."[57] T. Hobbes asserts there are three principal causes of quarrel among men and these are: competition, difference (mistrust), and glory.

World War I in 1914-1918 which had led to the death of 16 million people and World War II initiated by Dictator Adolf Hitler of German Nazis is fitting in the theory of egoistic urges to conquer Poland. A

---

57   D. Earl Miller, (ed.), *"Violence"* in the Dictionary of Pastoral Care and Counseling, (2005), p 1303-1305

country being recognized continentally as a nation, Adolf Hitler occupied it by force. With such an attempt, World War II broke out between Allis and Axis in which the Allies won the war in 1945-1963. This is considered the bloodiest war which that had led to the death of 40,000,000 -50,000,000 people. It was the war in which the United States used atomic bombs against Japan, leading to the death of 700, 000 in Hiroshima. The war which led to the death of 6,000,000 Jews was prompted by egoistic urges to control Poland.

It is confirmed that a stable social order emerges as to protective self-interest, not humankind's good nature. In this own view, E. Miller states that in Christian theology, violence is a product of the fall of mankind but the human proclivity toward evil is a widely held perception. He says, for example, Freud believed that the masses would destroy each other except for their fear of divine retribution or civil restraint.

3.3.4 Calculative Rational Theory of Culture of Violence

The fourth view on the calculative rational theory of culture of violence is rooted in social learning theory. This theory believes that individuals observe that strategically create violence which enables them to arrive at specific goals. It is asserted that thus, violence is rationally enacted as one pursues particular ends. This fourth view on the calculative rational theory of culture of violence affirms that violence is not an irrational or instinctual response in that an individual may be very calculative about rewards and punishments before performing a violent act. Miller states "In short, violence is viewed as a means to a specific end."[58]

This calculative rational theory of culture of violence seems to be the most common practice theory in our daily lives. Both personal and collective violence which fall under this theory are to be considered

---

58   D. Earl Miller, (ed.), *"Violence"* in the Dictionary of Pastoral Care and Counseling, (2005), p 1303-1305

mortal sins. This is because the agent studies, makes assessment, calculate the benefit, and gains and uses dirty means to achieve his/her goal or end. Therefore, all criminal activities fall under this category of a calculative rational theory of culture of violence. For example, all activity of robberies, snatching someone's phone, confiscating somebody's property and rape is to be well calculated by the agent for his/her benefit. Let us observe in our daily life to see how this calculative rational theory of culture of violence can be seen when we exercise "decision-making" to make sure that every decision must benefit us, for our gain and to achieve our personal goals.\

3.3.5 Frustration Reduction Theory of Culture of Violence

The discussed above theories are mutually exclusive but to some extent, they may complement each other in the sense that each theory discussed contains a toxin of violence. Some suggested that aggressive behaviour may reduce one's level of frustration or anger. According to this frustration reduction theory of the culture of violence, it is believed that "if one attacks, what one perceives to be the source of one's problems or some symbolic representative of it, then one may experience a reduction in the level of one's hostility even if one's attack does not make a substantial change in the circumstances causing the frustration."[59]

Given this frustration reduction theory of a culture of violence, it is believed that occasionally, the object of attack may serve as a scapegoat for frustrations that stem from a different source. For example, a wife is beaten by her husband, and she beats the children or a child is beaten by her mother and the child beats the dog. This theory operates to release tension and frustration. The name frustration reduction theory of culture of violence is fitting. Just let us observe in our contemporary

---

59   Ibid

society how this frustration reduction theory of culture of violence operates and has made others become victims of violence out of nothing. Have you ever become a scapegoat in your life? Have you ever experienced someone pouring violence on you for no reason at all? In those occasions, please, recall this frustration reduction theory of culture of violence. Or for example, what will you say when you see someone beating a pillow or a mattress or seeing somebody boxing on the air?

3.3.6 Cultural Conditioning Theory of Culture of Violence

The sixth theory namely, the cultural conditioning theory of culture of violence, believes that violence always occurs within a given cultural context of "values and norms." The sixth theory emphasizes that cultural values and normative principles related to belief, are to be respected otherwise, violating them will erupt into violence. Some say that beliefs of a religious or secular nature, play an enormous role in determining whether violence is justified, in what circumstances, and for what ends. It is asserted that "violence may be prescribed in all circumstances, as many sectarians, for example, held or its use may be carefully stipulated as belonging to the police or military."[60]

Some argue that these are culturally conditioned values and vary from culture to culture and subculture to subculture. Values are rooted in the belief systems related to the cosmological and historical myths of the people. According to this view, violence is legitimated and inspired according to the mythically based view of superiority and subordination, traditionally having affected women and racial minorities. For example, that is the case of altruistic suicide. With this cultural conditioning theory of the culture of violence, within the serves values and ideas are defended. Violence is respected and even rewarded, it

---

60   D. Earl Miller, (ed.), *"Violence"* in the Dictionary of Pastoral Care and Counseling, (2005), p 1303-1305

is performed by a legitimate authority or if justifiable according to publically approved goals.

3.3.7 Violence for Social Change

Historically, violence often accompanied concrete social change. For example, 'that revolutionary marks the history of every nation, as do revolts, strikes, and riots.' According to this belief, as expectations are raised through increased literacy, introduction of modernizing ideologies (missionaries being not infrequent source) programs of reform (especially those which are announced but not enacted), and including new elements within the political process, violence is often the instrument which forces those protecting tradition and personal self-interest to change. Such violence like riots, terrorism, and collective acts of culture of violence are to be communicative expressions whose goals need not be explained as wanton destruction, but as statements of subgroup plight of redress of grievances. "Violence is seldom the first attempt to articulate a concern; rather, it is more often born of desperation, a feeling that all other avenues of communication have failed."[61]

Conclusion

Chapter three elaborates and presents a conceptual analysis of the culture of violence and its social tangibility. Further, it has also presented the seven theories of the cause of culture of violence such as; relative deprivation, biological interpretation of instinctive violence, egoistic theory of culture of violence, calculative rational theory of culture of violence, frustration reduction theory of culture of violence, cultural conditioning theory of culture of violence and finally, violence and social change.

---

61   Ibid. p1303-1305

Chapter Four:
Sin as Culture of Death

Introduction

This chapter presents the general concept of sin, the nature and features of sin, and the definition of sin. It discusses two kinds of sins, the mortal and venial sins. It further examines three elements of mortal sin that is, matter, awareness and consent. This chapter also discusses seven capital sins and the causes of sin such as internal and external or remote causes. Finally, it presents the criteria for judging sin by moralists.

4. General Concept of Sin

When we talk about sin, we must remember as St. T. Aquinas argues "As a consequence of original sin our intellects are darkest, our wills weakened, and we are left with a strong inclination to sin."[62] In dealing with this disgraceful situation of sin foremost, our basic understanding of sin should come from the concept of original sin committed by our first parents, Adam and Eve. This sin of our first parents, as Richard

---

62   St. Thomas Aquinas, *Summa Theologica:* first Complete African Edition, Vol. 3. Benziger Brothers, inc. 1948, p. 3493

defines it "Original sin is the state or condition in which because of the sin of Adam and Eve, all human person is born."[63] Some state that even though our first parents denied the responsibility for the sin which they have committed, nevertheless, God held them responsible for it. Some argue that "Most theological discussions on sin have concentrated on original sin or sin,*the causal connection between Adam's first actual sin and our subsequent sin or sins."[64] One cannot avoid being responsible when one sins as St. T. Aquinas points out "the giving in" to this inclination constitutes actual sin, a sin for which we are directly responsible. Therefore, our actual sin can be both mortal and venial. When we sin, two things do occur in the very nature of sin: the first nature of sin is the voluntary act and its inordinateness which consists in departing from God's law. Based on this argument, sin has to proceed from the will, for man must be accountable before guilt may be imputed to him for instance, nobody can be accountable if he/she commits adultery in a dream unless it has been premeditated and contemplated with a clear picture of a specific woman being entertained before the actual sleep takes place.

Second, in sinning, there are essential things we need to consider: first, the thought, word, or deed not following God's law. As T, Aquinas fittingly divides the sins into thoughts, words or deeds: the beginning of sin is its foundation in the sin of thought: the second degree is the sin of word, in so far as man is ready to break out into a declaration of his though; while the third degree consists in consummating deed... for the angry man is first disturbed in thought; then he thoughts or (and) words are sinful without the deed following. Yet, the sin of thought

---

63 Richard McBrien, *Catholicism,* (ed.) Catholicism, London: Geoffrey Chapman, 1994, p. 184. The term has two references: the initial. "Originating" Sin of Adam and Eve (pecatum originale originans), and the subsequent "origininated" universality of human sin (pecatum originate originatum).

64 James F. Childress and John Macquarrie (ed.) *A New Dictionary of Christian Ethic,* SCM press, 1986, p. 585.

and words is not distinct from the sin of deed when united with it, but when each is found by itself.[65]

To make a contradistinction between mortal and venial sin, first T. Aquinas prioritizes the principle of the last end towards which the entire moral order gears. Therefore, some say that all men's actions are measured by closeness or lack of closeness to the source of heat. It is further asserted that "therefore, when the soul is so disordered by sin as to turn away from its last end, namely God, to whom it is united by charity, then there is a mortal sin; but when it is disordered without turning away from God, there is venial sin"[66]

According to H. Peschke, man is bound to strive after the ultimate end and not to offend in any of his actions against it. Some even argue that man acts badly if he disregards the obligations of the moral law and the commands of his conscience, which ensure the attainment of this end.

Therefore, disregard for moral law and the command of conscience are factors that amount to bad human acts as sin. If he freely and willfully infringes the moral law, which is understood in the wider sense that includes those personal obligations which result from a strictly individual call, this can be a mortal sin. Biblical and Christian thinking considers God as the author of the moral law; the disregard of the moral law is always simultaneously an offence against God. It is confirmed that "From this point of view sin can be described as disobedience against God's will and as an offence against him."[67] The gravity of sin according to this view, sin can be described as the infringement freely willed. i.e., it must occur knowingly and with free consent. Some state that, only then is wrongdoing a formal, imputable sin. This is called "formal breaking"

---

[65] Cf. St. Thomas Aquinas, *Summa Theologica*, p. 3493

[66] Ibid

[67] Karl H. Peschke, *Christian Ethics: Moral theology in the light of Vatican II, Vol. 1*, General Moral theology, Alcester, C. Goodlife Neale Ltd, 1986, p. 286

of the moral law and commands conscience. The material breaking of the moral law and commands conscience according to this belief, can be described as "An unintentional, involuntary offence against the moral law which is not sufficient to constitute a subjective, imputable sin."[68]

On the same area of culture of death by saying that though modern men know sin which is noticeable, however, where faith in God as a creator and redeemer vanishes, the awareness of sin as a disobedience against him must vanish. Other factors constitute to rejection of sin, where the autonomous man becomes the "measure of all things and consequently sin as an offence against a superior, divine authority is irrelevant. Still more facts constitute to rejection of sin and moral fault as the absorbing force of the anonymous masses, the determinists theory of certain psychoanalytic schools or revolt against morality which rightly or wrongly is rejected as too narrow-minded and too rigorous.

On the one hand, other positive factors of the culture of life constitute the realization of sin as an evil in the heart of men. Wrongdoing and human malice are obvious phenomena and man is anguished by evil and its terrifying power, the misery of sin and guilt occupies a large place in modern literature and philosophy, which trace human wretchedness, depravity and malice down to their most secret roots and unmask their intrigues in the conscious and unconscious depths of the human soul. It is said that another positive factor which constitutes the sense of moral offence and injustice is the sense of alertness for personal and social responsibility. It is even argued that Christianity is opposed to the unhealthy illusion of innocence that has become as widespread in contemporary society and to the practice of attributing guilt and failure if their presence is acknowledged at all to other and other…"We attribute success and victories to ourselves, but for the rest, we cultivate the art of denying our human conditions and are always in

---

68   Karl H. Peschke, *Christian Ethics*, p. 286

search of new alibi."[69] Furthermore, it is believed that change of heart and healing is possible only through honest recognition and admission of guilt which is the culture of life.

4.1 The Nature and Features of Sin

Sin has a double concept: first, it demonstrates disobedience towards God and second, it corrupts humans. Sin manifests itself as the distortedness or wrongness of human history it affects all humanity to participate in it. Its origin can be traced back specifically to our first parents aiming for self-determination (one of the seven spiritual capital sins, Pride) that ended with tragic results (original sin). The human predicament is firstly centrally and primarily a condition of sin that contains at least these four features as Hunter argues:

1. The problem of humans is determined by God, the transcendent, righteous Creator. When humans do not live from or are centred in the Creator, they invariable develop idolatrous or absolute relations to the world. 2. These idolatrous relations have disastrously distortive effects on the human. They invaded and corrupted reason, the emotions, the community, language, and embodiment. These effects concern moral experience because they disrupt the conditions and ways of being normatively and communally human and because they promote acts of voluntary human self-interest. 4. The effects of the idolatrous transformation accumulate not merely in the individual self-endures. 5. Because sin reaches and corrupts the deepest realities of human history and society, the human as we know, is formed in that corruption. Hence, sin is bondage which influences the will and an act is promoted by the will.[70] This is well explained by Hunter who asserts:

---

69 Karl H. Peschke, *Christian Ethics*, p. 287

70 Rodney J. Hunter (ed.), *Dictionary of Pastoral Care and counseling, Expanded Edition*, Abingdon press, 2005, p. 1173- 1174

Two issues were especially prominent and both obtained expressions weighted more on the Hellenistic than the Christian side. According to the first, human is radical slavery, universally and unavoidably present in all human history, it owes its origins to the ignorance, weakness, and miseries which constitute human finitude. In this Manichaean formulation, sin is only a mask for the deeper problem of finitude itself. According to the second, sin is a matter of human freedom and responsibility and there is nothing inevitable about it. In this Pelagian interpretation, sin is always a willful act, hence it is misleading to think of it as bondage.[71]

Sin has characteristics of the mark, and disguise, covering itself under the aspect of what is good. As Patricia and Paul claim, Heather King before her conversion..."narrative as testifies, often when we sin we do not seek to harm; rather, we pursue something that we (mistakenly) judge to be good or we seek good things but in the wrong ways"[72] sin also is closely related to the feeling of the sense of guilt. Moral guilt and sin signify the same nature, though under different aspects. Sin does involve moral guilt. Moral guilt and moral guilt always imply sin. Therefore, both moral guilt and sin exist together. On the one hand, sin is an offence against God while guilt signifies that a person is liable for the evil has done and that it is attributed to him/her as responsible against the agent. But guilt feeling can be differentiating from moral guilt as Peschke argues in his assertion that:

Moral guilt must be distinguished from guilt feelings. Depth psychology has called attention to this. Guilt feelings can also result

---

71 Rodney J. Hunter (ed.), *Dictionary of Pastoral Care and Counseling*, p. 1174

72 Patricia Lamoureux and Paul J. Wadell, *The Christian Moral Life: Faithful Discipleship for a Global Society*, Bangalore: Theological Publication India, 2011, p.88

from unwarranted prohibitions of the superego, resulting in wrong education and social taboos, or morbid psyche dispositions. They are therefore not unequivocal signs of moral offences. On the other hand, not every feeling of guilt is morbid. The more tender a person's conscience the more readily will react with guilt feelings at a person's sin. But not, every moral guilt comes with guilt feelings, especially if a person's conscience is dull. This, however, could hardly be elevated to an ideal. To this extent guilty feelings are irrational, they call for treatment ideal. To this here psychotherapy has a genuine task. But authentic guilt feelings have a positive function, and cannot be the aim of psychotherapy also to eliminate them.[73]

4.2 Definition of Sin

According to the Hebrew language, there is no exact word for sin, which can have the same meaning as theological sin. This is because Hebrew uses various words for sin and each word, has a profane use to signify sin. In Hebrew language, the word commonly translated sin is het'; *hatta't* lit like the Greek *hamaritia* the verb means "to miss the mark." Here it signifies not only merely an intellectual error in judgment but a failure to attain a goal. King Hezekiah uses the word sin in the sense of rebellion against his Assyrian overland (cf. Kg 18:14). It is also used with breach of an agreement between nations and people; for example, Jephthah denies that Israel has sinned by aggression (cf. Kg 11:27). Therefore, sin is described as failure of an interior to fulfil his obligations, (Gen 31:36; 42:22) or of the host to fulfil his duty of hospitality (Gen 20:9). Based on these descriptions, J. Pedersen remarks that "the kernel of sin is a breach of the covenant… the basic meaning of the miss the mark," failure to achieve an objective, that sin is a

---

73   Karl H. Peschke, *Christian Ethics*, p. 288

non-action.⁷⁴ Sin can also be defined as "Any word or deed or thought against eternal law."⁷⁵ The Catechism of the Catholic Church (CCC) defines sin as an offence against reason, truth, and right conscience; it is a failure in genuine love for God and neighbour caused by a perverse attachment to certain good.⁷⁶

According to T. Aquinas "A sin is a human act (it is, a deliberate thought, word, deed, desire and omission) contrary to right reason, and therefore contrary to God."⁷⁷ It also distinguishes vice from sin by arguing that "Vice is contrary to order and reason; it is opposed to the rational nature of man."⁷⁸ According to the Greeks, "Sin was an error, and ignorance or a foolishness, by which a person harms himself."⁷⁹

---

74   John L. McKenzie, SJ, *Dictionary of the Bible*, New York, 1965, p. 817

75   James F. Childress and John Macquarrie (ed.) *New Dictionary of Christian Ethics*, SCM press ltd, 1967, p. 585.

76   *The Catechism of the Catholic Church*, p. 406. It wounds the nature of man and injures human solidarity. It has been defined as "utterance, a deed or a desire contrary to the natural law. Sin is an offence against God: Against you alone, have I sinned, and done that which is evil in your sight. Sin set itself against God's love for us and turns our hearts away from it. Like the first sin, it is disobedience a revolt against God through the will to become "like gods," knowing and determining good and evil.

77   Cf. Paul J. Glenn, *A Tour of the Summa of St. Thomas Aquinas*, p. 151. A vice is a habit of sin. Vice is a morally bad habit: it stands contrasted with virtue which is morally good habit. A sin, which is a vicious act, is contrasted with a virtuous act, that is, a morally good act. In itself, a bad act is worse than a bad habit: for a bad act is deed done, whereas a bad is only stable disposition to commit bad deeds.

78   Karl H. Peschke, *Christian Ethics*, p. 288

79   Ron Highfield *"The Freedom to say "No"? Karl Rahner's Doctrine of Sin"* Pepperdine University, California, Theological Studies 55, (1995) 485-505. Human freedom is so radical and comprehensive, he argues, that it makes even God an object of choice, a choice which brings the human being to definitive completion as a "yes" or "no" to God. Modern people, however, find this claim incomprehensible, observes Raher, for it is difficult to imagine any human being uttering such a titanic "no" to God.

Highfields states that sin in its essence is a free and definitive "no" to God, a rejection of God's gracious offer of self-communication."[80] According to J. Gründel, sin is an act that is the free decision of the whole personality against the will of God as manifested in the orders of nature and grace and verbal revelation; it presupposes knowledge, free consent, and grave matter.[81]

4.4 Two Kinds of Sin

The two basic species of sins opposed to divine natural law are: mortal and venial. A mortal sin is the one which deprives the soul of the sanctifying grace and makes it deserving of hell. A venial sin does not produce these serious effects, although it weakens the action of grace in man and makes him deserving of temporal punishment.[82] The Catechism of the Catholic Church identifies the gravity of sin such as mortal and venial sin: first, mortal sin, destroys charity in the heart of a man by a grave violation of God's law; it turns man away from God, who is his ultimate end and his beatitude, by preferring an interior good to him, while venial sin allows charity to subsist, even though it offends and wounds it. Second, mortal sin, by distorting the vital principle within us- charity- necessitates a new initiative of God's mercy and conversion of the heart normally accomplished within setting the sacrament of reconciliation. As the Catechism of the Catholic Church asserts:

When the sets itself upon something that is of its nature incompatible with the charity that orients man towards his ultimate end. Then the sin is mortal by its very object...whether it contradicts the love of

---

[80] J. Gründel, *"Sins, Seven Deadly"* in the Concise Dictionary of Christian Ethics, Bernhard Stoeckle (ed.) London: Burns & Oates, 1979, (229-229), p. 229

[81] Pietro Palazzini (ed.), *Dictionary of Moral Theology*, the Newman press, 1962, p. 1134.

[82] Pietro Palazzini, (ed.), *Dictionary of Moral Theology*, the Newman press, 1962, p. 1134.

God, such as blasphemy or perjury, or the love of neighbour, such as homicide or adultery... but when the sinner's will is set upon something that of its nature involves a disorder but is not opposed to the love of God and neighbour, such as thoughtless chatter or immoderate laughter and like sins are venial.[83]

According to Patricia and Paul, "As the word suggests, mortal sin refers to actions habits and ways of being that bring death to our relationship with God, death of our relationships with others, and death to our souls and spirits."[84] Patricia and Paul claim that:

> There are acts, but especially habits and ways of being, whose cumulative effects are so morally and spiritually corrupting that they permanently separate us from our true good and turn us toward evil as if were our good. Mortal sin reminds us to take evil seriously. It calls our attention to habits of being and acting toxic for our souls. And it reminds us that if we give ourselves over evil, it will ruin us. At its most extreme, to settle into a state of deadly sin is to be so habitually given over to evil it is difficult for us not to do what is wrong. Not that we have lost our freedom to sin, but that we have so consistently misused it that we cannot, without grace, redirect it to the good. To speak of mortal or deadly sin to recognize that we can live "contrary to our nature" or " contrary to reason" for so long that from the innermost centre of our lives, we regularly choose evil over good exactly because evil has become our good.[85]

---

83   *Catechism of the Catholic Church*, no. 407.

84   Patricia Lamoureux and Paul J. Wadell, *The Christian Moral Life: Faithful Disciple*, p. 88

85   Patricia Lamoureux and Paul J. Wadell, p. 88-89

4.5 Three Elements of Mortal Sin

The Church's Magisterium asserts there are three elements of mortal sin. These three elements of mortal sin play a greater role when it comes to the judgment of human acts besides 'intention' 'acts' and 'object.' These elements of mortal sin determine the gravity of sin being committed by an individual.

4.5.1 Matter

A mortal sin consists of three important elements that qualify it to be mortal. The first element of mortal sin is that it should be a serious matter; the second element there should be sufficient awareness and the final element is that it should be carried out with full consent. Intention, object, and circumstance in human acts are the source of morality.

Matter, it is difficult to lay down a universal norm for determining its seriousness. Moralists limit themselves, to formulation it for individual commandments or sin. It may be noted, however, that certain violations always imply serious matter, but in others the matter may be serious or light, depending on the greater on the lest quantity involved.[86]

T. Aquinas has almost identified four elements for mortal sin to be a grave matter: first, a substantial violation of the natural law constitutes grave matter. According to him, the natural law regards the essential order, which one has to keep about God, oneself, and one's neighbour. What also substantially violates the natural as T. Aquinas argues "about the natural law."[87] This is seen when suicide occurs. This should be a

---

86 Pietro Palazzini, p. 1135

87 Cf. Thomas Pazhayampallil, (ed.), *Pastoral Guide: Fundamental Moral theology and Virtues,* Vol. 295. Secondly, we must stay that those objects constitutes grave matter which Scripture style as abominable and for which which one is excluded from the kingdom of God or fro which one deserves death, hell fire, etc. Example, if one oppresses the poor and commits robbery. Thirdly, those actions

direct violation of the principle of theological pillars which the matter must be judged not only on the object of the law but also on the end and circumstances that need to be considered.

4.5.2 Awareness

For any possible consideration of passing a judgment, a great amount of awareness is needed in the sense of intention involving no reflex action or long meditation. All that is required is attention that a normal individual, who is not distracted, employs in carrying out matters of ordinary importance.[88] It does not call for explicit intention to offend God. This awareness is always implicit in the conscience of anyone who adverts to the immorally of his action.

4.5.3 Consent

Consent is full if given with that ordinary liberty that we have when we are still exercising control over decisions, though we may be under the impulse of some passion.[89] This third element is often characterized by difficulty when one wants to establish especially if it involves a case of internal sins or sins involving a passion. The habitual dispositions of the individual, along with the circumstances surrounding the situation, will help us to arrive at a judgment with the greatest probability of being close to the truth.[90]

---

should be considered grave sinful which are punished by the church. Finally, when a unanimous opinion of the fathers and theologians of the church says that something constitutes grave matter; it is to be considered.

88	Pietro Palazzini, (ed.) *Dictionary of Moral Theology*, p. 1135.
89	Ibid.
90	Ibid.

4.6 Seven Capital Sins

The word capital sin is…"applied to sins to which man's fallen nature is more inclined and which are the source of other faults"[91] The name capital does not exactly, mean that each capital sin are mortal sin, however, sometimes the term capital sins are applied to tendencies toward sin; in this sense, we could speak of capital defects or vices. T. Aquinas quotes St. Gregory regarding the capital sin and states that:

Of the seven capital sins, five are spiritual and two are carnal. He is concerned with the distinction between the capital sins, not so much with the reason they are called capital. Sin is an inordinate desire for some created good; the possession of this gives inordinate pleasure. Pleasure is twofold: spiritual as when one takes pleasure in praise; and carnal as in bodily touch. Of the capital sins, five are spiritual: pride, covetousness, anger, envy and sloth: two are carnal; gluttony and lust. Those sins which consist in spiritual pleasure are called spiritual sins; while those consist in carnal pleasure, are called carnal sins, e.g. gluttony, which consists in the pleasure of the table; and lust which consists in sexual pleasure."[92]

St. Paul's letter to the Galatians demonstrates and articulates clearly the contra distribution between seven capital sins into works of flesh and fruit of the spirit. According to him, the works of the flesh are distinctively obvious immorality, impurity, licentiousness, idolatry, sorcery, hatred, rivalry, jealousy, outbursts of fury, act of selfishness, dissension, factions, and occasions of envy, drinking bouts, orgies and like. I warn you, as I warned you before, that those who do such things will not inherit the kingdom of God. The fruits of the spiritual are love, joy, peace, patience, kindness, generosity, faithfulness, gentleness, and self-control. Against such, there is no law (Cf. Gal 5: 19-23).

---

91 Pietro Palazzini, p. 1135.
92 St. Thomas Aquinas, *Summa Theologica*, p. 3493.

4.7 Causes of Sin

According to the teaching of the Church, there are various causes of sin. These various causes of sin demonstrate sin itself. Therefore, no one can ignore those causes of sin but everyone must pay attention to them otherwise.

4.7.1 Internal Causes

Internal causes may be referred to as egoistic selfish love. This is the basic source and principal cause of every sin and it is embedded in the soul, this egoistic selfish love is at the same time guided by three important elements: ignorance, concupiscence, and malice. Insofar, as one element may prevail on the others and exercise a particular influence in determining the commission of a sin, we have sins of ignorance, concupiscence, or malice.[93] P. Palazzini identified the following internal causes: first, sins of ignorance, the error which causes sinful acts, concerns not only the practical judgment on the opportunism but also the speculative knowledge that should be posed, second, sins of concupiscence have their source in the passions; the sins of malice is rooted in the perversity of the will. P. Palazzini concludes that the latter types are more dangerous sins than the former because they are more deliberate and persist more stubbornly in the soul.

4.7.2 External (Remote Causes)

External or remote causes along with internal causes, we have to consider external and indirect causes, such as the devil, scandal, and cooperation; or remote causes, such as habits, and loss of grace. The causality of the capital sins (pride, avarice, lust, gluttony, anger, envy, sloth) is remote;

---

93 Pietro Palazzini, p. 1135.

they derive their names not from being more serious than other sins, but from the fact that they are more likely to stimulate the appetite and thus more easily dispose and induce the will to committing other sins.[94]

4.8 Criteria for Judging Sin by Moralists

From the general rule to the particular rules used to determine the species of sins, moralists usually use the criterion of virtues because it is easier to grasp.[95] They continue to argue that acts constitute sins of different moral species if they are opposed: (a) to different virtues, or the same virtue but so it is (b) contrary, (c) or simply different.

Conclusion

Chapter four presents the general concept of sin, the nature and features of sin, and the definition of sin. It has elaborated and discussed two kinds of sins, mortal and venial sins, and three elements of mortal sin that is, matter, awareness and consent. The chapter has also discussed seven capital sins, and causes of sin such as internal and external or remote causes. Finally, it has presented criteria used for judging sins by moralists.

---

94 Ibid.
95 Ibid, p. 1136.

Chapter Five:
Freedom as a Culture of Life and Culture of Death

Introduction

Chapter five presents the definition of freedom, freedom as a personal responsibility, education to freedom, and restriction of freedom. It also briefly discusses grace as a culture of life and its general understanding of salvation. It presents its root meaning in the Greek language as "*charis*" which means divine gift or favour.

5. General Concept of Human Freedom

Freedom involves the possibility of undisturbed self-development and realization. But freedom is never unconditioned and unconditional because it survives through many challenges of life. Freedom is defined as the "absence of interference or impediment.[96] It is claimed that the ideas which are attached to freedom almost touch every aspect of its

---

96   Iain Mclean and Alistair McMillan, (ed.), *Oxford Concise Dictionary of Politics,* New York: Oxford University Press, 2003.

characterization as controversial. It is further argued that any controversial; dispute about freedom arises from three terms: 1. The disputes about freedom may refer to the agent, (specifically moral agent that involves: intelligence, will and free will), the obstacle, and the action or state to be achieved respectively. 2. Essentially, freedom has to do with a person's ability to do something and his/her freedom to do it. Therefore, it follows that ability is a condition of freedom. Here, ability and capacity are being referred more or less to physical regarding this respect of the conception of freedom. 3. Again, freedom can be defined as "the ability to affirm one's being despite all personal and material states and occurrences."[97]

B. Stockle has made two distinctions about first, traditionally, freedom was freedom of will or volition and action. In this idea, it presents the essential condition for the possibility of the very phenomenon of morality (responsibility and accountability). Whereas freedom of action means the possibility of making unfettered free decisions. Then freedom of will or volitional freedom is understood as the capability and ability of the will to act freely in an actual situation with several possible motives values or possibilities of action. Or self-determination without compulsion from outside.

5.1 Freedom as Personal Responsibility

B. Stockle argues that "freedom of action is grounded in the freedom of the will, and thus, brings into question the total personal and existential freedom of the human being."[98] Self- determination of the

---

[97] Bernhard Stockle (ed.) *Concise Dictionary of Christian Ethics,* London: Burn and Qates, 1979, p. 107.

[98] Bernhard Stockle (ed.) *Concise Dictionary of Christian Ethics,* London: Burn and Qates, 1979, p. 108. In this way, the individual always attains to a new existential stance: free decisions are among the prerequisites of any future decisions. Self-determination comes in here. But it is also a question of the surrender of

will does imply self-determination of the person. Freedom involves personal decision-making which according to B. Stokcle, "Free decisions are also decisions about one's nature and existence in the sense of personally responsible and conscious direction to what has been recognized as being morally valuable and appropriate, and what is therefore, striven for as such. Furthermore, N. Tripathi claims that "the progress of mankind has been achieved by seeking liberation from all kinds of bondage, and by overcoming all kinds of limitations."[99] some argue that the whole history of human civilization shows this assertion of the spirit of freedom in all areas of human endeavours such as in social, economic and political arrangements; in art and literature; in pure ideas and philosophies; in science and technology; in religious and spiritual movements.

Human freedom is not a selfish individualistic entity but it strongly involves social dimensions. As a common saying, "no man is an island." Therefore, humans will always find himself/herself next to his/her neighbour. To gain and preserve individual freedom, man needs in all stages of his life a basic orientation from others.[100] A human in his/her own

---

freedom in the very pursuit of freedom. This kind of free self-determination enables the individual to attain increasingly to a total freedom by growing in self-possession and reducing alien influence and susceptibility. This is anthropologically significant, since in the course of his personal history man forms himself: man is open to self and is not there, ready made from the start. The history of man's self-formation is the history of his freedom. It is the history of a freedom which is open to self and which realized self.

99   A. N. Tripathi, (ed.) *Human Values*, New Delhi, New Age international, (P) Limited Publisher, 2009, p. 191

100   Bernhard Stockle (ed.) *Concise Dictionary of Christian Ethics*, London: Burn and Qates, 1979, p. 109. Because of its social dimension, freedom also has a major political function. This consist above all of the fact that freedom is not restricted to the realm of thought (when it would become ineffective in the real world), but has to exercise an emancipator and critical form of control in regard to all human alienation, and all forms of freedom). True freedom is also against

freedom needs, true education, work, language, sex, and so on for his/her survival.

5.2 Education to Freedom

Since man is not a ready-made material, therefore, there is an urgent need to educate him. Education to his freedom should focus on the following: potential drives, strengths, weaknesses, external influences and how to counteract his challenging situations. Human needs education to discern, to appropriate the knowledge of moral values to acquire knowledge and to behave appropriately. B. Stockle claims that the form of education to freedom is opposed to all authoritarianism and is one prerequisite of human maturity and training for freedom that also includes awareness of those laws which govern group training and group behaviour.

5.3 Limits of Human Freedom

The restriction of freedom does include both individual and social levels. At the individual level of freedom, it ranks from personal difficulties and psychological deficits: Physical defect, depression, scrupulosity, excessive guilt, loneliness, and drug or other forms of addiction and all those compulsions and impulses which lie in the human psyche or can be traced to social causations: environmental imprinting, uncaring, and unloving upbringing and so on. At the social level, social restriction

---

the use of quite feasible technology of the laws of behavior intended on the basis of subtle knowledge of the laws governing behaviors to programme and in the end repressively to control that behavior. Freedom also is a political corrective role for man is subject to a number of social role and institutions in public and in private life. The requirement if freedom is nowadays of demand too for a certain distance-critical distance-in regard to roles and institutions (on the presupposition of full awareness of course, of course, of the task they imply).

of freedom includes any external compulsion, whether direct (threat, punishment, aggressions, repression of opinion using subtle means of repression whether in the media or elsewhere, dependence, or indirect, evil political structures and disadvantage of minorities. Exercising human freedom is limited to options and opportunities at his disposal. Therefore, there are other options and opportunities not at his disposal. For example, if he is born short, he remains short, if he is born tall, he remains tall.

There is also a theological significance of freedom. The access to self-determination which determines the history of human existence is not a human creation but an experience by man as given.[101] Humanity looks back at his/her history of freedom that traces its origin back to God as a Creator. Human freedom is a gift from God himself. The history of human freedom consists of many failures as a result of continuous disobedience to God's will. The Jewish people believe in this awareness which has led to the etiological determination of a general subjection of all men to original guilt or original sin, which disturbs if not destroys the human capacity for freedom.[102] Humanity needs to use freedom according to the commandments set before him/her by God. St. John Paul II expresses it in his Encyclical letter: *Veritastis Splender* "Certainly people today have a particularly strong sense of freedom.[103]

---

101   Bernhard Stockle (ed.) *Concise Dictionary of Christian Ethics*, London: Burn and Qates, 1979, p. 111

102   Ibid

103   John Paul II, Encyclical letter, *Veritatis Slendor*, The Splendour of the Truth, p. 34-35, in AAS 85((1993), 1133-1228. As the council's Declaration on Religious freedom dignitatis Humanae had already observed. The dignity of the human person is a concern of which people of our time are becoming increasingly more aware. Hence the insistent demand that people be permitted to enjoy the use of their own responsibly judgment and freedom, and decided on their action on grounds of duty and conscience, without external pressure or coercion. In particular, the right to religious freedom and to respect for conscience on its journey towards the truth is increasingly perceived as the foundation of the cumulative rights of the

Human freedom should find its fulfilment in God's law as John Paul II, teaches "God's law does not reduce, much less do away with human freedom; rather, it protects and promotes that freedom.[104]

Cowan concurs with this phrase as he asserts:

> With this understanding, how are we to understand the foe and how God parotids us as a way of escape in the face of temptations to sin? It is not, as Himes argues, by giving us foe power of contrary choice at foe point of foe temptation, Rather, it is by enabling us to progressively develop the virtues-habits of character-that will, when acquired/ motivates us internally to make the right choices. Rather than enabling us to make choices "regardless of (our) current value scale," foe very point that Paul seems to make is that we can avoid sin by working to acquire virtues that will naturally and inevitably lead to the right actions. Conversely, those who succumb to temptation are those who have failed to follow Paul's example of gently

---

person. The heightened sense of the dignity of the human person and of his or her uniqueness, and of the respect due to the journey of conscience, certainly represents one of the positive achievements of modern culture. This perception, authentic as it is, has been expressed in a number of more or less adequate ways, some of which however diverge from the truth about man as a creature and the image of God, the need to be corrected and purified in the light of faith.

104   John Paul II, Encyclical letter, *Veritatis Slpendor,* The splendor of the truth, p. 37-38. In contrast, however, some present-day cultural tendencies have given rise to several currents of thought in ethics which center upon an alleged conflict between freedom and law. These doctrines would grant to individuals or social groups the rights to determine what is good or evil. Human freedom would thus be able to "create values" and would enjoy a primary over truth, to the point that truth itself would be considered a creation of freedom. Freedom would thus lay claim to a moral autonomy which would actually amount to an absolute sovereignty.

pursuing acquire of such Hriues."[105]

But for us to understand the theological significance of human freedom, we need to cite three quotations from the Holy Scriptures, one from Genesis and two others from the New Testament. The three citations demonstrate and demarcate the limit of our freedom. As Jesus was starting on his way to Jerusalem, a man came running up to him, knelt and asked, "Good teacher, what must I do to inherit eternal life? (Mk 10:17-31-The Rich Man). "the Lord God commanded the man, saying, you may eat freely of every tree of the garden; but of the tree of the knowledge of good and evil, you shall not eat, for in the day you eat of it you shall die."(cf. Gen 2:17). "I am the vine; you are the branches." Remain in me, on the vine, do neither can you unless you remain in me. I am the vine, you are the branches if you remain in me and I in you, you will bear much fruit; apart from me, you can do nothing" (cf. Jn 15:4-5). If human freedom is understood in terms of freedom that would thus lay claim to a moral autonomy which would amount to an absolute sovereignty, as John Paul II expressed below in the Culture of Life:

That legislation in many countries, perhaps even departing from the moral principles of their constitutions, has determined not to punish these practices against life and even to make them altogether legal, is both a disturbing symptom and a significant cause of grave moral decline. Choices once unanimously considered criminal and rejected by the common moral sense are gradually becoming socially acceptable. Even certain sectors of the medical profession, which by its calling is directed to the defence and care of human life, are increasingly willing to carry out these acts against the person. In this way, the nature of the medical profession is distorted and contradicted and the dignity

---

105   Steven Cowan *"Does I Corinthians 10:13 imply Liberation freedom? A reply to Paul Himes"* JETS 55/4(2012)793-800

of those who practice it is degraded. In such a cultural and legislative situation, the serious demographic, social and family problems which weigh upon many of the world's peoples and which require responsible and effective attention from national and international bodies are left open to false and deceptive solutions, as opposed to the truth and the good of persons and nations. The result of this tragedy; the fact of the destruction is not only of so many human lives still to be born or in their final stage grave and disturbing, but no least grave and disturbing is that conscience itself, darkened by such widespread conditioning is finding it increasingly difficult to distinguish between good and evil in what concerns the basic value of human life[106]

5.4 Grace as Culture of Life

Etymologically, the word "grace" in the Greek language means "*charis*" and its religious usage means "divine gift" or favour. Thus grace can be described as a quality or power usually bestowed by God, a quality which could be exhibited by a mortal. Grace thus means the divine forgiveness of sin constituting the new creation, and it also means the power of God communicated to those who enter upon the new life of faith, hope and love[107] Grace is also defined as… a quality which makes a person amiable; also benevolence inspired by amiableness, or a favour done out of benevolence, or even gratitude for such a favour.[108] In theological language, it designates a gratuitous gift of God to an

---

106   Cf. Mark 10:17-31, the Rich man). "Why do you call me good? Jesus asked "only God is truly good."19 But to answer your question, you know the commandments: 'You must not murder. You must not commit adultery. You must not steal. You must not testify falsely. You must not cheat anyone; Honor your father and mother.

107   John Paul II, *Encyclical Letter: Evangelium Vitae, The Gospel of Life*, p. 8

108   John Macquarie (ed.) *Dictionary of Christian Ethic*, Philadelphia, The Westminster press, 1967, p. 139.

intelligent creature to effect his sanctification and the attainments of external life.[109]

Looking back at the historical background of grace up to the Second Vatican Council, where theology of race does reflect the general range of the word grace. For God's grace to restore original human freedom intoxicated by sin. Three categories of the usage of the word "grace." According to this view, first, grace to some extent refers to God's loving kindness. Second, grace refers to God's favour toward humans. Third, God's gifts themselves are referred to as graces and the thanks that fill the hearts of those who appreciate God's love and God's gift. These same three meanings of the Latin word gratia were singled out in the nineteenth century by T. Aquinas as the most important for theology.[110] The three theological concepts of grace are trying to summarize God's relationships with humans with special attention to the fact these relations of love, generosity and freedom are unexpected and undeserved. The New Testament expresses frequently the amazement, the deep appreciation, and the gratitude that the early Christians felt for God's salvation in Christ.[111]

The biblical words for "grace" are then (Hb) and Charis as we mentioned earlier (Greek). Sinclair and Ferguson argue that neither word carries the usual sense of the English word 'grace' implying personal virtue. They indicate rather an objective relation of undeserved favour by a superior to an inferior, which with divine grace towards making, accompanies the ideas of covenant and election.[112] (cf. Gal 1:15, Eph 2:8-9). According to McKenzie, grace means… "To find

---

109   Cf. Pietro Palazzini (ed.) *Dictionary of Moral Theology*, Maryland: Westminster press, 1962, p. 550-551

110   Cf. Pietro Palazzini (ed.) *Dictionary of Moral Theology*, p. 550-551

111   Joseph A. Komonchak, Mary Collins and Dermot A. Lane (ed.), *The New Dictionary of Theology*, New York, Gil and Macmillan, 1987, p. 437

112   Joseph A. Komonchak, Mary Collins and Dermot A. Lane (ed.), *The New Dictionary of Theology*, p. 438

favour in the eyes of God or man,[113] one who intercedes for another gives favour in the person to whom the intercession is made?[114] Grace in Christian theology refers to the unconditional, comprehensive, empowering love of God for the world. [115](cf. Jn 1:14; Rom 5:2).

St. Augustine of Hippo confesses the need for God's grace very clearly. He asserts that "Our hearts are restless until rest in you."[116] "Grace is an inner transformation that liberates our freedom to do good once more, whereas, without grace, it is impossible to do good at all.[117] St. Thomas Aquinas agrees with the above statement in his assertion that "as a creature would fall into nothing unless it was held fast by divine power, so also it would fall into nothing unless it was held fast by God. But it does not follow that unless it was held fast by God through grace, it would fall into sin, unless (this be true) only of fallen nature, which of itself inclines to evil.[118] In the same line, Abril claims that "however, if grace is understood in the fuller sense as an interior aid, then T. Aquinas believes that a person must be able to prepare him or herself for it.[119]

Martin Luther elaborates on the relation between grace and gift

---

113   John L. Mckenzie (ed.) *Dictionary of the Bible,* Milwaukee, The Bruce Publishing Company, 1965, p. 280

114   John L. McKenzie, p. 324.

115   Rodny J. Hunter (ed.), *Dictionary of Pastoral Care and Counseling,* Abingdon press, Nashville, 1990, p. 468.

116   Neil Ormerod, *The Grace-Nature Distinction and the Construction of a Systematic Theology,* Australian Catholic University, Theological Studies, Vol. 75 (3) (2014) 515-517

117   Ibid p. 518-519.

118   Joshua R. Brotherton, *"The Integrity of Nature in the Grace-Freedom dynamic: Lonergan's critique of Banezian "Thomism",* Catholic University of America, Theological studies, Vol. 75, (3)(2014) 537-563

119   Michael Anthony Abril, *Lamentation 5:25 within the Development of Thomas Aquinas' Theology of the Grace of Conversion",* international Journal of Systematic theology, Vol. 16, No. 3, July 2014

in his prefaces to the biblical texts. He stresses the importance of the sequence: first grace, then gift. Grace characterizes God's positive feelings toward humans and moves God to send Christ to us and to give us the gift of the Holy Spirit. Even though the gifts and the Holy Spirit are growing daily, human sin is still a reality.[120]

Conclusion

Chapter five has defined freedom, and it has expounded the meaning of freedom as personal responsibility, education to freedom, and restriction of freedom. It has also briefly discussed grace and explicated it as the culture of life and its general understanding of salvation. It has presented its root meaning in the Greek language as *charis* which means divine gift or favor.

---

[120] Peter Lodberg, Grace and Reconciliation as a gift: a journal of theology, Vol. 54, number 3 September (2014) 235-248.

Chapter Six:
Principles of Active Nonviolence

Introduction

Chapter six discusses the general concept of various principles of culture of life, Jesus' precepts on culture of life and culture of death, and its brief historical context. It presents the style and literary character of Jesus' teaching, and the need for a necessary correct interpretation of Christ's precepts of culture of life. The chapter also presents Pope John Paul II on the culture of life and culture of death, its historical background at Stapleton International Airport near Denver Colorado, the American political debate on the culture of life and culture of death, and the veritable structure of sin.

The chapter further presents the triple evils of cultural death according to Dr. Martin Luther King Jr., King's six principles of nonviolence, and Dr. King's six steps for nonviolence and social change. Finally, Mahatma Gandhi on principles of nonviolence.

6. Jesus' Precepts and Other Principles of Non-Violence

We should not assume to cover all the principles of culture of life which are presented by outstanding figures in human history. However, we shall present principles. Among the outstanding figures such as Jesus Christ, Martin Luther King Jr, and Mahatma Gandhi of India. Each person had developed the principles of nonviolence within his social context. Earlier, we emphasized the social tangibility of violence as the culture of death.

Jesus Christ developed the precepts of the culture of life within the Jewish context, specifically in the Jewish religious faith. Being sent by God to bring the good news of salvation to all humanity, his precepts of the culture of life are divinely inspired, and are focused on the interior, not on the exterior. They are characterized by rigidity, unchangeability and unchanged because their demands are based on 'righteousness and piety.' Their demands go beyond the morality and ethics of scribes and the Pharisees. Jesus taught not only those precepts of the culture of life to others but put his precepts into practice by his way of life in obedience to His Father's will. He presented his precepts of the culture of life as a way which leads to eternal life. Sometimes, their demands are very tough and they ought not to be interpreted literally.

Pope John Paul II used the phrase, "culture of life and culture of death" to the contemporary society of America. He referred to the phrases culture of life and culture of death as 'abortion' and 'euthanasia.' His usage of the phrases culture of life and culture of death has gained popularity in the American political arena.

While for Dr. King Jr, his context was one of racial segregation in America. The Negros were treated with racial segregation by the white majority in America. Segregation is the culture of death within the context of racial segregation. Therefore, in response to such a dilemma, Dr. King Jr developed the principles of nonviolence. He chose the principles of nonviolence life and developed a philosophy called, "The King Philosophy."

Mahatma Gandhi of India found himself in colonization. India was colonized by the British who were Christians. However, their way of administration contradicted the principles of a culture of life developed by Jesus their Lord. Within that context of colonization, M. Gandhi also chose a different approach to their colonizers. He developed the principles of a culture of nonviolence known as "nonviolence principles."

I would agree with Pope John Paul II, who coined the phrase "culture of life and culture of death" which follows the concept of nonviolence and violence. This is because where there is nonviolence, there is life and where there is violence, and there is death in its various forms. I wish the world would use the word "culture of life and culture of death interchangeably with nonviolence and violence.

6.1 Jesus' Precepts of Culture of Life

The moral and ethical teaching of Jesus on precepts of the culture of life is found in the synoptic Gospels of Mathew, Mark, Luke and John. These gospels bring us more closely to Jesus' own moral and ethical teachings. Some say that even though these evangelists were not the earliest New Testament writers, yet, they were the ones who deliberately committed themselves to handing down Jesus' teaching to the Church. The evangelists were the direct sources of the moral teaching of Jesus.

It is believed that on the one hand, Jesus shares many of his religious assumptions with the religion of his people. But he transcends its limitations. For example, "he ... breaks through the nationalist barriers of racial particularism and the narrow clinging to an obsolescent law."[121] In this view, "He lays the foundations for a religion of universal character, and sets men free for radical faith of an unhampered commitment to God."[122] He began the proclamation of the kingdom of God in the

---

121   Karl H. Peschke, *Christian Ethics,* p. 30.
122   Ibid.

synoptic Gospel of St. Mathew with this precept "The time is fulfilling, the kingdom of God is at hand; repent, and believe in the gospel" (Mt.1:15).

6.1 Style and Literary Characters of Jesus' Precepts

The ethical teaching of Christ is unique. He does not stipulate and articulate his precepts like the precepts of the Decalogue, or epistles. It is believed that Jesus uses metaphoric language which demands radical urge and to some extent, even exaggerated. His style of ethical instruction is essentially different from that of the epistles, Dr. King Jr and Mahatma Gandhi of India. When he uses metaphorical, figurative language and parables, there arises the necessity for correct interpretation of his commandments and precepts. Otherwise, any attempt to interpret them literally will be wrong and can lead to stupidity and irrelevance to what they mean. By comparison, Jesus' ethical teaching has a greater liveliness and pointedness than the epistles. His style of teaching creates a sense of alertness and provokes one to search for its meaning. It said that Jesus always in his precepts, uses poetical, and imaginative styles close to life in the figures and pictures he chooses, and is filled with dramatic power.

For example, the dramatic, stylistic, literary, poetic, metaphorical, figurative, parable and imaginative powers create a sense of alertness and provocative search for meanings of precepts, as found in his discourse from the Sermon on the Mount. In the synoptic Gospel of St. Mathew, Jesus says, "If anyone strikes you on the right cheek, turn to him the other also; and if anyone would sue you and take your coat, let him have your cloak as well; and if anyone forces you to go one mile, go with him two miles. Give to him who begs from you, and do not refuse him who would borrow from you" (Mt 5:39-42).

Other Christ's precepts which cannot be interpreted literally from written page to action are: "Give to everyone who asks. "Leave father and mother, wife and children, and hate your soul." "If your hand or your eye is leading you astray, cut it off and cast it away." Never worry about food or drink. Tomorrow will look after itself." "Do not invite your friends or your brothers." Invite the poor, the maimed, the lame, and the blind." Jesus said, "You have learnt how it was said: 'Eye for eye and tooth for tooth.' But I say to you, Offer the wicked man no resistance. If anyone strikes you on the right cheek, turn the other also; if a man takes you to law and would have your tunic, let him have your cloak as well. And if anyone orders you to go one mile, go two miles with him" (Mt: 5.38-41).

Here, are biblical citations of Christ's ethical teaching on the culture of life (nonviolence) of Christ as Pantocrator. Jesus said, "Blessed are you when people revile you and persecute you and utter all kinds of evil against you falsely on my account" (Mt 5:11). Jesus said, "You have learnt how it was said to our ancestors: 'you must not kill, and anyone does kill him must answer for it before the court.' But I say this to you: anyone who is angry with his brother will answer for it before the court" (Mt 5:21-22). Jesus said, "It is from within, from men's hearts, that evil intentions emerge: fornication, theft, murder, adultery, avarice, malice, deceit, indecency, envy, slander, pride, folly. All these evil things come from within and make a man unclean" (Mk 7:21-23). Jesus said, "You know the commandments: you must not kill..." (Mk 10: 18). Jesus said, "When you stand in prayer, forgive whatever you have against anybody, so that your Father in heaven may forgive your failings too" (Mk 11: 25).

But Jesus in his precepts points out clearly where the culture of death lies in human life. The emphasis in his precepts is on the interiority. "Do you not realize that everything that enters the mouth passes into the stomach and is expelled into the latrine?" But the things that come out of the mouth come from the heart, and they are defile. For from the heart come evil thoughts, murder, adultery, unchastity, theft, false witness, blasphemy. These are what defile a person, but to eat with unwashed hands does not defile" (Mt 15:17-20). "He summoned the crowd again and said to them, "Hear me, all of you, and understand. Nothing that enters one from outside can defile that person; but the things that come out from within are what defile" (Mk 7: 14-15). "A good person out of the store of goodness in his heart produces good, but an evil person out of a store of evil produces evil, for from the fullness of the heart the mouth speaks" (Lk 6:45).

6.2 Correct Interpretation of Christ's Precepts

These precepts or principles of culture of life according to Jesus require correct interpretation to arrive at their true meanings. The passage from the Gospel of St. Mathew is the most dramatic passage which puzzles many listeners and even his disciples. When they called him Lord and Master, but because they saw in him a unique way to convey the message of salvation. Christ's precepts of the culture of life reveal the mysteries of God to all humanity. Therefore; their correct interpretations are essentially a prerequisite.

Christ's precepts are not of general and moral principles which require verbal and literal translation into action but rather they stir his hearers and challenge them to a boundless generosity. Some state that their unique character is that they all enforce the unlimited scope of God's commands. They leave no room for complacency. For example, in this view, it is asserted that "It is impossible to be satisfied with ourselves when we try our conduct by these standards."[123] These principles of Christ's culture of life expose our need for forgiveness and constant conversion. They are mirrors, and standards, in which we reflect our own lives and signposts that lead us to God's kingdom.

It is believed that Christ deliberately uses an exaggerated, hyperbolic style of speech to enable men to recognize the radical demand of God's

---

123   Karl H. Peschke, *Christian Ethics*, p. 33.

calling to an ever-greater perfection. In this sense, Jesus wants to win acknowledgement of God's will in its original totality. It is believed that "The morality of Christ is characterized by precepts which claim man's total unconditional obedience and open up vista towards a surpassing and even inconceivable perfection."[124]

The precepts of the culture of life above-mentioned from the Gospel of St. Mathew, mean offer no resistance, set oneself against, oppose, resist, stand and stand one's ground. Jesus' commands about offering the other cheek and related actions are associated with discipleship and a missionary ethic. Jesus' command to love one's enemies is a revelation of Father's love. God causes rain to fall: "God's rain falls even on the witch" (African Proverb). The Father looks at us as his children and invites us to look at one another as brothers and sisters. This is the basis of the new kingdom established by Jesus and the only way of establishing true justice and peace in the heart of humanity.

An eye for an eye, Brown asserts that it is a legal rule (*talion*), regulating revenge and retaliation for damages. (cf. 21:22-25; Lev 24:20; Dt 19:21). He states that although the rule may sound, barbarous to our contemporary society, its original intention was humanitarian, to limit revenge (only one eye for one eye, not two or three). Some say that when first introduced, it constituted genuine moral progress."[125] It is believed that by the time of Jesus, the rabbis already felt it was too harsh and began commuting the penalty to fines, but the principle of corresponding restitution remains dominant in legal thinking. The etymological meaning of *talion* is in Latin, such as the same.

For example, the principle of the culture of life says "Do not resist" Jesus teaches the culture of life as non-resistance to evil in the sense of avoiding physical violence or damage. In this view, this indicates this attitude leaves open the possibility of psychological or moral resistance,

---

124   Ibid.
125   Raymond E. Brown, *The New Jerome Biblical Commentary*, p. 643.

"media is fighting," exemplified by Mahatma Gandhi or Martin Luther King. Jesus was using this strategy to show that his ethical teaching is for winning, not for passive resignation or indifference to evil. His goal is to shame the opponent into a change of heart which presupposes the prerequisite dispositions in the opponent, which are not always present. Therefore, in such an occasion, recourse to scripture appears to be necessary.

What is so admirable in Jesus' precepts of the culture of life is that he teaches them without contradicting them in practice. His actions and his precepts coherently follow each other. With no exaggeration, he put them all into action. Christ's precepts are called "love in action" which are exercised in the two commandments of love: Love of God and love of neighbour as love of oneself. It is necessary to give at least three examples of how Christ put his precepts into action.

One of the very disturbing principles of a culture of life taught by Jesus is "If somebody strikes you on the right cheek, turn your left cheek." This principle requires one to cross-check it with the action of Christ as it is in the Gospel of St. John. For example, Jesus answered him, "If I have spoken wrongly, testify to the wrong; but if I have spoken rightly, why do you strike me" (Jn 18:23). Another practical example is found in St. Luke, "And one of them struck the high priest's servant and cut off his right ear. But Jesus said in replied, "stop, no more of this! Then, he touched the servant's ear and healed him" (Lk 26:50-51). "And behold, one of those who accompanied Jesus put his hand to his sword, drew it, and struck the high priest's servant, cutting off his ear. Then Jesus said to him, "Put your sword back into its sheath, for all who take the sword will perish by the sword." Do you think that I cannot call upon my Father and he will not provide me at this moment with more than twelve legions of angels? (Mt 26: 51-53). Jesus said Father, forgive them, for they do not know what they are doing" And they divided up his clothes by casting lots." (Lk 23:34).

In inclusion, any attempt to compare the principles of culture of life and culture of death of Christ's ethical teaching with principles of other human models such as Martin Luther King jr, and Mahatma Gandhi of India, will be unbecoming and unreasonable. His ethical teaching on the culture of life and the culture of death surpasses all other human principles. His ethical teaching reflects God Himself incarnated him and is meant for human salvation in the establishment of God's kingdom. The emphasis of the ethical teaching of Christ is on the interior not on the exterior within the heart.

6.3 The Church's Magisterium on Two Ways

Although different authors use the expression "culture of life" however, the expression has entered popular parlance through Pope John Paul II, who first used it in a World Youth Day tour of the United States in 1993. Some state that while speaking to journalists at Stapleton International Airport near Denver Colorado, John Paula II denounced abortion and euthanasia, stating that "The culture of life means respect for nature and protection of God's work of creation." [126] The Doctrine of the Catholic Church on human life asserts that life must be respected and protected from the moment of conception as sacred until its natural death. The same website affirms that Cardinal B. Law reiterated the theme, urging Americans to "spread the culture of life over the culture of death." Jesus in his moral teaching presents the same doctrine of culture of life and culture of death such as the narrow door which presents the culture of life and the wider door presents the culture of death.

The Gospel of St. Luke confirms this by stating "Make every effort to enter through the narrow door, because many, I tell you, will try to enter and will not be able to. Once the owner of the house gets up and closes the door, you will stand outside knocking and pleading,

---

126   Pope ends visit with frank talk, "state Journal Register, Springfield, Illinois (August 16, 1993): en-wikipedia.org/Culture_of_life, retrieved as from 02/08/2018

'Sir, open the door for us.' (Lk 13:24-25). Furthermore, the book of Deuteronomy teaches the doctrine of the culture of life and culture of death as a necessary choice before Israel, "See, I have today set before your life and good, death and evil" (Dt 30: 15-20). What we said earlier demonstrates that the Sacred Scripture, one possible source for this philosophy of the two ways, is *Didache*. A first-century Christian document which exposes the doctrine of two ways: way of life and way of death. It is believed this philosophy is a part of the Church's Magisterium of the Catholic Church. Popes often cite *Didache*. By description, *Didache* as the philosophy of two ways of culture of life and culture of death, "*Didache* the Teaching of the Twelve Apostles state that "There are two ways, the Way of Life and the Way of Death, and there is a vast difference between them."[127]

The first example of the way of life from *Didache,* the Way means: first, you shall love the God who created you, and second, shall love your neighbour as yourself. And do not do to another anything that you would not have done to yourself. Now the message of these words is this: Bless those who curse you, and pray for your enemies, and pray for those who persecute you. If you love those who love you, what merit will you have? Do not even pagans do this? Love those who hate you, and you will have no enemy. Second example of the Way to Death from *Didache*: first, it is evil and accursed, involving oneself in murder, adultery, lust, fornication, theft, idolatry, black magic, charms, robbery, false witness, hypocrisy, duplicity, fraud, vanity, maliciousness, stubbornness, haughtiness, covetousness, foul speech, jealousy, arrogance, and boastfulness. Here, are the persecutors of the good, haters of truth, lovers of lies, those who are ignorant of the reward of goodness, those who do not adhere to good and righteous judgment...unmerciful to the poor, uncaring for the oppressed, ignorant of their creator, murderers

---

127 Luigi Antoni Clerical (ed), *A reader in Early patristic Writings,* Nairobi: Paulines Publications Africa, 2014, p. 17

of children, corrupters of the creatures of God, who turn away the indigent, crush the afflicted, are defenders of the rich and unjust judges of the poor, sinful. The *Didache*, the Teaching of the Twelve Apostles invoke, "My children... you be delivered from such as these ..."[128]

Joshua presents the doctrine of the culture of life and culture of death implicitly when he says, "If it is displeasing to you to serve the Lord, choose today whom you will serve, the gods your ancestors served beyond the River or the gods of the Amorites in whose country you are dwelling. As for me and my household, we will serve the Lord" Jos 24: 15-). But the people answered, "Far be it from us to forsake the Lord to serve other gods" (Jos 24:16). Furthermore, Jesus in his doctrine of his body and blood presents the unconditional choice to his disciples as the sacred scriptures assert, "Jesus then said to the twelve, "Do You also want to leave?" Simon Peter answered him, "Master, to whom shall we go? You have the words of eternal life. We have come to believe and are convinced that you are the Holy One of God" (Jn 60: 67-69). Here and now, is the matter of choice between life and death.

One of the great fathers of the Church in the West St. Augustine of Hippo once expressed an implicitly famous statement about the culture of life and culture of death in his great work entitled "Saint Augustine, The Great Confessions, The City of God on Christian Doctrine" asserting that "The thought of you stirs him so deeply that he cannot be content unless he praises you because you made us for yourself and our hearts find no peace until they rest in you."[129] St. Augustine through his personal experience knew what it means to pursue only the 'physical desires' which lead to dissatisfaction and what it means to seek for the Lord that only leads to satisfaction and resting of our hearts in Him. Further, in the book of Genesis, God says, "Let there be lights

---

128   Luigi Antoni Clerical (ed), *A reader in Early patristic Writings*, p. 17-18.

129   Mortimer J. Adler (ed), *Great Books of the Western World: Saint Augustine, the Confessions, the city of God on Christian doctrine*, Chicago: Encyclopaedia Britanninca, inc., 1961, p.1.

in the dome of the sky, to separate day from night. Let them mark the seasons, the days and the Years, and serve as lights in the dome of the sky, to illuminate the earth. And so it happened. God made the two great lights, the greater one to govern the day and the one to govern the night, and the stars. God set them in the dome of the sky, to illuminate the earth, to govern the day and the night, and to separate the light from the darkness. God saw that it was good" (Gen 1: 14-18). St. John's Gospel is very specific between light and darkness when he says, "Through him was life, and this life was the light of the human race; the light shines in the darkness, and the darkness has not overcome it" (Jn 1:4-5). Here, light symbolizes the culture of life found in Jesus Christ and the darkness symbolizes the culture of death.

Pope John Paul II reiterates in the same website cited earlier the theme of culture of life and culture of death in April 1995, focusing on the encyclical letter "*Evangelium Vitae*" ("Gospel"): In our present social context marked by a dramatic struggle between the culture of life and culture of death (dramatic struggle between darkness and light) there is need to develop a critical sense of discerning true values and authentic needs.

In moral theology, the phrase "culture of life" opposes the practical destruction of human life such as abortion, euthanasia, studies and medicines involving embryonic stem cells, contraception, capital punishment, unjust war, sadistic humiliation, narcissism, and excessive selfishness.

6.4 American Politicians on Culture of Life in 2000

According to the findings, it is asserted that in 2005, 68% of White evangelical Protestants in the United States opposed abortion, 58% opposed euthanasia, and 15% opposed the death penalty. After the pronouncement of Pope John Paul II, encyclical letter, the supporters of Culture of Life founded a Culture of Life Foundation and Institute in the United States to advocate the concepts behind *Envangelium Vitae* recognized by John Paul II and blessed its foundation in 1997.

The concept of culture of life entered the mainstream of United States politics on 3 October 2000, during the U.S. presidential election campaign. For example, former Texas Governor George W. Bush cited the term during a televised debate against Vice President Al Gore; expressing concerns that Mifepristone, then newly approved as an abortifacient pill, would cause more women to abort their pregnancies, whereas his goal was to make abortions rare and to "promote the culture of life. He said:

> This nation can come together to promote the value of life, we can fight off these laws that will encourage doctors or allow doctors to take the lives of our seniors. We can work together to create a culture of life, some of these youngsters who feel like they can take a neighbour's life with a gun will understand that that's not the way Americans do.[130]

George W. Bush used the phrase 'culture of life and culture of death' to convince moderate Catholics who oppose abortion without coming out strongly to denounce it. He used the phrases culture of life and culture of death to convince them to participate in the election. However, some Catholics criticized Bush for being inconsistent between his support of a "culture of life" and his adherent's support for the death penalty which Catholic social teaching only permits if there is no other means for society to protect itself. His inconsistency was manifested in his repeated authorized executions of convicted murderers. Although he was criticized for his inconsistency by some Catholics, yet, he reiterated

---

130   Bush Woos Catholic on abortion Nominee, Echoes Pope's culture of life' Phrase, Boston Globe (October 9, 2000): en-wikipedia.org/Culture_of_life, retrieved as from 02/08/2018.

the same theme on various occasions during his campaign, asserting that "I think the next president must talk about the culture of life."[131] Because he supported the culture of life, he narrowly won the election for the Presidency of the United States and assumed office on 20 January 2001. In the period of an eight-year Presidency, the American politicians repeatedly invoked the "culture of life." Notable instances included:

The summer of 2001, when a political controversy occurred over the position of the federal government on stem cell research, President Bush faced accusations of backtracking on his earlier "culture of life" rhetoric. (2) March 2003, when the United States Congress passed a bill prohibiting partial-birth abortion, which proponents cited as advancing the "culture of life.[132]

6.5 Veritable Structure of Sin as Culture of Death

Pope John Paul II in his doctrine on 'culture of life and culture of death' reaffirms his teaching in defence of human life and boldly asserts that good must be called by its name and evil likewise. He states that given such a grave situation, we need now more than ever to have the courage to look at the truth in the eye and to call things by their proper

---

131 Bush Woos Catholic on abortion Nominee, Echoes Pope's Culture of Life' 02/08/2018.

132 Bush Woos Catholic on abortion Nominee, Echoes Pope's Culture of Life' phrase 02/08/2018. (3) the unborn Victims of Violence Act in April 2004, which defined a violent attack on a pregnant women as two distinct crimes: one against the woman, the other against here fetus, politician promoted this act as imporving the right of the "unborn", hence advancing the culture of life (4) the US presidential election, 2004, when the Republican party incorporated the phrase into its official platform, referring to the opposition of the party against abortion, stem cell research involving he destruction of human embryos and euthanasia. (5) the Terri Schiavo controversy of March 2005, when the phrase was used in the support of legislative and leg efforts to prolong the life of a brain-damage woman in an alleged persistent vegetable state.

name, without yielding to convenient compromise or the temptation of self-deception."[133] Calling right and wrong in their proper places is nowadays reversed by the world's powerful leaders as K. Khandelwal states "It is for you to say then that the wrong is no wrong in the world which you rule, and so it is mended."[134] John Paul II warns against the danger of not calling things by their proper names by quoting the prophet Isaiah "Woe to those who call evil good and good evil, who put darkness for light and light for darkness" (ls 5:20).

The Church's Magisterium specifically mentions this attitude of ambiguity "Especially in the case of abortion where there is a widespread use of ambiguous terminology, such as "interruption of pregnancy," which tends to hide abortion's true nature and to attenuate its seriousness in public opinion." 132 He asserts that no word has the power to change the reality of things and he defines abortion by saying "Procured abortion is the deliberated and direct killing, by whatever means it is carried out, of a human being in the initial phase of his/her existence, extending from conception to birth."[135]

John Paul II reiterates his doctrine on culture of life and culture of death stating that the climate of widespread moral uncertainty can be explained by the multiplicity and gravity of today's social problems and these can sometimes mitigate the subjective responsibility of individuals. It is no less true that we are confronted by an even larger reality, which can be described as a veritable structure of sin. According to John Paul II, this veritable structure of sin is characterized by the emergence of a culture which denies solidarity and often a veritable "culture of death. It is believed that this culture is actively promoted by powerful cultural, economic and political currents which encourage an idea of society excessively concerned with efficiency.

---

133   John Paul II, Encyclical Letter: *Evangelium Vitae, the gospel of Life*, no. 58.

134   K. N. Khandelwal, *Shakespeare's Othello*, p. 139

135   John Paul II, Encyclical Letter: *Evangelium Vitae, the gospel of Life*, no. 12.

It is asserted that looking at the situation from this viewpoint; it is possible to speak in a certain sense of a war of the powerful against the weak: a life which would require greater acceptance, love and care is considered useless, or held to be an intolerable burden, and is therefore, rejected. Pope John Paul II says for example, that a person who, because of illness, handicap, or more just by existing, compromises the well-being or lifestyle of those who are more favoured is looked upon as an enemy to be resisted or eliminated. He states that in this way, a conspiracy against life is unleashed. The Church's Magisterium believes this conspiracy involves not only individuals in their personal, family or group relationships but goes far beyond to the point of damaging and distorting at the international level, and relations between peoples and states.

On the same line of argument, Cardinal Cormac Murphy-O'Connor reiterates *Evangelium Vitae*, by asserting that without morals "It is the strong who decide the fate of the weak," and "human beings therefore become instruments of other human being …We are already on that road: for what else is the termination of millions of lives in the womb since the Abortion Act was introduced, and embryo selection based on gender and genes."[136] Some say the advocates of culture life assert that a culture of death results in political, economic, or eugenic murder. However, they also point to historical events somewhere in chapter one. For example, those historical events such as the USSR's Great Purges, the Nazi Holocaust, China's Leap Forward and Pol Pol's Khmer Rouge as extreme examples of the devaluation of human life. Also, pro-life advocates or those who are called pro-life movement (supporters of embryonic stem cell research, legalized abortion and euthanasia) use the phrase, culture of life.

Pope Paul VI in his encyclical Letter *Humanae Vitae* states that "In

---

136   Bush Woo Catholic on aborton Niminee, Echoes Pope's culture of life, retrieved as from 02/08/2018.

the task of transmitting life, therefore, they are not free to proceed completely at will, as if they could determine in a wholly autonomous way the honest path to follow; but they must conform their activity to the creative intention of God, expressed in the very nature of marriage and of its acts, and manifested by the constant teaching of the Church."[137]

6.6 Techniques of Artificial Reproduction

Pope John Paul II in response to various areas of the culture of death such as: 1. Abortion. 2. Euthanasia (false mercy). 3. Reduction of human life to simple "biological material," 4. Eugenic abortion requires the acceptance of human life through certain conditions, such as efficiency, capability, and physical fit, contrary to these such as limitation, handicap or illness if discovered by "therapeutic diagnosis" will lead to abortion. In such cases infanticide is right. 5. The "incurable ill" is to be resolved by eliminating it at the root by the termination of one's life to avoid physical suffering. John Paul II confirms that all this is aggravated by a cultural climate which perceives no meaning or value in suffering, but considers suffering the epitome of evil, to be eliminated at all cost. 6. Sexual re-assignment. To undergo a surgical operation to change your sexual status as if God has made a mistake.

Among the general levels in contemporary society, there exists a culture of 7. A certain Promethean attitude or mentality asserts that people think that they can control life and death by taking the decisions into their own hands. An example of this is sometimes, supported by the utilitarian motive of avoiding suffering which costs bring no return and which weighs heavily on society. On the one hand, there is a phenomenon of. 8. "Demographic question" in which the rich and developed nations are disturbed by a decline or collapse of the birth rate

---

[137] Paul VI, Encyclical Letter: *Humanae Vitae, On Human of Life*, no. 10.

while the poorer nations have a high birthrate of population growth but because of low economic and social development that makes it difficult to sustain. Because of this imbalance, anti-birth policies continue to be enacted.

The decline in birthrate is due to the following such as 9 contraception. 10. Sterilization. 11. Abortion. 12. Lesbians. 13. Homosexuals and more increasingly the commonly known. 14. Campaigners of such activities always use the term "demographic explosion. The provisions of various means for licentious sexual activity are illustrated by J. Tab as follows: 15. Viagra: a synthetic compound used to enhance male potency. 16. Depo Provera: injection protects against pregnancy for up to 12 weeks. 17. Noristerate: injection is effective for up to eight weeks. 18. Sayan Press: injection is effective for weeks. An injection by a doctor or nurse into a muscle in the woman's arm or buttock. These injections must be given on time to stay protected against pregnancy. According to J. Tab, Benagaino and Mori ... "the contraceptive revolutions' of the 20th century (sex without reproduction, reproduction without sex, and reproduction in menopause and, one day, reproduction without gametes) are having a major impact on the life of individual couples and women."[138] Here and now, no one can doubt that sex has fallen into the hands of the wrong people, and the situation of sex supposed to be sacred is enormously dramatic and chaotic.

According to John Paul II, "The Pharaoh of old, haunted by the presence and increase of the children of Israel, submitted them, to every kind of oppression and ordered that every male child born of the Hebrew women was to be killed."[139]

---

138 Cf. J. Tab Charoa, *Ethics of human sexuality, A call for Christity in the Christian family,* Nairobi: CUEA press, 2018, p. 42

139 John Paul II, Encyclical Letter: *Evangelium Vitae, the gospel of Life,* no. 16

6.7 Legal Systems and Theories of Culture of Death

According to John Paul II, there are various legal systems to violate human life: 1. Legal justification which shows a certain tendency to claim it should be possible to exercise these rights with safe and free assistance of doctors and medical personnel. 2. There is another claim that the life of an unborn child is relatively good. Proportionalists argue that one of the sheer calculations; this good should be compared with and balanced against other goods. According to this view, only the person who is physically present and involved in a concrete situation can correctly judge the goods at stake. The proportionalists assert that only that person can decide on the morality of his choice.

3. According to civil law, o this view, the law should always express the opinion and will of the majority of citizens and recognize that they have, at least in certain extreme cases, the right even to abortion. This has increased illegal practices of such evil acts of the culture of death. When someone commits an abortion, the civil law is indifferent (neutral). 4. Radical views, according to a pluralistic society, it is claimed that people should be allowed complete freedom to dispose of their own lives and the lives of the unborn. This doctrine asserts that it is not the law to choose between different moral opinions, and still can the law claim to impose one particular opinion to determine others. 5. Ethical relativism characterizes much of present-day culture.

The discussions above-mentioned about various legal systems and theories lead us to two opposing tendencies. According to John Paul II, on the one hand, individuals claim for themselves in the moral sphere the most complete freedom of choice and demand that the State should not adopt or impose any ethical position but limit itself to guaranteeing maximum space for the freedom of each individual, with the sole limitation of not infringing on the freedom and rights of any other citizens. But it is held that, in exercising public and professional duties, respect for other people's freedom of choice requires that each one should set aside his or her convictions to satisfy every demand of the citizens recognized and guaranteed by law; in carrying out one's duties the only. The moral criterion should be what is laid down by the law itself. Pope John Paul II concludes that "Individual responsibility is thus turned over to the civil law, with a renouncing of personal conscience, at least in the public sphere."[140]

6.8 Dr King's Triple Evils of Culture of Death

As we have introduced earlier, the well-known initiator and innovator of principles of non-violence Dr. Martin Luther King Jr, has identified triple evils, in his article entitled "Where Do We Go from Here: Chaos or Community?" Dr. King argues that the triple evils are poverty, racism and materialism. These are forms of culture of death which require remedy. For their remedies, Dr. King Jr will outline six principles of culture of life also called "the Kingian model for social action on social change."

6.8.1 First Triple Evil of Poverty

According to Dr. King Jr, the first "triple evil" (poverty) entails the following: 1. Unemployment. 2. Homelessness. 3. Hunger. 4. Malnutrition. 5. Illiteracy. 6. Infant mortality. 7 Slum. He argues there is nothing new about poverty but what is new is to have resources to get rid of it. In that above-mentioned triple evil of poverty, it is emphasized that the world must come out to fight against poverty because it is the culture of death. Some further state that those who are blessed with riches, and security, should not become indifferent to poverty and deprivation. According to Dr. King Jr, "Ultimately a great nation is a compassionate nation. No individual or nation can be great if it

---

140 John Paul II, Encyclical Letter: *Evangelium Vitae, the gospel of Life*, no. 69

does not have a concern for the least of these."[141] It is believed that the above-mentioned issue such as the triple evil of poverty addresses the basic needs of all humans and each person deserves to enjoy the culture of life rather than the culture of death which is poverty.

6.8.2 The Second Triple Evil of Racism

The second "triple evil" racism consists of elements such as: 1. Prejudice, apartheid, ethnic conflict, anti-Semitism, sexism, colonialism, homophobia, ageism, discrimination against disabled groups, and stereotypes. Racism is described as a philosophy based on contempt for life; an arrogant assertion that asserts that one race is the centre of value and object of devotion before other races and others must kneel in submission. Some argue that racism is an 'evil dogma' because it claims that one race, claims the responsibility for all the progress of history and could determine the future progress. In this view, racism is an absolute total estrangement; it divides not only the bodies but also minds and spirits. It is asserted that racism "Inevitably...descends to inflicting spiritual and physical homicide upon the out-group."[142]

Dr. King Jr had developed this dogmatic doctrine of racial segregation between the whites and the Negros in which the Negros were looked upon by whites as inferiors and the whites as superiors based on colour and the ugly historical background of slavery. This is the culture of death which must be eradicated from the root. Unfortunately, sometimes in our contemporary society, we still see stupid people entertaining racism. To eradicate this culture of death called "racism" requires

---

141   www.thekingcenter.org/king-philisophy, retrieved as from 01/08/2018, Where do we go from here: Chaos or community? By D. Martin Luther King.; Boston press, 196

142   www.thekingcenter.org/king-philisophy, retrieved as from 01/08/2018, where do we go from here: Chaos or community? By D. Martin Luther King.; Boston press, 1967

a re-evaluation of the way we look at each other and to conclude that we all are naturally equal in the image and likeness of God.

6.8.3 The Third Triple Evil of Materialism

This triple evil of materialism consists of the following elements such as: 1. War. 2. Imperialism 3. Domestic violence. 4. Rape. 5. Terrorism. 6. Human trafficking. 7. Media violence. 8. Drugs. 9. Child abuse. 10. Violent crime. With such an illustration of issues related to materialism, one can never doubt that materialism is the culture of death. In this doctrine on the triple evil of materialism, it is believed that a true revolution of values will lay hands on the world order and say, 'this way of settling differences is unjust. According to Dr. King Jr, "This way of burning human beings with napalm, of filling our nation's homes with orphans and widows, of injecting poisonous drugs of hate into the veins of peoples normally humane, of sending men home from dark and bloody battlefields physically handicapped and psychologically deranged, cannot be reconciled with wisdom, justice and love."[143]

In favour of this argument, it is concluded that a nation that continues years after years to spend more money on military defence than on programs of social uplift is approaching spiritual death. There is a warning against materialism mentality which is the culture of death. Some say that this serious warning is to change our way of reasoning in favour of materialism. We are encouraged to embrace the culture of life and to eradicate the culture of death.

---

143   www.thekingcenter.org/king-philisophy, retrieved as from 01/08/2018, where do we go from here: Chaos or community? By D. Martin Luther King.; Boston press, 1967

6.9 Six Principles of Culture of Nonviolence

According to Dr. Martin Luther King Jr., to overcome the practice of a culture of violence, there is a need to put forward principles of a culture of nonviolence. Therefore, below are illustrated these principles of a culture of nonviolence:

1. First principle: nonviolence is a way of life for courageous people. This first principle of nonviolence is characterized by two strong pillars such as it is active nonviolence and resistance to evil and it is aggressive spiritually, mentally and emotionally. 2. Second principle: nonviolence seeks to win friendship and understanding. In line with this principle, some state that first, the result of nonviolence is redemption and reconciliation. Its purpose is the creation of a beloved community. 3. Third principle: nonviolence seeks to defeat injustice, not people. This principle is expounded by affirming that it recognizes that evildoers are also victims and they are not evil people. Meanwhile, a resister seeks to defeat evil not people.

4. Fourth principle: Nonviolence holds that suffering can educate and transform. The culture of life accepts suffering without retaliation and unearned suffering is redemptive and has tremendous educational and transforming possibilities. 5. Fifth principle: nonviolence chooses love instead of hate. It is illustrated that the culture of life resists violence of the spirit and the body and that love is spontaneous, unmotivated, unselfish, and creative. 6. Sixth principle: nonviolence believes that the universe is on the side of justice. "The nonviolence resister has deep faith that justice will eventually win"[144] and "Nonviolence believes that God is a God of justice."[145]

---

144 Based on Martin Luther Jr's Letter from Birmingham Jail *in why we can't wait,* Penguin books, 19963. www.thekingcentre.org/king-philosophy, retrieved as from 01/08/2018.

145 Ibid.

6.9.1 Dr. King's Seven Techniques for Social Change

'Love in action' is required for these principles of the culture of life. 1. Information gathering: The first step for the culture of life on social change is information gathering. It is emphasized that to gather information, it is better to understand and articulate an issue, problem or injustice facing a person, community, or institution, you must do research. In this sense, it is even believed that one must investigate and gather all vital information from all sides of the argument or issue to increase your understanding of the problem. Dr. King Jr highlights this requires from person to person to become an expert on your opponent's position. In this first step of the culture of life, it is recommended that serious analysis and diagnosis in question are required to become capable of understanding and gaining wisdom.

2. Necessity: the second principle of culture of life for social change, requires necessity. It is asserted that it is essential to inform others, including your opposition, about your issue to minimize misunderstandings while it gains you support and sympathy. 3. Personal commitment: the third principle of the culture of life for social change requires reaffirmation of personal commitment. This is needed for daily checks which affirm your philosophy and methods of culture of life. 4. Readiness to face suffering: It is even believed that thus, to eliminate hidden motives, be ready to prepare yourself to admit suffering in your work for justice. For example, Dr. King Jr died for love of truth and justice, Jesus and Socrates and others have suffered and died because of readiness to face suffering in the face of injustice.

5. Discussion and Negotiation are prerequisites: The fifth principle of culture of life for social change, states that both discussion and negotiation are prerequisites. It is emphasized this requires some styles of language such as "using grace, humour, and intelligence, confront the other party with a list of injustices and a plan for addressing and solving

this evil action."¹⁴⁶ In agreeing with Gandhi, Dr. King Jr reminds us not to seek to humiliate the opponent but to call forth the good in the opponent.

6. Plan of Action: In the six principles for social change, it is argued that direct action is needed. It is believed that these actions are taken when the opponent is unwilling to enter into or remain in discussion or negotiation. It has been pointed out that these actions impose a 'creative tension' into the conflict, supplying moral pressure on your opponent to work with you in resolving the injustice. These six principle of the culture of life for social change moves us from word and thought into action. This indicates that the culture of life is not passive but active.

7. Reconciliation: The last seven principles of culture of life is reconciliation which seeks friendship and understanding with the opponent. It is stated that the culture of life does not seek to defeat the opponent but rather is directed against evil systems, forces, oppressive policies, and unjust acts, but not against persons. It is argued that "Through reasoned compromise, both sides resolve the injustice with a plan of action. Each act of reconciliation is one step closer to the 'Beloved Community.'"¹⁴⁷

6.10 Mahatma Gandhi on Principles of Nonviolence

According to Sydney, Alternative Media-independent, community nonprofit, trustworthy, Mahatma Gandhi has identified these principles of nonviolence such as principles of a culture of life. These include the following: 1. Humiliating or deliberately provoking your opponent invites violence. 2. Knowing your facts and arguments will help to avoid

---

146   Based on Martin Luther Jr's Letter *from Birmingham Jail"* in why we can't wait, Penguin books, 19963. www.thekingcentre.org/king-philosophy, retrieved as from 01/08/2018.

147   Based on Martin Luther Jr's Letter *from Birmingham Jail"* in why we can't wait, Penguin books, 19963. www.thekingcentre.org/king-philosophy, retrieved as from 01/08/2018.

violence. 3. If you are open about your cause, your opponent is less likely to be violent. 4. Look for common ground between you and your opponents to promote trust and understanding. 5. Do not judge others. 6. Trust your opponent, they will sense this trust. 7. Compromise on inessential items to promote resolution. 8. Sincerity helps convert your opponent. 9. "By making personal sacrifice you show your sincerity; and 10, avoid exploiting a weakness in your opponent rather aim for integrity, not simply to win."[148]

Gandhi also wrote other seven principles of a culture of life besides the ten principles of a culture of nonviolence such as: 1. We each have a piece of truth and the un-truth. 2. Humans are more than the evil they sometimes commit. 3. The means we must follow ends. 4. We are called to celebrate both our differences and our fundamental unity with others. 5. We reaffirm our unity with others when they transform "us" versus when we transform their thinking and doing. 6. "Our oneness calls us to want and to work for, the well-being of all. 7. The nonviolent journey is a process of becoming increasingly free from fear."[149]

The principles of nonviolence of both Dr. Martin Luther King Jr and Mahatma Gandhi play a greater role within the context of social analysis. Both Dr. King Jr and Mahatma Gandhi do agree with Aristotelian traditional ethics about the analysis of social reality. According to Aristotle, social analysis implicitly involves three methodological moments. 1. Rational empirical study of reality. 2. Articulation of the general moral principles of right reason developed from the knowledge of that reality. 3. Prudential recommendation on how to proceed in action according to the right reason within that reality. Platonic tradition can be viewed in the form of his analysis of social reality in which he outlined two approaches to this social analysis. 1. The articulation of moral axioms,

---

148 Sydney Alternative Media-independent, community, non profit, trustworthy, Gandhi's 10 principles of nonviolence, www.sydneyalternativemedia.com/id73,html, retrieved as from 02/08/2018.

149 www.cpt.org/files/PW-Prinicples-Gandhi, retrieved as from 02/08/2018.

abstract values or ideal intelligible form. 2. Applying these ideals to the less real world.

Conclusion

Chapter six has discussed broadly the general concept of various principles of culture of life, Jesus' doctrine on culture of life and culture of death and its brief historical context. It has presented the style and literary character of Jesus' teaching, and the need for a necessary correct interpretation of Christ's precepts of the culture of life. The chapter also has presented Pope John Paul II on 'culture of life and culture of death', its historical influence at Stapleton International Airport near Denver Colorado, the American political debate on the culture of life and culture of death, and the veritable structure of sin.

The chapter has further indicated the triple evils of the culture of death according to Martin Luther King Jr, King's six principles of a culture of nonviolence, Dr King's seven techniques and steps for social change and finally, it presents Mahatma Gandhi's principles of nonviolence.

Chapter Seven:
African Contribution to Culture of Life and Culture of Death

Introduction

This chapter discusses the main forms of power, the classification of power, traditional power and kindly power. It also presents the colonial period, the depletion of natural resources and the slave trade. It withers discusses naked and revolutionary power. It also presents the Rwanda genocide and some areas of the culture of life on the continent. The chapter illustrates the post-colonial period and the ethics of power. Dialogue and negotiation as the culture of life. Finally, it discusses the four-day reports by National Dialogue and the identification of the stakeholders and criteria of selection.

7. Moral Evil as a Culture of Death

In discussing the culture of death in the African continent, one must look back to historical facts and the unfortunate tragedy that has presented a catastrophic disaster and loss of lives among indigenous people in the continent. Some of these unfortunate tragic events of the culture of death and were caused by the indigenous themselves, while some were caused by foreign invaders, some were caused by nature.

In the introduction, we said there were factors and tragic events of the culture of death inflicted upon the indigenous Africans by foreign invaders (colonizers). Historically the continent has undergone very unfortunate ugly events such as colonization which has resulted in the depletion of local natural resources and unfortunately the ugly experience of slavery and the apartheid in South Africa. The clash between the two cultures is, on the one hand, a superiority complex and an inferiority complex.

For example, in Sudan, the activities of slavery were very obvious and historically recorded. Diem Zubier was the famous market for the slave trade in Wau South Sudan. Suakin, the port of Sudan was the last station departure for slaves in Sudan. For example, St. Josephine Bakhita was forced to depart from Suakin port of Sudan to Europe by her slave master. Zanzibar was the big market for the slave trade in Tanzania. With such facts and catastrophic events, the continent was affected by the culture of death. This culture of death was initiated by moral agents who thought themselves to be superior to the indigenous people of the continent.

Among those tragic events caused by the indigenous people include the occurrence of ethnicity or ethnic cleansing, clan fighting between clans or over two clans against other clans using local tools such as clubs, spears, sticks, and machetes commonly traditional means of the culture of death in the content. It has to be mentioned that using these traditional tools for fighting takes fewer lives compared to using guns as it is nowadays in our continent. However, we must clarify that even the death of one person in such an unfortunate situation is unacceptable.

7.1 Main Form of Powers

A. Mugarura has classified power into either through influencing the individuals or through the organization involved. Some argue that individuals can be influenced in three ways namely: 1. First through physical power over the subject. For example, imprisonment; killing; and beating. 2. Others through rewards and punishments as inducements. 3. Third, is by option or propaganda. These three forms of power can be used for the culture of life or the culture of death in Africa.

The forms of powers mentioned above are different powers exercised by different organizations or institutions. Some say that the army and the police do exercise coercive power over the subjects. For example, economic groups use rewards and punishments as incentives and deterrents. The church school and political parties also influence options. Mugarura has clarified it because each organization or institution has its form of power. In these three forms of power, all are combined by-laws for exercising the power of the culture of life or the culture of death.

Emeritus Pope Benedict XVI states that in Africa, traditionally, exercising is administered by local chiefs. These "traditional chiefs have a very positive contribution to make good governance"[150] for the culture of life. It is believed that "the church for her part is committed to promoting within her ranks and society a culture that respects that rule of law."[151] The Church's Magisterium points out areas of the culture of death in Africa by asserting that "failure to respect the national constitution, law or the outcome of the vote when elections have been free, fair and transparent, would signal a grave failure in governance and lack of competence in the administration of public affairs.[152]

---

150 Benedict XVI Post-synod Apostolic Exhortation, *Africae Munus, Africa's Commitment,* no. 81.

151 Ibid.

152 Ibid.

7.1.1 Traditional Powers

From ancient times to our contemporary society there exist different types of powers. For example, some are secular and some are religious. Whether they are secular or religious if not exercised based on moral natural law, can be dangerous to human life and can be the source of culture death.

7.1.1.1 The Papal Power (Leadership)

Some argue that after a historical survey of the ancient and the main modern religion, Russell gave particular attention to the papacy. Exercising the papal leadership, it is acknowledged that the power of the church is a good example of propaganda. It is characterized by long and maintained moral standards respected by all believers in the church. It is believed this did not survive without putting it to the test, especially during the great papal leadership instigated by nobles, and princes who found a ground to rebel against the leadership of the papacy. The culture of death was inspired by economic aims. Some state that the breakaway of Protestants and heresies had led to the split of many believers from the Catholics, yet popes deserve respect and were morally convincing. The morality in public option and propaganda was very strong and above all, the popes of the 11th-13th centuries were learned men and better-informed than the kings.

Three reasons for the rise and instability of the leadership of the papacy in the middle are identified which include the followings: 1. First the pope is hereditary; he comes to power by merit of election, after long experience and normally through piety and they were considered above the average in one or more respects. 2. The continuity of the papacy is impersonal, if a pope dies, a new one would be elected. 3. Last, the church has the greatest strength of moral respect which inspired it.

The papal leadership is relevant to our situation in Africa. The African leaders should be inspired by papal moral authority and should exercise their authority within the boundary of laws such as natural, divine, positive, and other customary laws for the promotion of a culture of life. The culture of death initiated by the great schism is still yet to be seen in our continent. The great schism started by the Protestants has affected the universal church throughout its life. Our continent is witnessing the mushrooming of a thousand denominations which is a sign of the culture of death. Various denominations should embrace unity in diversity as the culture of life.

7.1.2 Kingly Power

We can trace the historical background of kingly power to pre-historic times which took full development in Hammurabi (2123-2081) BC of Babylonian, and by the great pyramid Egypt, i.e. by 3000 BC. Some argue that it existed throughout the history of the monarch, feudal system, commerce, and then nationalism. In this option, conflicts and tensions were the daily bread of these systems. At other times, destruction could come from outside. A. Mugarura argues that:

Traditional power, when not destroyed from without, runs, almost always, through a certain development. Emboldened by the respect which inspires it, becomes careless as regards the general approval, which it believes that it cannot ever be lost. By sloth, folly, or cruelty it gradually forces men to become skeptical of its claims to divine authority. Since these claims have a source no better than habit, criticism, once aroused, easily disposes of them. Some new creed, useful to the rebels, replaces the old one; or sometimes in Haiti when it won freedom from the French, mere chaos succeeds. During the period of every flagrant misgovernment is necessary before mental rebellion becomes widespread, and in many cases, the rebels transfer to themselves part or the whole of the old authority.[153]

The long misrule forces people to be critical and decide to act. According to N. Machiavelli, are hereditary in which the rulers have been for many years of the same family, or else they are of recent foundation.[154] This kingly power unfortunately has existed in the world for thousands of years and it still exists in our continent in some local tribes. On the one hand, we can take the recommendation of Benedict XVI positively which says that traditional chiefs have a very positive contribution to making good governance but also the other side of the coin, should not be ignored, the negative aspects of traditional chieftainship. Kings whether in our continent or other continents sometimes, do abuse their subjects brutally. They often practice castration as the culture of death. This is one of the negative factors in kingly power. Castration is carried out so male slaves do not engage in sexual activities with the king's daughters, wives, and female slaves. Jesus reflects this act clearly in the Gospel of St. Mathew saying, "Some of incapable of marriage because they were born so; some, because they were made so by others; some, because they have renounced marriage for the sake of the kingdom of heaven. Whoever can accept this ought to accept it" (Mt. 19:12).

For example, in Uganda, thirty-one young men excluding Charles Lwanga, were burnt in the great holocaust at Namugongo. Twelve were officially recognized as catholic martyrs, and nine were officially recognized by the Protestants, their names being inscribed on the memorial tablet in Namirembe Cathedral. According to F. Faupel, "It has generally been assumed that the remaining ten were pagans, who had been in prison under of death sentence for offences other than religion.

---

153   Augustine Mugarura, *Impulse to power according to Russell: a Critique Leading to a Principle of Integral Development*, Uganda, Fort, 1993, p.71

154   Niccolo Machiavelli, *The Prince and the Discourse,* New York: The Modern Library, 1950, p.5

However, at least five, and possibly more of these were protestant readers or catechumens, and Simon Sebuta mentioned one unknown Catholic."[155] This was the worst brutal culture of death inflicted by King Kabakamwanga on innocent lives in Uganda on June 3, 1886, out of this brutality culture of death (violence,) Africa as a continent is blessed with martyrs who sacrificed in obedience to their faith in Christ. Nowadays, Namugongo has become a place of pilgrimage for many. It has become the centre of culture of life, because of the blood of martyrs poured into it.

7.2 Two Types of Powers

It is believed that human experience in terms of the exercise of power has acknowledged the existing two notable powers. By their natures, one is brutal and the other is also brutal, gradual and progressive depending on how it is handled. Therefore, below is the descriptions of two type of powers. Humanity shares this naked power with animals.

7.2.1 Naked Power

It is believed that naked power can be compared to…"the butcher over the sheep, of the invading army over the vanquish nation, and of the police over detected conspirator."[156] Some say that naked power is

---

155   J. F. Faupel, *African Holocaust: The Story of the Uganda Martyrs*, Nairobi: Paulines Publications Africa, 1984, p.227. In two of his earlier lists of Catholic martyrs, James Mbiti mentioned an Ambrozio Kizito of the scaly Ant-Eastern Clan, One is the first tempted to identify this name with the unknown mentioned by Sebuta, But as Miti omits from these two lists the names of Ambrose Kibuka and Kizito, forced to assume that he has, in fact, run these two lists names together and produced Ambrose Kizito. Kibuba did in fact in fact belong to the Scaly Ant-Eastern Clan. Miti's final list of Catholic martyrs, in his history, tallis with the official cathoilic list.

156   Cf. Augustine Mugarura, *Impulse to Power According to Russell*, p.71.

characterized by psychological and transitory. It should be followed by a military conquest immediately, by a psychological conquest because this is the only way to stability. The people should be contented with the new leaders.

There are two types of naked power: 1. The first may come as competing of two or more fanatical creeds. 2. Second, it may come as a result of believing that all traditional beliefs have decayed and new ones must replace them and yet, when those in authority insist on ruling. 3. Third, because of unlimited personal ambition, those in power use a lot of force or naked power.

The period of naked power is always brief and lasts in three ways. 1. One way is by foreign conquest. 2. Second; by establishing a stable dictatorship which can soon result in traditional. 3. The third way is the rise of a new religion using the words in its widest sense. Power is naked when the subjects respect it solely because it is power, and not for any other reason.[157] Africa as a continent has gone through naked power which has led to the death of many people. Some examples of naked power such as naked power against defenceless victims, slavery and the slave trade, the exploitation of Congo, cruelty to children, judicial torture and many others.

During the beginning of industrialism, wages were not regulated by customs, nor were the workers organized the workers dependent on the mercy of the employers. The latter had naked power over the former when the workers organized themselves into unions and took part in politics, the relationship changed as the workers bargained with the employers.[158]

---

157   Ibid, p. 73.
158   Ibid.

7.2.2 Revolutionary Power

This revolutionary power can break out and be substituted by new conviction, and new creeds that involves new mental habits increasingly embraced by the citizens. Its characteristics differ from the traditional and naked power. A successful revolutionary could become a traditional one however; a severe and prolonged revolutionary struggle could easily degenerate into a struggle for naked power. Psychologically, the believers of the new creed are geared by ambitious adventurers and their effects are more important and permanent. For example, the French Revolution, nationalism, socialism and the Russian Revolution.

In our continent, we experience a culture of death through revolutionary powers for example, the Arabs springs in North Africa between 2011-2015. For instance the Egyptian revolutionary power by the civilians that threw President Hosni Mubarak and the humiliating overthrow of President Muammar Gaddafi of Libya, Tunisia's revolutionary power, Morocco's revolutionary power and Algeria's revolution power. The eruption of death after a disputed election in Kenya in 2007, the eruption of South Sudan cultural violence in 2013, the civil war in Sudan, the Boko Haram in Nigeria, and Al Shaba in Somalia and the culture of death going on in the republic of Congo.

Besides, there are also other areas of the culture of death in the continent which need attention such as poverty, corruption, lack of respect for the rule of law, diseases, unemployment, and human trafficking, whereby Rea Sea has become a graveyard for many African adventures injustices. We have poor governance characterized by a spirit of dictatorship. These challenges need to be addressed to find out their solutions.

7.3 Rwanda Genocide

In the African continent, the most brutal ever recorded as the culture of death was the Rwanda genocide which took place in 1994 between the Hutu and Tutsi. Some people call it "ethnic cleansing" which has the nation of accumulated hatred between the two tribes Hutu and Tutsi. It is believed that "about 85% of Rwandans are Tutu but the Tutsi minority has long dominated the country."[159] The Hutus overthrew the Tutsi monarch and tens of thousands of Tutsi fled to neighbouring countries, including Uganda. Some state that a group of Tutsi exiles formed a rebel group, the Rwandan patriotic front (RPF), which invaded Rwanda in 1990 and fighting continued until the 1993 peace deal was agreed.

What prompted this culture of death was also shooting plane carrying President Juvenal Habyarimana and his counterpart Cyprian Ntaryamiria of Burundi, in which everyone on board was killed. This allowed bilateral accusations between the two tribes which amounted to high tension. Some say that Hutu extremists blame the RPF and immediately started a well-organized campaign of slaughter while the RPF said the plane had been shot down by the Hutu to provide an excuse for the genocide. It is confirmed that:

With meticulous organizations lists of government opponents were handed out to militias who killed them, along with their families. Neighbours killed neighbours' and some husbands even killed their Tutsi wives, saying they would be killed if they refused. ID cards had people's ethnic groups on them, so militias set up roadblocks where Tutsi were slaughtered, often with machetes which most Rwandans kept around the house. Thousands of Tutsi women were taken away and kept as sex slaves.[160]

How this culture of death aroused at this level among two ethnic groups, one cannot wonder, the accumulation of violence among them has resulted in such atrocities. M. Adossi concurs with Butigan asserting that "Violence is emotional, verbal, or physical behavior which

---

159   www.bbc.com/news/world-africa-26875506, retrieved as from 26/07/2018.
160   Ibid.

dominates, diminished dehumanizes or destroys ourselves or others. Violence is often motivated by fear unrestrained anger, or greed to increase domination or power over others."[161] Some argue that violence can also be motivated by the desire for justice in the face of injustice: a longing to put things right to overcome an imbalance of power, to end victimization or oppression through wrong means.

As to the causalities, various documents state that the death toll of the Rwanda genocide increased from around 500,000-800,000 Tutsi killed (Prunier, 1998, p, 264), representing the annihilation of about 84% of the Tutsi population in 1994."[162] Some say that "just in 100 days in 1994, some 800,000 people were slaughtered in Rwanda by ethnic Hutu extremists."[163] Further, it is asserted that Tutu was targeting members of the minority Tutsi community, as well as their political opponents, despite their ethnic origin. For example, the unfortunate tragic event of the Rwanda genocide between Hutu and Tutsi in which they used local tools such as machetes which has led to the death of many lives. Can you imagine how people in the Rwanda genocide would have died if they used guns in 100 days? We can affirm that violence is more intrinsic in human nature.

We made Rwanda's genocide a point of reference to the culture of death but we also know almost every country in our continent has experienced violence such as civil war, the war between two countries; and proxy war. All these wars originated from moral agents and they are moral evils that is, evils by choice. Therefore, when we talk of violence; let us first look into ourselves to discover the areas of violence we have inherited in our human nature.

---

161 Cf. Foffissan Mathias Adossi, *Conflict Resolution and Transformation: A participation Approach for Youth*, Nairobi: Paulines Publications African, 2009, p. 23.

162 www.cairn-int.info/article-E_POPU_504_0401--- retrieved as from 26/07/2018.

163 www.bbc.com/news/world-africa-26875506, retrieved as from 26/07/2018.

7.4 Colonial Period

During the colonial period, the culture of death was inflicted upon the continent through the depletion of natural resources and the slave trade. The demarcations of geographical location within the continent based on interest were the main strategy for such activities. The superiority complex and the inferiority complex were the characteristics of this period. Indigenous people of the continent became part of natural resources as it did happen elsewhere in the world. A mixed policy which consisted of political conquest of the continent and religious activities that is, Christianity and Islam were competing over new converts. The colonial period can be described as a period of exploitation in which both natural resources and indigenous people were disappearing. There were also other causes of culture of death in the continent from nature such as diseases, famine, drought, earthquakes, volcanoes, fires, and floods.

For example, somebody says, the missionaries said to their converts, 'Let's close our eyes and pray, after the prayer, the land is gone, who took the land? These are funny things about the culture of death that happened during the colonial period. The colonizers massacred the indigenous people through slavery and by confronting their resisters with guns. An example of this colonial period is what Egypt experienced as indicated in that, "Egypt passed from the rule of the polemics to that of Rome almost imperceptibly"[164] from year -237. G. Mokhtar asserts that the Roman emperor, however, copied the polemics administration of Egypt as a vast personal estate, the whole income from which was managed by the crown. Such a policy of colonial conquest of the culture of death that began with Egypt in North Africa was implacable to many African countries.

---

164   G. Mokhtar, (ed), *General History of Africa: II Ancient Civilizations of Africa,* Nairobi: UNESCO, 1990, p.131.

After Egypt liberated itself from the Roman Empire, it massacred the indigenous people of Sudan with a foreign policy called "Angelo-Egyptian condominium rule" thus allowing the activities of slavery to operate through Arab traders. The culture of death continued with the British's conquest of Sudan and Uganda. The indigenous people were massacred by the Colonizers and after Sudan gained independence in 1956, the Sudanese people also massacred themselves. The scenarios and spiral of the culture of death continue. This had created a spirit of difference between the Arabs of Sudan and the Southerners of Sudan by then. This culture of death is expressed by A. Akol asserting, "In 1898, Sudan used to belong to the Sudanese; after that Sudanese took its ways from the Egyptians, misgoverned themselves and massacred themselves and everyone else; and then in the end either England helped win it back to Egypt or Egypt helped to win it for England."[165] According to H. Idris,

> Alienated by their use of force the Africans remained, with a few exceptions, impervious to the appeals to Mahdism preached by the Arabs and resisted attempts by the Arabs to force Islam upon them. The failure of the Mahdists to spread Islam up the Nile is one of the most significant aspects of the Mahdiya. A generation of interaction between the Africans and the Arabs in the Northern Sudan had produced not the acceptance of Islam or Arab culture by the African tribesmen, but a legacy of distrust and fear and tradition of resistance to the imposition of alien ideas and customs upon them.[166]

---

165   Deng D. A. Akol Rauy, *The Politics of two Sudans: The South and the North, 1821-1969*, Motal-Sweden: Motala Grafiska, 1994, p.11.

166   Amir H. Idris, *Sudan's Civil War: Slavery, Race and Formational identities*, Lewiston: The Edwin Mellen press, 2001, p.44.

7.5 The Dilemma of Post-Colonial Period

After the post-colonial period, somehow the continent experienced independence from foreign invaders. The civil authority is in the hands of indigenous people both in society and in the Church. For example, the local hierarchy is exercised by the local bishops usually in the continent. The Urban cities have brought indigenous people closer to one another though with serious challenges. Both Christianity and Islam have brought the indigenous people together as brothers and sisters.

Although the continent has experienced figures of dictatorship, nevertheless, there are at least two African leaders who can take as excellent models such as the late President Nelson Mandela of South Africa and the late President Julius Nyerere of Tanzania who initiated *Ujamaa*-African socialism. The post-colonial period also experienced developments of various political ideologies such as black consciousness, and negritude as R. Rwiza concurs with Lēopold Sèdar Senghor affirming that:

First negritude was a history lived and was expressed in written poetry and prose. It was born out of the denial of the dignity of the black people. It was born out of their struggle for freedom. It emerged from their own lived experience of protest, defence and inspiration, an elaboration of their situation and hope.[167]

R. Rwiza and Sneghor assert that negritude is the fact of being black, implying the concept of a spiritual return to the original homeland to regain an authentic back identity, in terms of cultural heritage and the spirit of communitarianism. Pan-Africanism according to Rwiza and Nkrumah denotes a moment initiated to claim equal rights, self-government, independence, and unity for legitimate bodies formed after the colonial period such as the pan-African moment from 1900-1945, which we have mentioned before, the organization of African Unity as

---

167   Ibid.

from "May 26, 1963"[168] which has its limitations.

Some of these limitations were pointed out by President Godfrey Binaisa of Uganda who took the floor at the 1979 Summit in the apartheid era. Condemning the racial regime in Liberia said, "There is no use to criticize other's human rights records when we are doing the same thing."[169] The naked power was exercised by some African leaders as Okoth states "At the same time Emperor Bokassa had just beaten 80 disrespectful school children to death, and Macia Nguema Biyongo of Equatorial Guinea had murdered about one-eighth of his country's population."[170] Okoth said for example, leaders like Idi Amin of Uganda, Kamuzu Banda of Malawi, and Mobuto Sese Sako of the Now DR. Congo massacred their civilians and looted the wealth of their nations with impurity. It is said something had to be done to make the OAU more meaningful. African Union was formed on July 9, 2002, in Durban, South Africa and Regional Economic Cooperation was also formed.

Conclusion

Chapter Seven has discussed the main forms of power, the classification of power, traditional power, the power of the leadership papacy, and kingly power. It also presented colonial the period, and depletion of natural resources and the slave trade. This chapter has further elaborated on the naked and revolutionary power. It has also presented the Rwandan genocide and some areas of the culture of life on the continent. The chapter has illustrated the post-colonial period.

---

168   Assa Okoth, *A History of Africa, Volume II: African Nationalism and the Decolonialsation Process,* Nairobi: East African Eduactional Publishers, 2006, p. 319.

169   Ibid, p.324.

170   Augustine Mugarura, *Impulse to Power According to Russell,* p. 85.

Chapter Eight:
The Covid-19 Pandemic

Introduction

Chapter eight deals with a matrix of covid-19 pandemic and its definition. It discusses various hypotheses (or theories of the origin of Covid-19; its infectiousness as a contagious and transferal disease; its symptoms and its ethics). The chapter also presents the responses of world leaders to the COVID-19 pandemic including medical professionals through various social principles; such as public health guidelines for U.S. citizens; presidential guidelines for Ugandans; and presidential guidelines for South Sudanese. Furthermore, the chapter also explains covid-19 pandemic, as a disease for everybody; its impacts on the world and the incredible fight against it. The chapter also presents general concepts of myths; myths vs. realities by Jackie Powder; quiz-myths according to W.H.O. on COVID-19; and finally, the local myths in South Sudan about COVID-19.

8. Pre-Epidemic and Covid-19 Pandemic

Historically, human life has experienced different types of viruses, each with its degree of contagiousness; complexity; delicacy, unique behaviour and deadly consequence. According to C. Lennox, after all, we seem to have little difficulty accepting the annual influenza death statistics. For example, Public Health estimates that, on average, 17,000 people in England have died annually from flu in the past five years; in the US, the Center for Disease Control and Prevention puts the figure for October 2019 to March 2020 at 23,000-59,000."[171] They also estimated that in 2019, 1.35 million people died on roads worldwide.

C. Lennox argues that there have been similar pandemics in the past. According to him, the most ancient recorded instance is probably the so-called Antonine Plague or Plague of Galen in AD 165-180. The cause of this disease was uncertain but was thought to have been measles or smallpox. It killed around five million people. It is believed that there was also the Plague of Justinian (AD 541-542). This was a bubonic disease which was spread from animals (rats) via fleas to humans. The causalities of this disease were over 25 million. It is argued that there was a further bubonic plague, known as the Black Death in the 14th century (1346-1353), which killed an estimated 70-100 million people living in Eurasia, reducing the world population by around 20 per cent. C Lennox further states, that much later in history, there were several cholera pandemics in the 19th and early 20th centuries in which over a million died. He asserts, that a flu pandemic took 20 million lives in 1918-1920. C. Lennox gives his testimony by stating "In my lifetime, two million died of Asian flu in 1956-1958 and a further millions of Hong Kong flu in

---

[171] Cf. John C. Lennox, *Where is God in A Coronavirus World?* United Kingdom, The Good Book Company, 2020, p.10.

1968-1969."¹⁷² The HIV/AIDS pandemic, which was at its peak in 2005-2012, has had a death toll of around 32 million.

On December 8, 2019-2020, human life was once again attacked by the most complex, and deadly delicate type of virus called 'Covid-19' (coronavirus by the World Health Organization (W.H.O.). It is affirmed that the 'Covid-19 pandemic' is the name given by the World Health Organization (W.H.O.), on February 11, 2020, for the disease caused by the novel coronavirus SARS-CoV-2."¹⁷³ It is further stated that it started in Wuhan, China in late December 8, 2019. Furthermore, the coronavirus pandemic is described as an 'acronym' that stands for coronavirus disease of 2019-2020. Furthermore, it is affirmed that Covid-19 is the name of the disease caused by the SARS-CoV2 virus. The World Health Organization (W.H.O.) also states that the viruses and the diseases they cause have different names. For example, AIDS is a disease caused by the human immunodeficiency virus (HIV). It is asserted that covid-19 in its full form, stands for coronavirus disease of 2019.

On December 31, 2019, a strange new pneumonia of unknown cause was reported to the Chinese WHO Country Office. A cluster of these causes originally appeared in Wuhan, a city in the Hubei Province in China. It has been asserted that "These infections were found to be caused by a new coronavirus which was given the name "2019 novel coronavirus" (2019-CoV)."¹⁷⁴ Furthermore, the World Health Organization states that it was later renamed "severe acute respiratory coronavirus 2," or SARS-CoV-2 by the International Committee on Taxonomy of Viruses on February 11, 2020. Again, it was named SARS-CoV-2 because the virus is a genetic cousin of the coronavirus

---

172   John C. Lennox, *Where is God in A Coronavirus World?* P. 10.

173   https:// www.goodrx. Com/blog/what-does-covid-19-mean-who-named-it, retrieved as from 13/04/2020.

174   https:// www.goodrx. Com/blog/what-does-covid-19-mean-who-named-it, retrieved as from 13/04/2020.

caused by the SARS outbreak in 2002 (SARS-CoV). It is asserted that the unofficial name for the virus is '*The Covid-19 virus*. The World Health Organization also defines coronavirus as mild to severe respiratory illness that is caused by coronavirus (severe acute respiratory syndrome coronavirus 2 of the genus Beta coronavirus) and is transmitted chiefly by contact with infectious material (such as respiratory droplets). Its symptoms are fever, cough, and shortness of breath that may progress to pneumonia and respiratory failure.

The new pneumonia of 'unknown cause' that was reported to the Chinese W.H.O. Country Office, coincided with information that Dr Li Wenliang who first whistled about the unique abnormal behaviour of the coronavirus in Wuhan, was however, warned by the Chinese authorities not to spread rumours. Consequently, he contracted covid-19 in a hospital and died as a victim of it, in Wuhan the capital Province of Hubei on February 7th /2020, at 02:58 on Friday (18:18 GMT). Consequently, Dr. Li was considered a hero by the Chinese in Wuhan for proclaiming the truth. Some people say that COVID-19 is not the first of its kind in China but rather the second type in its appearance.

In early January 2020, the Chinese authorities passed a piece of information to the United States of America about the imminent threats of the pandemic which Mr. Trump's administration ignored. This was confirmed by Dr. Anthony Fauci the US Director of the National Institute of Allergy and Infectious Disease. He is characterized as the trusted voice in the United States in separating fact and fiction. Dr Fauci states that if "We had, right from the beginning, shut everything down, it may have been a little different," Dr. Fauci told CNN, but added that making the decision had been complicated."[175] Dr. Fauci says US 'could have saved lives with earlier action. Other US top Health Officials state that U.S. "could have saved lives" if it had introduced measures

---

175   https:www.bbc.com/news/world-us-canada-52264860, retrieved as from 16/04/2020.

to stop Covid-19 earlier. According to Dr Fauci, "no one is going to deny" that logically, earlier mitigation could have saved lives. He said, when we make a recommendation, often the recommendation is taken and sometimes it's not. But it is what it is. We are where we are right now."[176] Dr Fauci adds by using a metaphor from the fastest-moving sports to describe his strategy on the outbreak by stating that 'you skate not to where the puck is, but to where the puck is going to be.'

Hypotheses of Covid-19 Pandemic

1. The majority of ordinary people including some few experts believe that coronavirus is a disease of bats. This theory is in the process of investigation by the scientific community. 2. Dr. Fauci who specializes in infectious diseases and member of the 'White House Coronavirus Task Force" for Covid-19 in America, states that "markets selling wild animal meats must be banned due to their health status." 3. The majority of people believe that coronavirus was a bioweapon leaked in the lab of Wuhan. 4. Some people believe that it might be revenge from nature against us or retaliation (fighting back or hitting back. 5. Others believe that coronavirus was a response to our complaints about our number here on earth. For example, Cairo's Conference which proposed for an artificial family planning in 1994. Furthermore, some whizzed experts use the word "population explosion" to exaggerate our number and to terrify innocent people. 6. Some people believe that coronavirus came to disapprove of our false exploitive dominion over nature (disregard for nature). 7. Furthermore, others believe that coronavirus came as a consequence of the battle between good and evil and naively justify it in the book of Revelation (Cf. Rev 20:7-10). 9. Some people believe that COVID-19 came to disprove our illusion of claim of "absolute freedom" or our claim of "absolute autonomy" without limitations over nature.

---

176   https:www.bbc.com/news/world-us-canada-52264860, retrieved as from 19/04/2020.

10. Some people do not even believe Covid-19 exists. 11. Others say that coronavirus may originate either from one type of animal as defense mechanism for their lives or from one type of plant or insect as a defense mechanism for their lives. In principle, we are not allowed to eat everything and we are also not allowed to touch everything because our experiences tell us that certain creatures or plants or insects are poisonous. 12. The team of experts from the World Health Organization and other experts made an investigation about the possible origin of the virus in China. They concluded their findings with four possible scenarios about the origin of the virus such as 1. Direct spillover from animals to humans. 2. Spillover from animals to humans through the intermediate host. 3. Introduction through refrigerated or frozen foods. 4. Unlikely possible from the laboratory leak. As to the exact origin of Covid-19, attempts are on the way by the Chinese high scientific universities to establish the cause of it, but CNN on April 13, 2020, reported that "China imposes restrictions on research on Covid-19 pandemic." It is reported that Chinese authorities warn that any publication of its origin must be restricted by Beijing. This restriction prompts a lot of questions and suspicions as to whether China was aware of its origin or not.

8.2 The Blame Game Between America and China

There were 'counter-blames' between U.S. and China concerning the origin of Covid-19. Each of these two countries suspected the other of being behind the cause of COVID-19. United States blames China for two reasons; by accusing her of lack of transparency about COVID-19, and by suspecting that COVID-19 may be related to Chinese lab mishandling or intentional handling in Wuhan. There was a claim by the Washington Post that two cables were sent in 2018 as lab research bat coronavirus in Wuhan. China on her part, suspected the U.S. for being behind the origin of Covid-19. Based on those counter-blames between the two countries, so far, there is no scientific evidence as to whether Covid-19 is a bioweapon or not.

For example, in World War II, on August 6, 1939-1945, an American B-29 bomber dropped the world's first atomic bomb over the Japanese city of Hiroshima, the explosion wiped out 90 per cent of the city and immediately killed 80, 000 people; tens of thousands more would later die of radiation exposure. It is affirmed that…"three days later, a second B-29 dropped another A-bomb on Nagasaki, killing an estimated 40,000 people."[177] This second atomic A-bomb on Nagasaki forced Japan's Emperor Hirohito to announce his country's unconditional surrender in World War II in a radio address on August 13, citing the devastating power of a new and cruel bomb.

In that cruelest incidence of World War II, our common sense permits us to conclude that there is no vaccine or "antibody for any bioweapon." Every person is liable to bioweapon. Should Covid-19 originate from the lab, scientists would have revealed to the world that it is so. Scientists all over the world, including in the U. S. and China are still doing research on vaccines and antibodies for Covid-19. Perhaps, this could mean that COVID-19 is one of the new infectious diseases as appears in its descriptions. Then, let the establishment of scientific facts about Covid-19 be left to scientists and not to politicians. Therefore, only a scientific finding will prove the degree of authenticity of the origin of the COVID-19 pandemic.

The chronological dates and years recorded below demonstrate that the U.S. blames China for not being sincere in its handling of COVID-19. The accusation is related to the following chronological dates: A Chinese epidemiologist together with the Chinese Centre for Disease Control and Prevention: article on 20th Jan 2020. The first cluster of patients with 'pneumonia of an unknown cause, was identified on 21st Dec. 2019.

---

177   Cf. J. Tab Charoa, *The Dramatic Clash Between the Culture of life and Culture of Death, Its Relevance to the African Context*, Juba, Universal Printers Company Ltd, 2018, p.25.

On December 31ˢᵗ 2019, it was argued that the Chinese confirmed they were treating cases of pneumonia of an unknown cause. Days later, researchers in China identified a new virus that had infected dozens of people. No evidence that the virus was spreading from a human. China contacted their WHO and informed them of a case of pneumonia of unknown etiology' detected in Wuhan. On Jan 2ⁿᵈ 2020, it was reported that the central hospital of Wuhan banned its staff from discussing the disease publicly or recording them by using text or images that can be used as evidence. On Jan 8ᵗʰ 2020, it was affirmed that the Chinese agreed to accept a WHO scientific team to assist their researchers. On Jan 11, 2020, it asserted that Chinese state media reported the first known death of an illness caused by the virus. A 61-year-old man who was a regular customer of the market in Wuhan. He had been previously found to have abdominal tumours and chronic liver disease.

On Jan 14 2020, Reporters from Hong Kong took to a police station after trying to film the situation in Wuhan hospital. On *Jan 20 2020*, the First cases were confirmed from outside mainland China which occurred in Japan, South Korea, and Thailand according to the World Health Organization. On Jan 21ˢᵗ 2020, the first case of the virus was confirmed in Washington State, U.S.A, where a man in his 30s developed symptoms after returning from Wuhan. However, on was discovered that COVID-19 was already in the U.S. by February 6ᵗʰ/2020 than it was thought to be. Jan 22 2020, Public Health in England announced that it was moving the risk level to the British Public from' very low' to' low'. On *Jan 23ʳᵈ 2020,* Wuhan (population over 11 million) was cut off by the Chinese authorities. Planes and trains leaving the city are cancelled, and buses, subways and ferries within the city are suspended. 17 people had already died at this point. Already 570 were infected in Taiwan, Japan, Thailand, and South Korea including the U.S.A.

Figures compiled by the Chinese Railways Administration show that approximately 100,000 people had already departed from Wuhan train station by the dateline. Construction had begun in Wuhan for a specialized emergency hospital which was opened on the 3rd of February 2020. Just after seeing and reading these chronological dates and years, it is your duty as a reader to judge whether the blame of the U.S. against China for lack of transparency in its handling of the COVID-19 pandemic was genuine or not.

8.3 Covid-19 Pandemic as a Transferal Disease

As we have mentioned earlier, Covid-19 started in China, in Wuhan the capital city of Hubei Provence. It has spread worldwide with unprecedented rapid speed and infected the whole world from January 20th to April 5th 2020. We refer to the worldwide spread of the COVID-19 pandemic in all 195 countries within the five continents which are; Africa, America, Europe, Asia and Australia. Within 195, 193 countries are members of the United Nations, and 2 states are non-members of the United Nations namely, the Holy See and, the State of Palestine. About 29% of the world's countries are located in one continent, Africa. The continent of Africa alone has a total number of 54 countries as of April 19, 2020.

Out of the five continents, only 16 countries were freed from Covid-19 that is, Comoros; Kiribati; Lesotho; Marshall Islands; Micronesia; Nauru; North Korea; Palau; Samoa; Sao Tome and Principe; Solomon Islands; Tajikistan; Tonga; Turkmenistan; Tuvalu, and Vanuatu. All the remaining 177 countries plus the 2 states that are non-members of the United Nations were afflicted or infected by the Covid-19 pandemic. These above-mentioned 177 countries plus the 2 non-members of the United Nations were attacked by Covid-19 without exception beginning with developing and most advanced nations to the poorest ones. In this sense, Covid-19 has made all countries that have become candidates to it as members of it. Below are the descriptions of COVID-19 and how it got transferred from one country to another.

The coronavirus pandemic is described as a transferal contagious disease. It is also described as an "imported disease." It is further described as an "invisible enemy" which creates economic chaos worldwide. It is also described as a terrible, invisible disease with abnormal complicated behaviour. Dr. Siddhartha Mukherjee a cancer physician described it as a challenging disease which has two characteristics, "one infected person can infect hundreds of people, and that an "infected person does not know that he/she is infected by Covid-19. This seems to be the dilemma of Covid-19, that everyone is not sure of his/her status. Dr. Armand Dorian the Chief Medical Officer at USC Verdugo Hills- Hospital, confirms that within one month, one person who is infected with COVID-19 can infect one thousand persons.

On the other hand, Dr. Anthony Fauci warns us of the danger of delaying the testing result of Covid-19. According to him, you want to know exactly what you are dealing with; at the time you are dealing with it. Dr. Fauci added that it is better "to identify, to isolate an infected person. He asserts that if the number of cases has reduced, it is because social distancing is working. According to Priti Patel, the British Home Secretary in her briefing on Covid-19 on April 11, 2020, states that it is better to take the right step at the right time. Dr. Richard Howard highlights two dimensions of the level of suffering of COVID-19 patients within two weeks. According to him, one week is for constant coughing, and the other week is for deterioration of the patient's health which will determine either for his/her survival or for his/her death in the last stage of the shortness of breath.

Covid-19 was transferred to other countries first by those who were infected by it in Wuhan. If its contagiousness lives for "72 hours" (three days) on an object, and respiratory droplet through coughing or sneezing lives for 3 hours in the air according to the experts, and if some infected persons travel by the same flight taking into consideration the means of its transmission with those who are not infected yet, then, it should be very clear that majority of passengers might have been infected in that flight.

How many passengers do the intercontinental flight take? For example, after the official declaration of COVID-19 by the Chinese authorities to the World Health Organization after the suspension of all international flights by the U.S.A., experts said that within that period, *13,000* flights flew from Europe and landed in New York City. Consequently, it is believed that the coronavirus pandemic came to the U.S. through Europe and not from China to the U.S. Therefore, 13,000 flights with many infected persons flew from Europe and landed in New York City should be a good reason to justify the greater number of confirmed cases and the death toll in New York City more than any other States in the U.S. However this could have been prevented if the voices of the experts were listened to or heard by their politicians in the United States of America.

One can also imagine; how many infected persons were there on each flight. What about the circulation of oxygen in the flight' when its atmosphere is already infected by COVID-19 patients? What about the seats; the belts that were touched by infected persons and the shared toilets with handles touched by infected persons in the flight? These questions seem to resolve the dilemma as to why Covid-19 has spread rapidly worldwide in a short time according to my view. Therefore, those who were infected have unknowingly contributed to the transfer of COVID-19 to those who were not yet infected. By being so terrible and a killer, according to some people, Covid-19 that can be compared to World War II. The Americans also compared it to the September 11, 2001 attack.

Consequently, all the airlines or aviation companies all over the countries worldwide whether free from COVID-19 or candidates for COVID-19, were economically affected more than any other institutions on earth. The 'social distancing measures' both national and international were applied to various airline aviation companies without a time limit. The airline companies worldwide as we stated before, have contributed so much concerning the transfer of Covid-19 ignorantly to all the countries in the world and eventually, paid the high price.

8.4 Covid-19 Pandemic Symptoms and Its Ethics

According to the World Health Organization, the five symptoms of coronavirus are as follows: 1. Fever. 2. Cough. 3. Shortness of breath. 4. Pneumonia. 5. Respiratory failure. 6. Loss of consciousness. 7. Sudden onset of confusion. It has also other symptoms such as sneezing; running nose; diarrhea; vomiting; headache; and rise in body temperature; chill; muscle pain and sore throat. 8. Specifically, Covid-19 causes blood clotting and stroke in young people.

Therefore, because of the symptoms of coronavirus mentioned above, and with its capacity of contagiousness; COVID-19 has compelled medical doctors to propose general public health information or public service announcements (public health measures or right measures) such as the following with their heading *STAY HOME. SAVE LIVES.* Help stop coronavirus. 1. Stay at home as much as you can. 2. Keep a safe distance. 3. Wash your hands often. 4. Cover your cough. 5. Sick? Call ahead. Social physical distancing tolerates only one meter or two meters of distance. This will also depend on the direction of the wind according to medical doctors.

It is argued that Covid-19, as we all now know, is a contagious disease that can be deadly to certain groups of people. Many patients infected by the COVID-19 virus may experience mild to moderate symptoms and older people have reduced serious symptoms. According to the World Health Organization, the symptoms of Covid-19 range from mild to severe. It takes between 2-14 days after exposure to develop symptoms. Those with lower immunity may develop severe symptoms, such as bronchitis or pneumonia.

The World Health Organization asserts if you have the symptoms mentioned above or if you have possibly been exposed to the virus, medical advice should be sought. For responsible contact tracing purposes, inform your doctor of your travel or contact history. Let your doctor know if you have had close contact with anyone who has been recently diagnosed with the virus. Based on your signs and symptoms, your doctor may determine whether to conduct the diagnostic tests or not.

According to the World Health Organization, in most cases, doctors consider factors such as: Whether you have had close contact with someone diagnosed with the virus and if you have travelled or lived in areas with the ongoing spread of COVID-19 in the last two weeks. It is affirmed that your doctor may take samples of saliva (sputum), a nasal swab, and a throat swab to send to a laboratory for diagnostic tests.

The World Health Organization confirms that the most effective way to prevent or slow transmission is to be well-informed about the disease and how it spreads. As a recommendation, it is asserted that you must protect yourself and others from infection by washing your hands or using an alcohol-based sanitizer. Rub frequently and do not touch any part of your face.

Apart from those recommendations mentioned above, there was also a recommendation from medical personnel for citizens to wear non-medical face masks and medical doctors to wear medical masks. The famous international principle of COVID-19 which says 'stay at home' simply means stop spreading the virus. Recommendations to wear non-medical masks by citizens and medical masks by physicians and nurses and social distancing measures became the most adopted three principles worldwide as COVID-19 intensifies its attack on human life.

Yet, amidst this crisis of COVID-19, physicians have to prioritize patients who have more chance for survival over those who have less chance for survival, which requires a legal and ethical dimension otherwise, the value of each person takes priority. Physicians have also testified that among patients themselves, some voluntarily offered their ventilators to those who had more chance for survival than themselves. This is to be considered a heroic act and ethics of altruism.

Apart from the general guidelines which were provided by experts for COVID-19, there are other ethical principles which require observation and attention to Covid-19. These principles are as follows: 1. Avoid information overloaded. 2. Name your fear and prepare. 3. Think outside of yourself that is, in this period of the coronavirus pandemic which is a very contagious disease, one needs to care about the lives of others in terms of respecting social distancing. 4. Seek help from experts wisely. 4. Never feel a sense of guilt about your worries instead face them with courage. 4. Routine. Do your usual work. 6. Have a sense of hope for better days to come, that is, it is not the end of everything. The Governor of New York, Andrew Cuomo, in his daily briefing and updates on coronavirus, always ends with articulation and stipulation of the New Yorkers' ethics that is, to "be tough in being smart, in being disciplined, in being unified, and in being loving."

This situation mentioned above requires messages of hope from high-profile leaders in the world both political and religious. Her Majesty, Queen Elizabeth in her unusual address to the nation on April 05th 2020, calls for the implementation of the principle of social distancing during this period of isolation. She states that the people of the United Kingdom … "must be self-disciplined" and be united to defeat Covid-19. The Queen in her final speech, delivers a message of hope, she promises "better days to come." His Holiness, Pope Francis, on Palm Sunday, on April 05th of 2020, called for "creativity of love" during this time of Covid-19. Michael Howard, the former British Home Secretary states that, in this critical situation of COVID-19, we need critical decisions which will involve criticisms, yet with perseverance; patience; and wisdom.

8.5 The World Responses to Covid-19 Pandemic

In response to the coronavirus pandemic, world leaders including medical professionals formulated various social restrictions for the implementation of morality and ethics of "social distancing measures." They are as follows: 1. Guidelines. 2. Public Health guidelines. 3. Presidential Guidelines.4. Coronavirus Restrictions.5 Social restrictions. Federal Guidelines. 6. Social Distancing Measures. 7. Lockdown Restrictions. 8. International Guidelines. 9. National Guidelines. Uniformed Guidelines. World Health Organization Guidelines. 10. U.S. Center for Diseases Control (CDC) Guidelines. 11. The Executive Office issued: Initial 15-day Self-Isolation Guidelines. 12. Travel Restriction. 13. Strict Measures. 14. The White House Coronavirus Task Force Guidelines. 15. Stay-at-home orders.

One must question himself/herself as to why the ethics and morality of 'social distancing measures are formulated in various ways by different authorities that promulgated them and the implications they have on human life during the coronavirus pandemic. Nobody should ignore the different ways in which the 'social distancing measures' are formulated. Sometimes, there are clashes between politicians and experts who articulate and stipulate them. With such various terminologies, one can conclude that Covid-19 is so delicate and complex. Therefore, it requires stringent complex ethics and delicate morality. CDC Director states that Social Distancing is the most powerful measure for Covid-19. It is asserted that social distancing and good hygiene are key to limiting illness' reach. Harvard Researchers affirm that "Social Distancing may last until 2022."

Consequently, world leaders including religious leaders of various religions adopted disciplinary social distancing recommended by experts such as suspension of all social gatherings; suspension of all flights; suspension of all border crossings; and suspension of all religious gatherings including the celebration of Sunday masses or other forms of prayer. In short, all citizens in each country, are asked to stay at home. This has led to social isolation both for an infected dying; infected persons, and for the uninfected persons. In this *status quo,* even a funeral mass is allowed to be celebrated with attendants of only five members of the deceased person. Therefore, below are examples of three countries that have articulated and stipulated very clearly the implementation of the principle of social distancing which has repercussions in every aspect of human life. Yes, COVID-19 is so a complex and delicate disease, that also requires complex and delicate morality and ethics to combat it.

8.5.1 Public Health Guidelines for the U.S. Citizens

We may not be able to write down the healthcare measures for COVID-19 for every country. We shall only take three countries as examples for the rest, since all the guidelines for covid-19, are implacable to any situation with the same measure of rigidity. These countries include South Sudan, Uganda and the United States of America. First, the healthcare measures for the United States of America are presented below. There are other guidelines for stopping the spread of COVID-19 from the "White House Coronavirus Task Force" for COVID-19 in the U.S.A such as; 1. If you feel sick, stay home. Do not go to work. Contact your medical provider. 2. If you are sick be at home and if your children are sick, keep them at home. Do not send them to school. Contact your medical provider. 3. If someone in your household has tested positive for the coronavirus, keep the entire household at home.

Do not go to work. Do not go to school. Contact your medical provider. 4. If you are an older person, stay home and away from other people. 5. If you are a person with a serious underlying health condition that can put you at increased risk (for example, a condition that impairs your lungs or heart function or weakens your immune system) stay home and away from other people. 6. Even if you are young, or otherwise healthy, you are at risk and your activities can increase the risk for others. You must do your part to stop the spread of the coronavirus: 6.1. Work or engage in schooling from home whenever possible. 6.2.

If you work in a critical infrastructure industry, as defined by the Department of Home Security, such as healthcare services and pharmaceutical and food supply, you have a special responsibility to maintain your normal work in seclusion. You and your employers should follow CDC guidelines to protect your health at work. 6.3. Avoid social gatherings in groups of more than 10 people. 6.4. Avoid eating or drinking in bars, restaurants, and for courts-use drive-thru, pickup delivery options. 6.5. Avoid discretionary travel, shopping trips and social visits. 6.6. Do not visit nursing homes or retirement or long-term care facilities unless to provide critical assistance. 7. Practice good hygiene: 7.1. Wash your hands, especially after touching any frequently used items or surfaces. 7.2. Avoid touching your face. 7.3. Sneeze or cough into a tissue, or the inside of your elbow. 7.4. Disinfect frequently used items and surfaces as much as possible.

8.5.2 Ugandan Presidential Guidelines for Covid-19 Pandemic

In Uganda, President Yoweri K. Museveni for the implementation of social distancing guidelines prioritized the following in his address: 1. We are happy that we took critical decisions early enough, like closing schools and centres of worship. This will greatly reduce points of contact. 2. The government is suspending public transport for 14 days. This directive affects taxis, coasters, minibuses, buses, all passenger trains, tukutu buses, (tricycles) and bodda-boddas carrying passengers. This rationale is to minimize movement and contact among people. 3. Only private vehicles are allowed to operate and should not have more than three passengers, including the driver, at any single time. Therefore, let us not see families of more than three packed in private care. 4. Other vehicles that are not affected by this suspension are the trucks

(Lorries) delivery vans, and pick-ups delivering essential commodities and food. None of these vehicles should be used to ferry passengers.

5. Hospital ambulances, vehicles belonging to the security forces and some key government institutions doing essential work, plus those offering sanitary services are also exempted from this suspension. 6. Therefore, the government will not close markets, there will be some adjustments. With immediate effect, markets should only be used for the sale of foodstuff such as matooke, sweet potatoes, cassava, rice, beans, beef, chicken, vegetables, etc. 7. Trading of non-food items in the markets is suspended immediately. There should not be sales of items like clothes, necklaces, phones, sandals, shoes, etc. We expect this to greatly reduce numbers in the markets and help enforce social distancing. "I have also directed government ministries, agencies and departments to work out plans where only essential staff report for duty in the offices. The non-essential staff should work from home."[178] Critical agencies like the Uganda Revenue Authority will continue in full operation.

8.5.3 South Sudan Precipitation on Covid-19 Pandemic

Until March 30th 2020, South Sudan was among the three countries worldwide that were declared free of coronavirus or COVID-19. However, the leadership of the government of South Sudan was precipitating the eventuality of the coronavirus pandemic while it had already attacked all the bordering countries to South Sudan. Besides, the South Sudanese citizens were constantly watching various channels to see for themselves the attack of the coronavirus pandemic on human lives in other parts of the world. On April 05th 2020, the first case of COVID-19 was confirmed by U.N. staff of 29 women. On April 6th 2020,

---

178 www.statehouse.go.ug/media/news/2020/03/25/presidents-address-covid-19-new-guidelines, retrieved as from April 13, 2020.

another case of coronavirus was confirmed from another U.N. Staff. At this point, South Sudan became a candidate for Covid-19.

At this juncture, the South Sudanese began to wonder and say to themselves "If coronavirus can overwhelm developing or advanced nations such as the United States of America, Italy, China, Britain, Germany, etc., with enough facilities and medical personnel, what will happen to us now if it comes?

Can you imagine! Until this time in South Sudan, the machines for testing suspected cases of COVID-19 were offered voluntarily by South Africa, China, and Germany. Moreover, there are not enough facilities (hospitals), no electric power over the whole country that can operate ventilators; (respiratory machines for patients) and medical masks in the country; and not enough qualified medical personnel. Vice-President Dr. Riak Machar confirmed it when he said "South Sudan, with 11 million people, currently has four ventilators and wants to increase that number. Dr. Machar emphasized that people should stay three to six feet apart from others."[179] He added that 'the only vaccine is social distancing.

Nevertheless, in response to this imminent threat to human life by the coronavirus pandemic, the government of South Sudan has adopted all other world disciplinary measures or right measures to be on the safe side and to trust in God's care and protection. The leadership in the country calls these guidelines "Presidential Guidelines" articulated and stipulated by the High-Level Task Force Committee for COVID-19, appointed by President H.E. Salva Kiir, headed by Vice-President Dr. Riak Machar. Hence, those "Presidential Guidelines" for South Sudanese are articulated and stipulated below.

179　　https://time.com/5815838/south -sudan-africa-coronavirus-covid-19/ retrieved as from 15/04/2020.

8.5.3.1 Presidential Guidelines for the South Sudan

1. South Sudan's President Salva Kiir has urged all citizens to avoid handshakes and hugging each other as a protective measure against COVID-19. 2. He encouraged non-physical contact but said that citizens could opt for elbow and foot bumps as greetings if they have to make physical contact. 3. Suspension of all flights to countries affected by a novel coronavirus, effectively Friday midnight such as Egypt; Tunisia; Togo; Middle East; US; Canada; Brazil; Chile; Ecuador, Costa Rica, Peru; Paraguay; and some countries in Europe. In Asia, China; Korea; Japan; Singapore; Malaysia; Australia; Philippines; Vietnam; New Zealand, Cambodia; and India have been listed. Others are Thailand; Indonesia, Maldives and Bangladesh. 4. The ministry also added that all travellers in the country are being screened for COVID-19. 5. "South Sudan's President on Monday banned all social gatherings, including sporting events, religious events; weddings and political activities, due to coronavirus."[180] 6. President Salva Kiir also temporarily postponed international conferences slated to take place in South Sudan.

7. All planned social gatherings like sporting events, religious events, socio-cultural ones such as weddings, and political events must be postponed. 8. Caution must be exercised to reduce and avoid crowding at places of work. 9. Workers sharing an office space must ensure they are seated at least one meter apart. 10. We have directed security and law enforcement agencies to support the Health Ministry in enforcing self-quarantine, removing COVID-19 suspected cases, and relocating them to isolation centres for 14 days said the President.

11. Travelers arriving in South Sudan from affected countries and areas with established local transmission will be self-quarantined for 14 days said the President. 12. Non-essential travellers to affected countries

---

180   https:www.aa.com.tr/end/Africa/coronavirus-south-sudan-bans-socail gatherings/17/68378, retrieved as from 13/04/2020.

must be called off or postponed to a later day said the President. 13. We have ordered restrictions on the movement of people including declining to issue new visas, revoking visas and resident's permits and denying admission to ports of entry added by the President. 14. Suspension of all the training of unified forces. 15. President Salva Kiir ordered the closure of all border crossing points and shut down commercial flights, including imposing stringent measures on public transport and trade.

16. Imposing a night curfew from 8:00 p.m. to 6:00 a.m. except in emergency cases that require health services. 17. The spread of COVID-19 in the region has further halted the return of millions of displaced people both internally and externally to their homes. 18. The only vaccine is social distancing", said Machar. Protect yourself and stop the spread of Coronavirus in South Sudan: 1. Wash your hands frequently with soap and water. 2. Avoid shaking hands and close contact with anyone 3. Maintain physical distancing in markets, churches, mosques, funerals, marriages, health facilities and other public sites. 4. Use face masks in public places. 5. Avoid group eating and gatherings. 6. Cover your mouth and nose with tissue or cough and sneeze into a flexed elbow 7. Stay home and avoid travel when you have flu-like symptoms.

8.6 Covid-19 Pandemic: A Disease for Everybody

Experts assert that Covid-19 does not discriminate, old and young all are liable for infection. However, physicians underscore that some are susceptible to COVID-19 and those who show no signs or are asymptomatic to COVID-19. Because of these variations, Doctors are making some hypotheses on essential issues such as antibodies or genes of each individual may play greater to susceptibility or asymptomatic. Nevertheless, coronavirus is a disease for every person, rich, and poor alike. Even the high profile world leaders such as British Prime Minister Boris Johnson; Prince Charles of England' and Prime Minister of Israel

Benjamin Netanyahu were the first to be infected by Covid-19 before other world leaders.

Consequently, they were quarantined. In a normal situation of war, such leaders only command others to fight and do not go to the front line, and should the situation of normal war get worse, they will be the last to die. However, with Covid-19, this is not the case. Covid-19 can attack any commander in chief without his/her notice in any country wherever, and whenever it wants. The first female U.S. former Secretary of State Madeleine Albright when interviewed by Fareed Zakaria on CNN on April 19, 2020, affirmed that "coronavirus knows no boundaries."

It is not a normal war that we are used to, it is a war that is waged against human beings by an "invisible enemy" and as if, and nature is revenging on us. It is a spiral of violence if you wish, because sometimes we inflict more violence on nature, and sometimes, nature comes to revenge on us. Historically, this has repeated itself several times in various events of our lives. The aggressiveness and contagiousness of the coronavirus pandemic put all people at an equal level. There is no longer rich; poor; white; black; old or young as we have indicated before.

8.7 Humanity in Solidarity with Each Other

The role of technology in fighting against our common enemy, the "coronavirus pandemic" is an amazing one. In this specific *status quo* of the coronavirus pandemic, through technological means, we were able to receive the latest news updates about the COVID-19 pandemic. Technology provided various means of video plays for COVID-19 patients to cope with social distancing or social isolation. It facilitates work from home such as meetings, conferences and lectures for developing nations. According to Richard Quest, "working from home" (WFH) has become a 'new reality' imposed by the Covid-19 pandemic.

Pope Francis says, that if the struggle against COVID-19 is a war, then you are truly an invisible army, fighting in the most dangerous trenches; an army whose only weapons are solidarity, hope and community spirit, all revitalizing at a time when no one can save themselves alone. Pope Francis states, 'To me, you are social poets.' We see in this chaotic situation of COVID-19, each government in each country has tried its level best to provide means or instruments for healthcare workers. Such instruments are needed by physicians and nurses like medical masks for doctors and nurses, and ventilators for respiratory breathing for Covid-19 patients in various hospitals in each country. Each government provided non-medical masks to citizens of each country. This is all done through the "High-Level Task Force for COVID-19" in some countries while the rest adopted other models. Each government in each country provides some guidelines for COVID-19 with the help of medical experts. Various journalists both in newsrooms and in frontlines give daily news updates on Covid-19 patients in different hospitals worldwide.

Medical doctors and nurses deserve to be given distinction in their incredible fight against the coronavirus pandemic. Their heroic act will be unforgettable in this war. Some medical doctors lost their lives due to a lack of personal protection equipment (PPE) that could protect them from this rampant contagious disease. In Italy alone, 51 physicians and 50 priests lost their lives in the U.S.A. 100 hundred doctors lost their lives, the list can go on. Each citizen in each country acknowledged this amazing life support from medical doctors and nurses and they were applauded for their heroic acts worldwide. His Holiness Pope Francis on his part said, if we act as one people, even in the face of other epidemics that threaten us, we can make a real impact. He continues, may we find within us the necessary antibodies of justice, charity and solidarity. Pope Francis also states, as the tragic coronavirus pandemic has taught us, we can overcome global challenges only by showing solidarity with one another and embracing the most vulnerable in our midst.

Other institutions which did charitable work such as various football teams or associations in Europe turned their various facilities into Covid-19 patients' facilities. Military facilities in the U.S. were given to Covid-19 patients and various security organs joined the front line in fighting against our common enemy "the Coronavirus Pandemic." Various companies and engineers also joined this fight by making ventilators and other necessary instruments such as medical masks for doctors and nurses.

The fight against Covid-19 was both national and international. Human beings were united together both enemy and friend to fight the common enemy "Covid-19. The biggest Evangelical Church was turned into facilities for COVID-19 on the eve of the Easter Celebration. Masses were celebrated for the Covid-19 victims and the recuperation of infected persons. There was daily individual adoration in front of the Blessed Sacrament for the defeat of Covid-19. An old man of 99 years of age, British veteran captain Tum moved around 100 times by pushing his wheel cards before celebrating his 100 years. By that exercise, he raised 66 million for the healthcare workers as a work of charity. During the celebration of his Birthday of one hundred years, he received 125,000 congratulatory cards. Miss. Alicia Keys composed a song for all those who did charitable works during the coronavirus pandemic regardless of race; religion' color; background; and status. It is affirmed that Alicia Keys honours unsung heroes in the new song "Good Job."

The British Prime Minster Boris Johnson in his briefing after he recuperates from Covid-19, states that "we have put a lot of money for mental healthcare charity, because of the increase of suicide cases during Covid-19. He added that the objective of the government is to minimize death and maximize life. The Congregation for Divine Worship and the Discipline of the Sacraments states that "The plague that prowls in the darkness you will not fear (Cf. Ps 90, 5-6). The above-mentioned Congregation asserts that "In these days, during which the whole world has been gravely stricken by the COVID-19 virus, many requests have come to this Disaster to be able to celebrate a specific Mass to implore God to bring an end to this pandemic."[181]

It is affirmed that this Congregation, in virtue of the faculties granted to it by the Supreme Pontiff (Pope Francis), is permitted to celebrate the Mass in Time of Pandemic, on any day except Solemnities, the Sundays of Advent, Lent, and Easter, days within the Octave of Easter, the Commemoration of All the Faithful Departed (All Souls' Days), Ash Wednesday and the days of Holy Week). In the Archdiocese of Juba, South Sudan, a prayer for consolation and healing during covid-19 pandemic was prepared to be recited before the final blessing after the Holy mass. It reads; God, our creator, you who are all power and might, you are indeed the Father of all in the Universe, listen to our prayer. We, your children, are daily faced by the fear of COVID-19, the fatal disease. We cry unto you to intervene on our behalf, sparing us of all evils.

Almighty Father, we thank you for the gift of life, good health and peace that we enjoy. We pray for consolation, healing and wholeness for the sick. Protect the elderly and save the lives of the little children. In your great mercy receive all the dead into your heavenly home. In this time of trials, give us the vision that enables us to see your hand at work in the world, despite our human weakness. Let our hope and goodness grow as often as we are assailed by doubts and fears. We pray for those who are involved in the Medical Research on COVID-19 that you bless them and bring their work to fruition. The prayer concludes, we make our prayer through Jesus Christ Your Son and our redeemer and saviour: Amen. These prayers are offered for good reasons as Pope Francis asserts "This disease has not only deprived us of human closeness, but also of the possibility of receiving in person the consolation that flows from the sacraments, particularly the Eucharist and

---

181 From the Congregation for Divine Worship and the Discipline of the Sacraments, *DEGREE on the Mass in Time of Pandemic,* 30, March 2020.

Reconciliation."[182] Furthermore, Francis asks 'How many are praying, offering and interceding for the good of all? Prayer and quiet service: these are our victorious weapons.

8.8 The Deaths of COVID-19 and Recent Events in the Globe

Globally, as of 5.57 pm CEST, 25 October 2023, there have been 771,549,718 confirmed cases of COVID-19, including 6,974,473 deaths, reported to the World Health Organization. As of 22 October 2023, a total of 13,533,465,652 vaccine doses have been administered. The recent earthquake in Morocco killed 2,900 people.

Around 11,000 people are believed to have died, according to the Red Crescent, though Derna mayor Abdulmenam Al-Ghaithi fears that up to 20,000 people perished in the port city alone thousands more have been displaced after entire neighbourhoods were washed away when two dams burst under pressure from Storm Daniel's intense rainfall. The ongoing war between Russia and Ukraine about the people who have died and who will die on both sides cannot be determined because the war is ongoing. The same is true for Israel and Palestine

Conclusion

Chapter eight has dealt thoroughly with a matrix of the COVID-19 Pandemic and its definition. It has discussed various hypotheses (or theories of covid-19 pandemic; its infectiousness as a contagious and transferal disease; its symptoms and its ethics. The chapter also has presented the responses of world leaders to covid-19 pandemic including medical professionals through various social principles such as public health guidelines for U.S. citizens; presidential guidelines for Ugandans; and presidential guidelines for South Sudanese.

---

182   Francis, *Life After Pandemic*, p. 25.

Furthermore, the chapter has explained also covid-19 pandemic, as a disease for everybody; its impacts worldwide' and the incredible fight against it.

Chapter Nine:
The Mythological Confusions of Covid-19 Pandemic

Introduction

Chapter Nine presents general dramatic concepts of myths; myths vs. realities by Jackie Powder; quiz-myths according to W.H.O. on the Covid-19 pandemic; and finally, the local myths in South Sudan for COVID-19. This chapter discusses thoroughly the role of myths during uncertainty and fear.

9. The Role of Myths About Covid-19 Pandemic

Myth is described as a story, handed down from olden times, especially concepts or beliefs of natural events, such as the seasons. However, myth is not limited to the origin of religion alone, but it plays a greater role in human life. Broadly, myth tries to explain certain dilemmas or uncertainties of situations where the answer becomes impossible through human reason or human logic. According to J. Mbiti, "A myth is a means of explaining some actual or imaginary reality which is not adequately understood and so cannot be explained through normal descriptions."[183] He argued that myths do not have to be taken literally, since they are not synonymous with facts. It is asserted that they are intended to communicate and form the basis for a working explanation about something. J. Mbiti argues that some myths are more important and meaningful than others, and some myths have a longer history than others. He further affirms that myths continue to be formulated all the time.

It is difficult to prove the authenticity of a myth or its facts. Nevertheless, myth tries to answer such questions of uncertainty and fear. It is only a trial which requires investigation and enquiry. Therefore, in this situation of Covid-19 where experts are unable to get medicine for Covid-19, myths are created to resolve and answer questions about "uncertainty and fear'. In this time of the coronavirus pandemic, myths have become international and local. Are they created by a person (creativity) or by some people? One of the debates among the experts during the period of COVID-19 was "malaria drugs (cardiology). Because some people believe that it can cure Coronavirus. Experts do say that there is no scientific evidence which proves that malaria drugs (cardiology) can cure Covid-19. Unfortunately, Mr. Trump, the president of the United States of America who is not an expert in the field of medicine said, "he is for it." India was ready to supply the U.S. with malaria drugs while experts objected. Mr. Trump also made another blunder by suggesting that ingesting or disinfectants could cure Covid-19 which he was also criticized by the experts.

If among the experts, a debate can be raised about this theory which says that 'malaria drugs'(cardiology) can cure COVID-19, how worse would it be for ordinary people when they propose myths to deal with the dilemma of Coronavirus that they believe could be the solutions to cope with it? Here, uncertainty and fear are the motives behind myths.

---

183   John S. Mbiti, *Introduction to African Religion*, Second Revised Edition, East Africa Educational Publishers, Kampala, 1991, P. 82.

In this specific chaotic situation of Covid-19, myths have become both international and local and each myth requires careful analysis. To dismiss them completely could mean not reading between the lines. Each myth whether international or local has its message to convey, that is why, and they are to be answered by experts. When there is no solution to the problem, myth works as a consolation while waiting for a real answer to come. Below are some international myths during the Covid-19 pandemic

9.1 Myths Versus Realities

According to Jackie Powder, the swiftly novel coronavirus continues its relentless spread around the world; upending life as we know it and creating a breeding ground for misinformation. Some rumours are harmless, while others can be dangerous, stoking fear and threatening health. Therefore, Jackie Powder prioritizes the following myths versus. Realities with various doctors are listed below.

1. *Myths*. The novel coronavirus is a bio-weapon. *Reality*: "At this point, there is no genetic evidence of anything other than a naturally occurring virus. There is indeed a major laboratory in Wuhan that studies coronavirus and has a large collection of coronavirus. But from the analysis that has been done…there isn't any evidence that this virus has been engineered or different from something that has been found in nature."[184] 2. *Myths*. The coronavirus remains in the throat for 4 days, causing sore throat and coughing before it reaches the lungs. 3. Drinking a lot of water and gargling with warm water and salt or vinegar can eliminate the virus. *Reality:* "While it is true that coronavirus can cause a sore throat and gargling with warm water may make it feel better, it has no direct effect on the virus."

---

184 https:/www/hsph/edu/covid-19/articles/coronavirus-facts-vs-myths.html, retrieved as from April 13, 2020.

4. *Myths*. Children are immune to the coronavirus. *Reality:* "We have seen (in a study conducted in China) that children are being infected in the same distribution as other age groups. They're just not symptomatic. Unless you were carefully doing contact tracing, you would miss those kids and might have the impression that kids just aren't getting infected. So the good news continues to be that so far no reports have come that kids are getting severe illness in high numbers, but it does appear that kids are getting infected in the same way as other age groups get infected."[185]

5. *Myths*. You can boost your immune system and lower your risk of getting Covid-19 by eating sweet potatoes and taking certain vitamins and supplements, or taking colloidal silver. *Reality:* "There is no evidence that you can boost your immune system by eating sweet potatoes, taking specific vitamins or supplements, or ingesting silver." 6. *Myths*. You can avoid the virus by drinking warm water every 15 minutes. *Reality:* I've seen this kind of meme going around the internet. There's also a claim that if possible drink cold water so that patients' lungs will become fibrotic. I want to stress there's no evidence at all to support these claims." 7. *Myths*. You can self-treat for COVID-19 by taking chloroquine phosphate, an additive used to clean fish tanks. *Reality:* Although chloroquine and hydroxychloroquine have been mentioned as a possible treatment for COVID-19, fish tank cleaning products that contain chloroquine phosphate are not intended for human use. While chloroquine phosphate can be used to treat malaria, it is a dangerous, lethal poison if not used correctly by a physician. Neither hydroxychloroquine nor chloroquine have been proven to definitively work for Covid-19. Primary data suggest a small benefit but this has to be validated.

---

185   https:/www/hsph/edu/covid-19/articles/coronavirus-facts-vs-myths.html, retrieved as from April 13, 2020.

9.2 Quiz-Myths According to W.H.O on Covid-19 Pandemic

Question 1. Can Covid-19 be transmitted in areas with hot and humid climates? *Answer:* Based on the evidence, COVID-19 can be transmitted in ALL AREAS. This includes places with hot and humid weather. *Question 2.* Can spraying alcohol or chlorine all over your body kill Covid-19? *Answer:* No. Spraying alcohol or chlorine all over your body will not kill viruses that have already entered your body. Alcohol and chlorine can be useful as surface disinfectants but need not be used according to recommendations. *Question 3.* Can taking a hot bath reduce the risk of infection? *Answer:* No. There is no scientific evidence of that kind. *Question 4.* Can cold weather kill the Covid-19 virus? *Answer:* There is no reason to believe that cold weather can kill the new coronavirus or other diseases. The normal human body temperature remains around 36.5 degrees Celsius to 37 degrees Celsius, regardless of the external temperature or weather. *Question 5.* Can the Covid-19 virus be transmitted through mosquito bites? *Answer:* There is no evidence to suggest that the coronavirus could be transmitted by mosquitoes. *Question 6.* Can an ultraviolet disinfection lamp kill the Covid-19 virus? *Answer:* UV lamps should not be used to sterilize hands or other areas of skin as UV radiation can cause skin irritation. *Question 7.* Are hand dryers effective in killing the new coronavirus? *Answer:* No. Hand dryers are not effective in killing the Covid-19 virus.

Question 8. Do vaccines against pneumonia protect you against the Covid-19 virus? *Answer:* No. vaccine against pneumonia such as pneumococcal vaccine and Influenza Type B vaccine, do not protect against Covid-19 virus. The virus is new and so different researchers are still trying to develop a vaccine. However, vaccinations against respiratory illnesses are highly recommended. *Question 9.* Can regularly rinsing your nose with saline solution help prevent infection of the recommended? *Answer:* No. no evidence that regularly rinsing the nose with saline solution has protected people from infection with the

COVID-19 virus. However, there is some evidence that regular nose rinsing with saline solution can help with quicker recovery from the common cold. *Question 10.* Does the Covid-19 virus only affect older people or are younger people also susceptible? *Answer:* People of all ages can be infected by Covid-19. However, older people, those with pre-existing medical conditions appear to be more vulnerable to the virus.

Question 11. Can antibiotics be used as a means of prevention? *Answer:* No. Antibiotics do not work against viruses, only bacterial infections. Therefore, antibiotics should not be used as a means of prevention or treatment. *Question 12.* Are there any specific medicines to prevent or treat the Covid-19 virus? *Answer:* As of today, there is no specific medicine. However, those infected with the virus should receive appropriate optimal supportive care to relieve and treat symptoms. Some specific treatments are under development and are being tested through clinical trials. *Question 13.* How effective are thermal scanners in detecting people infected with the Covid-19 virus? *Answer:* Thermal scanners are effective in detecting people who have developed a fever because of infection with the COVID-19 virus. However, they cannot detect asymptomatic people. It takes between 2-10 days before those who are infected become sick and develop a fever.

In conclusion, the World Health Organization (W.H.O.) states that safety in numbers is the opposite ideology of what COVID-19 containment is all about. It asserts that avoidance of crowded and interpersonal contact is the best practice and that knowledge of the facts will help to avoid confusion. Stay safe and healthy at all times is the best policy.

9.3 Other False Myths for COVID-19 Pandemic

It was believed that if someone violates social distancing by standing close to you and if he/she begins to cough and sneeze, you just run away immediately to avoid infection of COVID-19. It is further encouraged that there is no need for you to reason as to whether it was normal coughing or normal sneezing. 2. In South Sudan, somebody circulated a message through social media saying if you drink tea early in the morning without sugar; Covid-19 will not infect you. 3. It was believed that black men don't get Coronavirus. 4. Some people believe that Coronavirus is a disease for rich people. 5. Others believe that home remedies can cure or prevent Coronavirus. 6. Everyone should wear a mask. 7. It was believed that people who are infected by coronavirus will die.

Conclusion

The chapter has presented general dramatic concepts of myths; myths vs. realities by Jackie Powder; quiz-myths according to W.H.O. on the COVID-19 pandemic; and finally, the local myths in South Sudan for COVID-19. This chapter has discussed and explained thoroughly the role of myths during uncertainty and fear.

Chapter Ten: Evaluation and Conditions for the Reopening

Introduction

Chapter ten deals with assessments concerning how world leaders should manage the Covid-19 pandemic. Finally, the chapter will treat the criteria for the reopening of lockdowns and the marathon between scientists all over the world to develop vaccines and antibodies for the COVID-19 pandemic, the disinformation about vaccines; and when the will COVID-19 pandemic end.

10. World Leaders' Management on Covid-19 Pandemic?

Our general evaluation, first and foremost, is based on the days in which the information about the COVID-19 pandemic was received by each country in the world. The quick response to the COVID-19 pandemic determines how each country in the world handled the coronavirus pandemic. The response in each nation is about immediate implementation of the 'social distancing measures, face masks, washing hands, that were promulgated, articulated, and stipulated, by the leader of each nation to the citizens. Our assessment concerning the effect of the COVID-19 pandemic on some countries can permit us to conclude that those nations such as Italy, the UK, the U.S. France, Spain, Japan, and the rest were unable to implement social distancing guidelines with immediate effect. However, Chris Whitty, the Chief Medical Officer for England states that the number of death tolls in each country should not be used as a judgment because each country has its challenges.

Lack of preparation in some countries was related to not having enough medical personnel; ventilators; medical masks for doctors and nurses (healthcare workers) and facemasks for citizens. In short, there was not enough 'personal protection equipment' (PPE). There were not enough hospitals and other countries have no ventilators at all. These are some of the major challenges being observed during the coronavirus pandemic. Due to this level of unpreparedness by some nations, the number of confirmed cases and death toll are higher in some countries compared to the rest. The WFP. Chief warns "Famines Biblical Proportions" during this pandemic time. It was reported that one of the States in America, the State of Missouri will sue China for Covid-19 handling.

During the coronavirus pandemic, the earth pollution was dramatically reduced while the locusts launched attacks on East Africa. There was disrespect to 'social distancing guidelines' specifically in the U.S. For example, some people in some States in the United States of America protested against 'social distancing guidelines. Unfortunately, Mr. Trump supported them and consequently, called them "liberated" Michigan etc. The coronavirus pandemic has brought the highest rates of unemployment in the whole world. Some people compare the period of Covid-19 to 'Great Depression (recession.' It was said that politics should be separated from science that is, politicians should listen to the advice given by the experts instead of silencing them. They ought to act on the information they receive from the experts and not to get odds with them.

10.1 The Impacts of the COVID-19 Pandemic on the World

According to medical records, Italy and China in the initial stages of the spread of the coronavirus pandemic, were leading in the list of the death toll and infected cases. Later on, Italy took the lead in terms of death toll followed by Spain and the U.S.A. As the COVID-19 pandemic intensifies its attack on human life, China dropped from the list and became the first country to reopen Wuhan, the capital of Hubei Province where the Coronavirus had started.

Transitory records of the death toll of the COVID-19 pandemic by Johns Hopkins University; apart from those who died and were recorded in hospitals for the COVID-19 pandemic, there were other cases of death at home for other diseases such as diabetes; high blood pressure; low blood pressure and kidney failure. It is reported that these categories of patients categorically refused to go to hospitals for fear of infection. Medical professionals reported that for pregnant women, there were no record cases of infection of an infant in the womb of her mother. This seems to be a mystery over the Covid-19 pandemic. There were also survivors of the COVID-19 pandemic, because of their antibodies which was also a victory over the COVID-19 pandemic example, even a man who lived for 106 survived the COVID-19 pandemic.

The scientists draw some hypotheses as to why some people are susceptible and some are asymptomatic to Covid-19 pandemic. According to them, this may be related to the antibodies of an individual and the genetic code of the person. However, it is medically recorded that among the survivors of the Covid-19 pandemic, there are dramatic serious consequences such as the loss of smell and taste. The World Health Organization states that there is "no evidence of immunity after Covid-19 pandemic infection." It is affirmed that even with those who have been tested with antibodies, nobody knows how long and how strong they are to resist the Covid-19 pandemic.

The lockdowns of everything in some countries and the

implementation of the principle of social distancing have made megacities look like ghost towns. The isolation of everybody has turned some people into nightmares with consequences of various dreams at night. The economic breakdown has led to serious uncertainty; anxiety, distress and fear of what is to come next. Apart from the COVID-19 pandemic, hackers and criminals who were fighting on the side of coronavirus have made the situation worsen. For example, they use the *status quo* of isolation for their benefit by intimidating the isolates by threatening their lives.

10.2 Guidelines and Criteria for the Reopening

With lockdowns which have led to economic collapse worldwide, the pressures from businessmen/businesswomen upon politicians and experts became tougher and sometimes dramatic in some countries specifically in the U.S. The slogan to 'ease or lift; the lockdowns has become too pressing and burning issue. On the one hand, the scientists emphasized doubling the testing depending on the capacity of each country and cautioned that any lifting of the lockdowns without proper scientific assessments on the ground would lead to square one. On the other hand, scientists marathon to develop vaccines and antibodies for Covid-19. Some politicians gave in to the pressures and eased the lockdowns. In reality, people were tired of social distancing measures' anxiety and they wanted those restrictions to be lifted.

According to Patrick Vallance, the Chief Scientific Advisor to the British Government, the guidelines for reopening are not uniform in all countries. The concern for the reopening of each country after lockdown seems to call for a proposal for gradual reopening. Testing and contact tracing efforts are emphasized by physicians and world leaders. Contact tracing means to stop the spread of Covid-19. Testing means: 1. to identify those who are infected and to isolate (quarantine) them from society. 2. To find out symptomatic and asymptomatic.3. Those with antibodies can donate their blood to susceptible ones.4. To find out the rate of infections in society or country at large. It is argued that the criteria for the reopening of the lockdowns require mitigation guidelines. Some countries propose that social distancing guidelines will be maintained to some degree. Others strongly proposed that the Covid-19 experience will change our ways of life for good.

For example, Dr. Anthony Fauci strongly recommended that handshakes must never be practiced again. Some countries recommended greeting with bent elbows and bumps and legs. Large social gatherings will not be there to some degree. Harvard Researchers assert that "Social distancing may last until 2022." CDC Director says that social distancing is "one of the most powerful weapons" for Covid-19. The world leaders were very cautious about the quick reopening. The majority of them proposed a careful and slow reopening of the lockdown. Some leaders recommend that there should be no large gatherings but with a few, social distancing guidelines are to be maintained. Facemasks were strongly recommended in some countries. Some say that our lives will never be the same again. Bill Gates the Co-Chair of, the Bill & Melinda Gates Foundation recommends that we need to develop testing capacity in case of any eventuality of either pandemic or epidemic in future.

10.3 Vaccine and Antibodies

As to the progress on vaccine and antibody, "researchers around the world race to develop a vaccine." This was reported by CNN on April 16, 2020. Prof. Robin Shattock affirms that scientists around the world funded by the World Health Organization (W.H.O) are working hard to discover a vaccine for the COVID-19 pandemic. He added that there is competition among the scientists, however, he asserted that competition is good among the scientists to produce good quality vaccines for the Covid-19 pandemic. The World Health Organization (W.H.O) states that the Covid-19 pandemic could probably come from bats. When will the vaccine for the COVID-19 pandemic be out? He declined to mention the date. Some scientists say it may take months or a year for the vaccine to be ready.

Scientists are also working to discover the antibodies for Covid-19. On April 24, 2020, CNN reported that "scientists start human trials for the potential vaccine in the UK". Two people were reported tested and the result was not harmful. When will it be out? Some talk of months or a year from now. These are good signs for us. However, the Centre for Disease Control cautions that there will be a "Second wave of COVID-19 and it will be "more difficult" with potential and complicated consequences. This was reported by CNN on April 22, 2020. Dr. Anthony Fauci asserts that the second wave of coronavirus will come, he said, "I am convinced". On April 24, 2020, CNN reported the start of the second Covid-19 in Singapore and Japan.

While scientists worldwide are working hard to discover the vaccine and antibodies for the COVID-19 pandemic, also they are expected to trace the origins of COVID-19 in cooperation with the Chinese authority. Earlier, it was mentioned that there was a marathon among scientists to develop a vaccine and antibodies for COVID-19 to produce good quality. However, there is another danger of cyber-attacks on this process among scientists. It was reported by CNN on April 27, 2020, that the U.S. 'blames China for cyber-attacks on Covid-19 pandemic research.' This ought to be pointed out as a negative aspect of technology. We thought all of us were fighting the common enemy (the COVID-19 pandemic), yet because of envy and jealousy over this marathon which aims at discovering and developing a vaccine and antibody for the COVID-19 pandemic scientists, however, have turned against each other. Concerning the treatment of the COVID-19 pandemic, it was reported by CNN on April 28, 2020, that "heartburn drug has been tested and studied as coronavirus treatment." However, it is in the process and not yet scientifically confirmed.

10.3.1 Earlier Positive Updates on Vaccines

Good News! On April 30, 2020, Dr. Anthony Fauci announced on CNN that he is "Optimistic about early data on the drug Remdesivir" as a possible treatment for Covid-19. The trial has proved to reduce the Covid-19 patient from 15-11 days. The drug "Remdesivir" was also tried for Ebola but did not work for it. Therefore, a placebo is 15 days for Covid-19 patients and remdesivir reduces it to 11 days for COVID-19 patients. According to Dr. Fauci, Remdesivir shows a "significant effect for Covid-19 patients. Remdesivir trial shows "positive effect on recovery time. Remdesivir shows 31% improvement. However, Dr Fauci cautions that the vaccine would take 12-18 months to develop.

Oxford University's vaccine trial results may be ready by mid-June. For Oxford University; several people are being vaccinated as a trial. UK researchers could know the vaccine's effectiveness by mid-June. On September 11/2020, the American Company Pfizer announced that early data shows covid-19 vaccine than 95% effective and another American Company Modena, early shows covid-19 vaccine than 94 % effective. AstraZeneca: Coronavirus vaccine 79% effective in U.S. trial.

Points for consideration on the following updates on the COVID-19 pandemic 1. On December 01, 2020, according to CNN, a Chinese document shows chaotic early COVID-19 responses such as misinformation which includes the number of people infected by the virus and the death toll in the early stage of the virus. 2. Types of violence against women during covid-19 pandemic. Genital mutilation, rate of unintended pregnancies, early child marriages and domestic violence. 3. On December 1, 2020, the W.H.O. traces the Origin of the virus: the W.H.O. stresses that "don't politicize the origin of the virus."

10.3.2 Scientific Achievements of Vaccines

4. On December 2, 2020, the U.K. became the first country to approve the use of the Pfizer Biotech vaccine for the categories of people such as healthcare workers (essential workers), people with pre-medical conditions, and old age of 80 years old. On December 9, 2020, Margaret Keenan, the first person in the West to get a COVID-19 vaccine, called the experience a "whirlwind" and said other people should get it too. Keenan, a grandmother of four who turns 91 that week, after she had gotten Pfizer and Biotech's shot at the University Hospital in the English city of Coventry on Tuesday morning.

On December 10, 2020, another first man to get the new coronavirus vaccine in the UK was named William Shakespeare-inspiring a veritable flurry of Bard-worthy puns. The 81-year-old gained fame when he got his historic shot early. However, The U.K. reported two cases of serious allergic reactions from two healthcare workers on December 10, 2020, after vaccination. Consequently, experts warn that: people with allergic reactions to the vaccine should avoid getting the Pfizer Biotech vaccine. Experts said that Pfizer Biotech has side effects such as fatigue, achiness, and fever that last about one day.

On the same date, the U.S. was already preparing for vaccine distribution. Experts assert that both Pfizer Biotech and Modena are characterized by safety, efficacy and immunization. Consequently, On December 11, 2020, the Food and Drug Administration (FDA) Panel recommended authorization of the Pfizer vaccine in America. The team consists of independent experts of which 17 voted in favour of the authorization of vaccine. Four voted against the authorization of the vaccine due to unforeseen side effects of the Pfizer Biotech vaccine upon the categories of people such as those with previous serious allergic reactions, children under 16, and old, pregnant women and breast-feeding mothers.

As to whether the Pfizer vaccine came as pressure from political leaders, Stephen Hahn Commissioner for Food and Drug Administration asserts that 'science and data' guides our decisions. On December 13, the first COVID-19 vaccine shipments left the Pfizer facility in U.S. Michigan State for distribution of the Pfizer vaccine to other states. Furthermore, the Centers for Disease Control and Prevention, the Director accepts advisory committee's recommendation; covid-19 vaccine can now be administered in the United States of America. Consequently, President-elect Joe Biden was grateful for the authorization of vaccines by independent scientists.

On Monday, December 14, 2020, before the first healthcare worker got a vaccination, the Governor of New York Andrew Cuomo addressed the healthcare workers by saying "Today is the beginning of the end of the last chapter of the book and it is the beginning of the new chapter of the book of life. After he finished, one of the doctors gave a brief speech which was immediately followed by the vaccination of the first healthcare worker in New York.

Warning against the abuse of nature: the secretary general of the U.N. Antonio warns "We are waging war against nature and nature will fight back. On December 9, 2020, CNN reported that China is preparing for large-scale vaccination distribution. For example, the United Arab Emirates (UAE) reported that the Chinese Sinophma vaccine is safe 86% and effective. The Russian 'Sputnik' vaccine is 91.6% effective against Covid-19 pandemic.

10.4 New Variants of Delta & Omicron of Covid-19 Pandemic

While experts and the majority of people celebrate the hope for the defeat of the COVID-19 pandemic due to the discovery of various vaccines, nevertheless, the deadly virus seems to change its techniques and styles in the form of variants. This has raised an alarm and concern for experts and people globally. The newly detected variant has been termed a 'variant of concern' by the World Health Organization

(WHO). The experts have warned that the Delta variant which had its origin in India in October 2020 is spreading rapidly surpassing all the other previous strains of novel coronavirus. 5 Things to Know About the Delta Variant such as.1. "Delta is more contagious than the other virus strains."[186]

Delta is the name for the B.1.617.2. 2. Unvaccinated people are at risk. 3. Delta could lead to 'hyperlocal outbreaks. 4. There is still more to learn about Delta. For example, Top experts have likened the COVID-19 "Delta Variant" to the common cold and hay fever. This comes as people like Anthony Fauci, Boris Johnson, and the WHO are pushing for more social distancing, lockdowns, mask mandates, and vaccinations. Experts explain 'hay fever' as an allergy caused by pollen or dust in which the mucous membranes of the eyes and nose are itchy and inflamed, causing a runny nose and watery eyes.

Covid symptoms linked to the new 'Omicron variant' have been described as "extremely mild" by the South African doctor who first raised the alarm over the new strain. Dr. Angelique Coetzee, chair of the South African Medical Association, told the BBC on Sunday that she started to see patients around Nov.18 presenting with "unusual symptoms" that differed slightly from those associated with the delta variant, which is the most virulent strain of the virus to date and globally dominant. Although it was described as 'extremely mild, nevertheless, it killed a person on December 12, 2021.

"It started with a male patient who's around the age of 33 ... and he said to me that he's just [been] extremely tired for the past few days and he's got these body aches and pains with a bit of a headache," she told the BBC. The patient didn't have a sore throat, she said, but more of a "scratchy throat" but no cough or loss of taste or smell-symptoms that have been associated with previous strains of the coronavirus.

---

186   https://www.yalemedicine.org/news/5-things-to-know-delta-variant-covid retrieved as from 16/07/2021.

The Technical Advisory Group on SARS-CoV-2 Virus Evolution (TAG-VE) is an independent group of experts that periodically monitors and evaluates the evolution of SARS-CoV-2 and assesses if specific mutations and combinations of mutations alter the behaviour of the virus. The TAG-VE was convened on 26 November 2021 to assess the SARS-CoV-2 variant: B.1.1.529.

The B.1.1.529 variant was first reported to WHO from South Africa on 24 November 2021. The epidemiological situation in South Africa has been characterized by three distinct peaks in reported cases, the latest of which was predominantly the Delta variant. In recent weeks, infections have increased steeply, coinciding with the detection of the B.1.1.529 variant. The first known confirmed B.1.1.529 infection was from a specimen collected on 9 November 2021.

On 26 November 2021, WHO designated the variant B.1.1.529 a variant of concern (VOC), based on advice from W.H.O's Technical Advisory Group on Virus Evolution. The variant has been given the name Omicron. Early data shows that Omicron may be contagious but less severe. Scientists reportedly identify the "stealth" Omicron variant.

Omicron is a highly divergent variant with a high number of mutations, including 26-32 in the spike, some of which are concerning and may be associated with immune escape potential and higher transmissibility. However, there are still considerable uncertainties.

The main uncertainties are (1) how transmissible the variant is and whether any increases are related to immune escape, intrinsic increased transmissibility, or both; (2) how well vaccines protect against infection, transmission, clinical disease of different degrees of severity and death; and (3) does the variant present with a different severity profile. Public health advice is based on current information and will be tailored as more evidence emerges around those key questions.

WHO Chief Scientist Soumya Swaminathan urges people not to panic over omicron. She added that we need to wait, let's us hope it's milder…but it is too early to conclude about variant as a whole."

The World Health Organization's (WHO) Chief Scientist on Friday, November 3, 2021, urged people not to panic over the emergence of the Omicron Coronavirus variant, and she said it was too early if COVID-19 vaccines would have to be modified to fight it.

Speaking in an interview, Soumya Swaminathan also said it was impossible to predict if Omicron would become the dominant strain. However, Omicron has gained a foothold in Asia, Africa, the Americas, the Middle East and Europe and has reached seven of the nine provinces of South Africa, where it was first identified. Consequently, governments have tightened travel rules to keep the variant out.

Mss. Swaminathan said that the right response was to be ready. "How worried should we be? We need to be prepared and cautious, not panic because we're in a different situation to a year ago" she said. Concerning the degree of the severity of Omicron, a recent study of South African scientists shows that 2 doses of Pfizer/Biotech are 33% effective Vs Omicron.

10.5 Campaign for the Third Booster Shot.

The war that we waged together at the beginning of the Covid-19 pandemic, ought to lead us to equal distribution of vaccines proportionately. However, instead, some rich countries such as Israel was the first country to offer a third booster shot to people over 60 years followed by the United States of America. Imagine! The majority of poor countries did not have access even to the first shot of the vaccine. In response to the disproportion of vaccines, the Watchdog group states that wealthy countries hoarding covid-19 vaccines. Furthermore, apart from the rebound of the COVID-19 pandemic in many countries, the situation is aggravated by delta variants because even with the availability of various vaccines, nevertheless, the variants have become very challenging and even the vaccines are not enough for the rich nations, forget about the poor nations. There is a constant re-emerging of the virus in many countries.

Beneficiary of Pfizer/Biotech: According to Bill Gates the Co-Chair, of and Melinda Gates Foundation, Bill Gates Co-founder, Microsoft, during the interview on CNN with Jake Tapper that the administration of Pfizer/Biotech does not mean who is to be vaccinated first or who is to die last. According to him, the Pfizer/Biotech vaccine is about the protection of human life regardless of race, religion, nationality and region.

10.6 Conspiracy Theories Concerning Vaccines

Even with the availability of different types of vaccines and the struggle for scientists to encourage vaccination, nevertheless, there is skepticism. For example, on December 3, 2020, CNN reported that some people do have prejudices based on misinformation about the vaccine. There seems to be a lack of trust in the scientific community. Some people opt to be anti-science based on misinformation which the scientists should address. However, in U.S. Pew Research poll shows that 60% of Americans say they would get the vaccine. It is believed that vaccine hesitancy could undermine vaccination campaigns as some experts assert that "discrimination and distrust may hamper COVID-19 vaccination in the minority community.

However, it is argued that the spread of misinformation in public health and science is not a new problem, nor are the concerns raised in health research and communication, said by leading author Dr. Lisa Parker, from the Charles Perkins Centre and School of Pharmacy at the University of Sydney.

According to Dr. Lisa Parker, the goal of this study was to explore the views and experiences of science researchers and communicators about misinformation. It showed widespread concern about the ongoing problem of misinformation, which has been such a prominent feature in the current pandemic. Dr. Lisa further states that there is a huge public interest in scientific discovery the need for adequate funding, and growing awareness about the problem of misinformation.

The paper articulated what "Triggers" of misinformation: Using the insights from the participants, the paper mapped out the pathway of scientific information from the health research community to the general public. The authors also collated an extensive list of causes of misinformation collected around particular points along the pathway: science production, science communication and target audience access and interpretation.

The University of Sydney has identified the following conspiracy theories which triggered misinformation. Key points included:

- Science production can be of poor quality or biased; triggers for 'bad science' include:
- Institutional pressure to publish academic papers.
- High competition for academic science jobs.
- Systemic bias from widespread industry funding.
- Questionable research practices, such as recruiting participants until results are statistically significant then stopping.
- Science communication and access problems include:
- Inadequate access- Lack of access to high-quality research that is free, understandable and timely.
- Publication bias, such as only publishing results favourable to funders or political leaders.
- Impenetrable language and concepts and loss of specialist science journalists and communicators to translate for the public.
- The peer review system is inefficient and lacks transparency.
- Academic journal publication paywalls.
- Conflicting views on whether pre-prints (papers released before formal peer-review) are part of the problem.
- Audience access and interpretation issues:
- Many use unreliable and algorithm-driven resources for science news.
- A need for better education for the public about where to find and how to evaluate good science.

- Scientists are not always trained to use engaging communication tools.
- More could be done to encourage greater public understanding of the scientific process.
- People expect certainty and immediate answers in science.

This information about misinformation concerning vaccines was provided by the University of Sydney.

10.7 The Inconclusive Origin of Covid-19 Pandemic

As to the origin of the Covid-19 pandemic, CNN reported that the W.H.O. team went to trace Covid-19 origins in China. China claims that COVID-19 can be imported into frozen foods, such as goods imported from other countries, and contaminated foods which include cement. Experts negate that the virus does not live longer on the surface. U.S. and China politicized the issue related to the origin of the virus and consequently, played the blame game we have mentioned earlier. While other experts such as Bill Gates warned that there will be another pandemic, what is needed is good leadership to prepare and respond to the pandemic with scientific data and facts. As to the origin of the virus, nobody knows whether we shall arrive at any conclusion.

On August 28, 2021, CNN reported that the U.S. released inconclusive intelligence on the Covid-19 pandemic. In other words, the U.S. intelligence report on the Covid-19 pandemic origins is inconclusive. The classified document prepared by the U.S. in a summary form of indefinite inconclusive, came up with two theories about the possible origin of the virus. First, the virus might have originated from the lab in Wuhan-China or animal to human beings through physical contact. China on her part, criticizes and calls it "a fabrication by the intelligence community" and consequently, dismisses it.

However, the uniqueness and the particularity of this virus will not depend on its complexity and dynamism alone, but even the dilemma of lack of its origin will remain a mystery and puzzling to experts. Consequently, it will make it unique compared to the other viruses that came before it. I am not sure, whether there was any virus whose origin was never traced by experts in the past. Therefore, a lack of assessment of its origin will always disturb our comfort zone including experts. Consequently, even with a vaccine to defeat it, it will look as if experts did not address the root cause of the problem of the COVID-19 pandemic. For example, it will be like healing the wound, without knowing its cause.

10.8 When will the Covid-19 Pandemic End?

The dramatic clash between humanity and the COVID-19 pandemic is inconclusive. Dr. Anthony Fauci says coronavirus turned 'out to be my worst nightmare' and it 'isn't over. 'Key Points from Dr. Anthony Fauci: White House health advisor Dr. Anthony Fauci said Covid-19 turned out to be his "worst nightmare" come to life as the coronavirus continues to rapidly spread across the globe. The virus is "highly transmissible. ... In a period you just think about it in four months, it has devastated the world," said Fauci, director of the National Institute of Allergy and Infectious Diseases.

Dr. Anthony said that's millions and millions of infections worldwide. And it isn't over yet. And it's condensed in a very, very small time frame," he said. "You know, first notice at the end of December, hit China in January, and hit the rest of the world in February, March, April, May, and early June. The coronavirus, which emerged in Wuhan, China, in late December, has infected more than 7 million people worldwide and killed at least 408,244, according to data compiled by Johns Hopkins University.

Other information concerning confirmed cases and deaths is reported by the WHO Coronavirus (COVID-19) Dashboard WHO

Coronavirus. COVID-19 Response Fund Donate Globally, as of 5:51 pm CET, 2 December 2021, there have been 262,866,050 confirmed cases of COVID-19, including 5,224,519 deaths, reported to WHO. Therefore, Dr. Fauci was right when he said "And it isn't over yet."

Experts recommend that covid-19 pandemic will be eradicated only by vaccination otherwise. Dr. Soumya Swaminathan the Chief Scientist of the World Health Organization (WHO) asserts that primary vaccinations are key to stopping new variants from forming. Everyone is recommended to be vaccinated. Those who have received the first vaccine either from Pfizer, Modena, or AstraZeneca, are recommended to receive the second shot. Experts also recommend that people receive a vaccine from Johnsons & Johnsons which is one shot. The third is recommended by experts to boost the immune system. While everyone is not vaccinated, experts urge everybody to be vaccinated with available vaccines. Handshakes are to be avoided and facemasks are required in social gatherings even for those who are vaccinated. The experts assert that testing and contact tracing will continue as long as the COVID-19 pandemic is not over.

10.9 My Testimony on the Day of My Vaccination

As I conclude this last subtopic, I cannot ignore my unique personal experience concerning vaccines. If you ask me "Are you vaccinated? The answer is "yes." However, here is the scenario of my hesitancy concerning vaccines. On May 13, 2021, we were invited to Rajaf by Rev. Jackson Yuggusuk, Rector of St. Lawrence Minor Seminary of the Catholic Archdiocese of Juba. The occasion was about the visit of Friends of St. Lawrence Minor Seminary to the Seminary. His Lordship Bishop Santo Loku Pio, the Auxiliary Bishop of the Catholic Archdiocese of Juba was the guest of honour. A good number of priests were present including some lay faithful.

The program started with the Holy Mass followed by speeches.

After a few speeches, we were invited for lunch under the shade of a big tree nicknamed "the Ancestral Tree" by the staff and seminarians of St. Lawrence Minor Seminary. It is located to the north of the seminary's campus. There we took our lunch with different types of delicious food prepared by well-qualified cooks. It was accompanied by various types of drinks and spontaneous cordial conversations. Inexpertly, Doctor James Alphonse interrupted our appetites and spontaneous cordial conversation with sensitive questions related to vaccination. He asked us, "Are you vaccinated?" We all kept silent as if we heard the sad news.

Consequently, our modes changed from enthusiastically cordial conversations to coldness. We all became like people who saw the brightest sudden lightning during rain while waiting for a thunderbolt. After a long period of silence, Doctor James further asserted," I am vaccinated with AstraZeneca." Regardless of our intentional silence to doge the question concerning vaccination, Doctor James further went made by adding that tomorrow, I want all of you to come to 'Juba Teaching Hospital Campus' to be vaccinated with AstraZeneca. Can you imagine? Not everybody among us knows something called 'AstraZeneca.' For example, for some, it does not exist even in their vocabularies or if it exists at all, it was because they heard of it as 'a type of vaccine' that kills people. However, the persistence of Doctor James made us more passive and every priest was pretending as if he was not aware of what he was talking about or as if he were talking to us in his tongue.

At the bottom of our hearts, our silence was due to various conspiracy theories against the vaccine created out there. Based on that, we considered the question of Doctor James as irrelevant to us or non-essential to us. I knew that each of us had a different reason concerning vaccine hesitancy and reservation. Finally, it was His Lordship Bishop Santo Loku Pio who broke our silence by saying to Doctor James, "We shall arrange it next time." Instantly, we all felt a sense of relief because the tension was very high.

However, one cannot dismiss the concern and persistence of Doctor James. Thus, we could read from his facial expression. He was seriously concerned about our lives, nevertheless, none of us were concerned about vaccination as the majority of people were. After some months, I reflected on whether I should be vaccinated or not. Then I asked myself "Why should I document the COVID-19 pandemic if I am not ready for vaccination?" Even throughout the various TVs, every expert is urging people to get vaccinated. Another reason which finally convinced me to be vaccinated was the hearing of the constant siren of an ambulance from time to time in Juba. I said to myself, hi! If I continue resisting vaccination, next time, it will be the turn of other people to hear the siren of an ambulance carrying me.

However, an opportunity came on November 21, 2021, the Sunday of the celebration of Our Lord Jesus Christ, King of the Universe. I was the main celebrant at St. Augustine Chapel under the Parish of St. Kizito in the Archdiocese of Juba. Before the final blessing, I heard the announcer saying 'Next Sunday 28, the first Sunday of Advent, at the Parish Main Centre, there will be a vaccination at the school campus. On November 28, 2021, after I finished the Holy Mass at Mercy Centre, which belongs to St. Kizito's Parish, I was taken immediately by the Chairman of the Chapel Mr. Christopher Akim to the Main Parish Centre. To my surprise, when we arrived at the school campus, I saw roughly something like 12 persons including the medical personnel. There I concluded that the majority of faithful did not turn up for vaccination even though 'Johnsons and Johnsons' was brought to them to the Parish Main Centre.

I went straight to the place of vaccination accompanied by Mr. Christopher. When the lay faithful who came to be vaccinated saw me sitting and ready for vaccination, they gave me applause as if I were performing a miracle. However, before I received the vaccination, I was asked by a nurse to fill out the form which I did. The nurse asked me after I filled out the form whether I had preexisted diseases or not.

I replied no. Instantly, I was vaccinated with 'Johnsons and Johnsons on November 28, 2021.

During my vaccination, I could see that everybody was busy taking my photo. One woman asked me softly to listen to my body for five minutes before I talked to anyone which I did. That advice, although it was out of concern, nevertheless even increased the degree of the temperature of my body as to what would happen to me after five minutes. Fortunately, nothing bad happened in my body. After that, Mr. Christopher took me to the studio for my photo to be put in a frame which was done. Consequently, he brought me back home. The only side effect which I experienced was that in the following night, I could not sleep till morning, but there was no pain in my body

My hesitance concerning AstraZeneca and Johnsons and Johnsons' was they caused death to few people. You can imagine! It took me exactly 6 months and 19 days to be vaccinated after that question from Doctor James Alphonse. Here and now, as scientists urge you to get vaccinated, I also urge you to get vaccinated before it is too late. Please, do away with all conspiracy theories and be smart.

In conclusion, as the origin of the COVID-19 pandemic is inconclusive, the pandemic itself seems to be inconclusive for now, and the issues of conspiracy theory concerning vaccine hesitancy continues, this book ought to be conclusive otherwise, its message will not be heard.

However, we ought to point out that though the confirmed cases of the COVID-19 pandemic is 262,866,050 and the death toll of the COVID-19 pandemic is 5,224,519 as of December 6, 2021, these numbers will keep on increasing due to two factors such as conspiracy theories concerning vaccines and lack of vaccines for the poor nations.

Conclusion

Chapter ten has dealt with the COVID-19 pandemic blame games between the U.S. and China; it has also assessed how the world leaders managed the COVID-19 pandemic and the impact of the COVID-19 pandemic worldwide. It has treated the criteria for the reopening of lockdown and the marathon between scientists all over the world to develop vaccines and antibodies for the COVID-19 pandemic, the third offer of booster shots by some countries. Finally, the chapter has discussed the pending origin of the COVID-19 pandemic, the disinformation concerning vaccines; and when the will Covid-19 Pandemic end.

Chapter Eleven:
Theological Reflections

Introduction

This chapter discusses theological reflection on the COVID-19 pandemic taking into consideration the fragility of human perfection; the principle of preferential option for the vulnerable; and eschatology. It will also present the doctrine of the last things concerning the future of God's people such as the Pilgrim Church (people of God); the second coming of Christ (Parousia); the faith in the second coming of Christ, the time of the second coming of Christ is the concept of Antic-Christ (Serpent); the Sacred Scripture on the signs of anti-Christ and the Signs of anti-Christ in the course of our lives.

The same chapter also deals with death and resurrection; the significance of the problem; the Sacred Scriptures on resurrection; the Church's Magisterium & and liturgy on resurrection; theological problems about the resurrection; the judgment of the world, and, the nature of the final judgment. Finally, the chapter recommends that every human person take care of himself/herself.

11. The Purpose of Theological Reflections

As we read through those chapters that dealt with the COVID-19 pandemic, no wonder, even in the 21st century, humanity has been attacked once again by deadly catastrophic contagious diseases. The COVID-19 pandemic is affecting and is infecting everyone here on our planet Earth. The impact of the COVID-19 pandemic on each person is undeniable and perceivable in the eyes of all. Consequently, people feel as if they are abandoned by God based on the fact that it is taking many lives. It is out of concern that we ought to theological reflections on the Covid-19 pandemic.

This unfortunate great evil, the COVID-19 pandemic (the serpent, Satan, the Lucifer) is demonstrating or manifesting the signs of the end of anything on this planet earth. However, we do hope and believe that God cannot abandon his image and likeness to the hand of the evil one. With this conviction in mind, the decision to give theological reflections on the COVID-19 pandemic as one of the signs of Antic-Christ is based on the fact that we followed it from the onset. These reflections are focused on eschatology, the doctrine about the last things. It neither focuses on proctology, the doctrine about the last things (creation, the fall), nor it treats the last things concerning the future of the individual such as death; and immortality; the particular judgment, purgatory, hell and heaven.

The theological reflections on the Covid-19 pandemic concentrate on the "last things" concerning the future of all the people of God, such as the pilgrim Church, the second coming of Christ, (Parousia), the death and resurrection, and the judgment of the world. These reflections on those areas of the last things are not limited to the COVID-19 pandemic; they go beyond it because the word of God is timeless and not like medicine for a specific cure. In addition, we consider the Covid-19 pandemic as one of the signs of Antic-Christ.

The choice of theological reflections about the last things on the

Covid-19 pandemic is based on the fact that it is through this militant Church that the Covid-19 pandemic has inflicted pain on human life and consequently, has affected the lives of many people including the loss of many lives. It is through this pilgrim Church that the proclamation of the second coming of Christ is ongoing; it is through this militant Church that the dead are mourned and are buried; it is through this pilgrim Church that the doctrine of the resurrection is proclaimed; it is through this Church that the gospel's virtues and values are proclaimed to Christians, such as hope, faith and love in this situation of Covid-19 pandemic.

The pilgrim Church does this in obedience to God's command and under the mandate of Christ through his love for the salvation of humanity. It is through this Church that the signs of the second coming of Christ are experienced daily, including the Covid-19 pandemic. The pilgrim Church does this by imitating the paschal mysteries that is, suffering, death and the resurrection of Christ. Here in the pilgrim Church, we experience our fragility and constantly seek God's protection upon us. As we deal with theological reflections on the COVID-19 pandemic, we also refer to previous signs of Antic-Christ as they happened in the course of human history. Importantly, these theological reflections aim at consoling, comforting and giving hope to every Christian in every situation in the course of human history.

11.1 The Centrality of Christ in Creation

The COVID-19 pandemic requires that all of us ought to look back to our origin, both believers and non-believers (atheists) and people of indifferences. We must do this because we believe that nothing happens by chance. Nobody came into existence by his/her will, somewhere, somebody has decided for the existence of all. This leads us to the understanding of proctology which is the doctrine about the last things (Creation, the fall). However, according to M. Schmaus, "This entire work has been shaped by the conviction that the work of Christ was just a beginning, that Christ unleashed a development whose full force was directed towards the ultimate future."[187] It is believed that the creation of the world was itself already the beginning of a vast evolution, its pre-ordained direction was towards the emergence, through Christ, as a movement destined towards the perfection of all creation in the absolute future.

The fall of Adam and Eve will permit us to conclude that somewhere, something has gone in the wrong direction. Consequently, we see no perfection in all creatures including Mother Earth. Our experience does permit us to see two types of evil that is, physical and moral evil. Moral evil is further divided into 'formal' and 'material' evils.

11.2 Human Progress in the Course of History

The first chapter of the book of Genesis states "Then God said: Let us make human beings in our image; after our likeness. Let them have dominion over the fish of the sea, the birds of the air, and tame animals, all the wild animals, and all the creatures that crawl on the earth" (Gen 1:24-26). "God created mankind in his image; in the image of God he created them; male and female he created them. God blessed them and God said to them: Be fertile and multiply; fill the earth and subdue it. Have dominion over the fish of the sea, the birds of the air, and all the living things that crawl on the earth" (Gen 1: 1:27-29).

This is the perfect picture of creation that is demonstrated in the book of Genesis which requires serious analysis if full understanding is to be achieved. This creation puts humanity at the centre of creation (summit of creation). For example, our observation and experience permit us to conclude that human beings are truly created in the image

---

187   Michael Schmaus, *Justification and the Last Things,* London, Sheed and Ward Inc., 1977, p.149.

and likeness of God in terms of progress, development, and participation in creation. This can be seen through four periods of progress such as: 1. During the prehistoric period that describes free man as a forger of tools. 2. The ancient period depicts man's use of others as living instruments for family production. 3. The modern period was the beginning of business of the familial type or the artisan, where there was a different structure between work and the other three factors, that is, direction, prime material, and capital. 4. It is stated that…"the last period is the contemporary times between the 19th and 20th centuries, which is characterized by the struggle between work and capital, and thus between communism and capitalism."[188] These four periods of human progress, and development have already indicated the existence of formal and moral evil. For by making use of others as tools (or instruments for the benefit of the rest (masters and slaves).

The claim to subdue the earth and to have dominion over it, is undeniable. This is based on the progress and development of human life. Human beings consider themselves the most advanced creatures here on Earth. Consequently, they even try to discover life on other planets. Human beings can modify nature and consequently, such modification ranges from building giant towers full of excellent beds; bed sheets, pillow cases' cushions, supper chairs; and toilets, taking showers with beautiful soaps; using perfumes; wearing different types of shoes; wearing different types of clothes including under wears; brushing his/her teeth with sensondyne or signal toothpaste; covers himself with blankets during the cool weather; combing his/her hairs; make watering systems as to drink purified water through electric power.

From a technological perspective, humanity has advanced in terms of communication by using various sophisticated tools for social communication through social media. Human beings have made different types

---

188 J. Tab Charoa, *The Key Principles of the Catholic Social Teaching Their Relevance to the African World View,* Nairobi, Press, 2019, P. 84.

of cars to facilitate movement from within and outside the country. For example, you can see human people flying like a bird in airplanes day and night, from one continent to another. Humanity has made progress in terms of infrastructure such as the building of hospitals, roads, and bridges to connect one state to another and one country to another. What a marvelous achievement! The Sacred Scripture has put it right when it says "You made him a little lower than the angels…" (Ps 8:5). Look! He/she cooks food full of ingredients and drinks different types of wines.

Whatever effort we make to describe the achievements of human person's progress, will be beyond our capacity. However, all these achievements are the products of 'human intelligence' which will always make mankind resist fragility and liability. From a philosophic point of view, a person is defined as a 'rational animal.' We can affirm with certainty that the rest of the creatures do not need advanced developments for their survival but rather they simply need life guided by instinct, yet they seem to preserve and conserve their species.

Despite such excellent progress, development, and dominion over nature, however, still there is a dimension of human fragility. We could even say that human beings are the most liable and most fragile creatures compared with other creatures.

11.3 Biblical Origin of Original Sin

The Sacred Scripture says, "They strengthened the spirits of the disciples and exhorted them to preserver in the faith, affirming, "We must undergo hardships to enter the kingdom of God" (Acts 14:22). St. Paul's exhortation is relevant to the situation of Covid-19 pandemic. He never uses that exhortation out of the blue but rather through his personal experience of hardships which according to him, are necessary before entering the kingdom of God. Paul speaks like a madman, with far greater labours, such as imprisonments, with countless beatings near to death. Five times received forty slashes at the hands of the Jews, beaten with rods, once stoned; three times shipwrecked, in dangers: from rivers; from robbers, from both gentles and his people; in city; at sea, from false brethren; hunger and thirst, sometimes without food; in cold and exposure, in toil and hardship with sleepless night apart from the daily pressure upon me of my anxiety for all the churches (cf.1 Cor 18.21b-30).

Even during the Covid-19 pandemic, we ought to be courageous like St. Paul who said "I completed well; I have finished the race; I have kept the faith. For from now on the crown of righteousness awaits me, which the Lord, the just judge, will award to me on that day, and not only to me, but to all who have longed for his appearance" (2 Tim 4:7-8). In all these, Paul boasts because of Christ's power. In this dilemma of the COVID-19 pandemic, Christians ought to take St. Paul as their excellent example to bear hardship and preserver consider it as a necessity before entering God's kingdom.

For Christians, the COVID-19 pandemic can be compared to a great storm of wind which aroused the waves beating the boat almost filled with water. The master was asleep on the cushion while his disciples were anxious about their safety. They awoke Jesus saying, teacher! We are almost perishing. Instantly, Jesus awoke; rebuked the wind and commanded the sea to be peaceful and be still. Consequently, the wind ceased and there was a great calm. Jesus asked us during the Covid-19 pandemic as he asked his disciples, why are you afraid? Have you no faith in me? We would ask like his disciples, who then is this, that even the Covid-19 pandemic of a greater storm of wind and sea obey him? (Cf. Mk 4:35-41).

Furthermore, the militant Church is compared to a ship or a boat in the ocean and sea, jostled on all sides by all types of great storms of wind, yet never give in. Thus, the divine power of God guides her in the course of history. The COVID-19 pandemic is one of those great storms of wind putting the militant Church into temptation.

Jesus would repeat the same questions as he did his disciples, why are you afraid of the COVID-19 pandemic? Have you no faith in me? Furthermore, the disciples asked Jesus about their worries about perishing as a group, however, Jesus emphasized that each Christian is required to put his words into action. Otherwise, to temptation to lose hope in God during the COVID-19 pandemic is very imminent. Some might have already lost hope in God. Jesus stresses at individual level "Everyone who listens to these words of mine and acts on them will be like a wise man who built his house on rock. The rain fell, the floods came and the winds blew and buffeted the house. But it did not collapse; it had been set solidly on rock" (Mt.7:24-25). Jesus warns us about the consequence of the opposite of instruction.

The catastrophic situation of the COVID-19 pandemic has brought death and chaotic situations in areas of economic, cultural and political arenas. It has put all human beings at the same level, rich and poor alike. In the minds of people, both believers and atheists (non-believers) many questions have been raised. For the believers, the questions are simple but difficult to answer by anyone. For example, is God punishing human beings with the Covid-19 pandemic? Is it sleeping while innocent people are dying? Where is he in this catastrophic situation of the Covid-19 pandemic? He is still loving his creatures whom he has created in his image and likeness? Can his divine power not overcome the Covid-19 pandemic? Can he bring good out of the Covid-19 pandemic? These questions, and others, are prompted in the minds of believers based on the threat of the Covid-19 pandemic to human life. At least, for the believers, those questions were addressed to someone whom they trust while, for the atheists, they might have addressed purely human reason.

Why such questions were raised to God by the believers and to purely human reason by atheists? In each group, there is a need to find a solution to the problem of the Covid-19 pandemic, because it has exhibited radical hostility to human life. However, in all those questions raised to God, the King of the ages; the King of kings; and the Commander in Chief of commanders will simply answer us as he did to Job. "The Lord answered Job out of the whirlwind: "Who shut in the sea with doors, when it burst forth from the womb; when I made clouds its garment, and thick darkness its swaddling band; and prescribed bounds for it, and set bars and doors, and said, thus far all you come, and no farther, and here shall your proud waves be stayed?" (Job 38:1.8.11).

During the COVID-19 pandemic, the Psalmist on his part reminds us about the majesty of the Lord and Man's dignity saying, O LORD, our Lord, how majestic is your name through all the earth! Your majesty is set above the heavens, from the mouths of children and of babies you fashioned praise to foil your enemy, [COVID-19 pandemic], to silence the foe and rebel. When I see the heavens, the work of your figures, the moon and the stars which you arranged, what is a man that you should keep him in mind, the son of man that you care for?" Ps 8: 2-5).

The mentioning the divine power of God to defeat both physical and moral evils, nevertheless COVID-19 pandemic has reminded us that our human body is fragile and liable to infection from various diseases ranking from non-contagious to contagious diseases. In this sense, we ought to make sure that our body requires serious medical care that includes daily hygiene and other medical attention. If our body is liable to different types of disease due to its fragility, consequently, we must make sure to have constant medical tests should we suspect anything, and take strict measures in this regard.

For example, Sr. Dr. M. Martinelli advised that there is a need to introduce health screening tests for admission to seminaries and communities also the test for hepatitis A and B. According to her, if the tests are negative, a vaccination course should be scheduled; if the test for hepatitis B (HBsAg) is positive, the Bishop must discern seriously if it is to admit the candidate, considering the possible implications for the health of the candidate himself. According to Sr. Dr. M. Martinelli,

"My advice is to consider such persons not fit to live in community and for long studies. This may change in a few years, according to the progression of treatment."[189]

We ought to be aware that whatever effort we can make in terms of progress and development, will never be perfect. Our progress and development are also liable to fragility if done without moral and ethical principles. The tools we make such as cars and airplanes are subject to fragility. For example, we witness a lot of accidents in our lives. Our progress and development ought not to lead us to ourselves ego but to depend on God in the spirit of prayer. His Holiness Pope Francis proposes in the following prayer: to recognize that we are not self-sufficient and therefore to entrust ourselves to God; to be committed to the Lord's body to be permeated by his way of doing, to dialogue with him to welcome, accompany, support as he did; to learn from Jesus to take up the cross and together with him to take on the suffering of many; to imitate him in our frailty so that, via our weakness, salvation enters the world; and to look to Mary, Health of the People and Star of the stormy Sea and ask her to teach us to say "Yes" every day and be available, concretely and generously.

11.3.1 Sacred Scripture on the Contagious Diseases

The Sacred Scripture presents us with life as a mystery. Only God knows how life begins in us and with other lower-living organisms. We can admire such life both for higher living organisms and lower organisms. The Sacred Scripture whether it is in the *Yahwistic* or *Elohistic* tradition in the book of Genesis, presents us the marvelous and splendour picture of Creation. When we look around, we see millions of living organisms living second by second; minute by minute; day by day;

---

[189] Sr. Dr. Maria Martinelli, Provincial Superior CMS in South Sudan, *Enlightenment on Hepatitis*, p. 2.

night by night; week by week; month by month; and year by year from the time of creation to this day. However, on the other hand, we see millions of living organisms dying second by second; minute by minute; day by day; night by night; week by week; month by month; and year by year from the time of creation to this day. Nevertheless, still-living organisms both higher and lower species continue to survive throughout procreation. It seems that nobody knows the mysteries of life except God who is the Creator of all.

For example, in the case of leprosy, the Holy Scriptures affirm, "If, however, the blotch on the skin is white, but does not seem to be deeper than the skin, nor has the hair turned white, the priest shall quarantine the affected person for seven days" (Lev.13: 4). In these days of coronavirus pandemic, we hear every time that we should wash our hands, the Holy Scriptures recommend the same hygiene and ethics for example when it says, "Whoever sits on an article on which the man with the discharged was sitting shall wash his garments, bathe in water, and be unclean until evening" (Lev15: 6). In the Gospel of St. Luke, we are told … "They stood at a distance from him, and raised their voice, saying, "Jesus, Master! Pity us! When he saw them, he said, "Go show yourselves to the priests" (Lk 17: 12-14). The ten lepers in the Gospel of Luke exercised social distancing guidelines by calling Jesus at a distance.

Somewhere, we said that some faithful explained the coronavirus pandemic as the end of the world by quoting the book of Revelation. Christians ought to read the Sacred Scriptures well and they ought to be informed about the depths of its meaning. As to the end of the world, what is required from each Christian is preparedness (readiness) in the Sacred Scriptures. St. Mathew asserts "But of that day and hour no one knows, neither the angels of heaven, nor the Son, but the Father alone" (Mt 24: 36).

The Old Testament prioritized priests to have double functions, that of spiritual function and that of a physician without having a divine power to heal. For example, the priest declares someone unclean and sanctions that person for quarantine. In the New Testament, Jesus acts as God by not sanctioning a person with an infected disease but rather healing the person and sending him back to the community through the testimony of a priest. The case of ten lepers is a good example that God brings good out of evil. Jesus combines both roles of being the physician and a high priest with the divine power to heal. He manifested these two divine powers during the Covid-19 pandemic explicitly and implicitly in the lives of all Christians. Jesus heals us both spiritually and physically as he did to the ten lepers even during the Covid-19 pandemic.

In our theological reflections, we must know that both contagious and non-contagious diseases which contribute to the death of many living organisms including humans, are not foreign to Sacred Scripture. During the Covid-19 pandemic, we heard resistance from some denominations especially, pastors who tried to resist Covid-19 pandemic guidelines stipulated by their own countries. Instead of saving lives, they contributed to the death of their members by conducting public prayers without respect to COVID-19 pandemic health measures. For such pastors and other denominations, one can question their reading of the Holy Scripture. Religious leaders and pastors all over the world ought to respect social distancing guidelines during any pandemic or epidemic. In general, Christians must understand that the Sacred Scriptures recommend social distancing guidelines in case of any 'infectious disease' either on the person or object.

11.4 Holy Scripture on Physical and Moral Evil

In our theological reflections, the COVID-19 pandemic ought not to be explained as a punishment from God. We are aware of the presence of evil in the world both physical and moral evils. These are evils and are considered as a lack of perfection in something or deprivation of something. Theologically, we perceive both physical and moral evils as fighting against good or absolute good. Physical and moral are not necessary to exist, they are contingents. In the book of Genesis, we are told that God appreciates himself after he saw everything he had created. "God looked at everything he had made, and found it very good" (Gen 1:32). Neither does God condone physical or moral evils. God is not neutral when he sees physical or moral evil. He condemns and negates both of them. The Psalmist puts it right "You are not a god who delights in evil; no wicked person finds refuge with you; the arrogant cannot stand before your eyes. You hate all who do evil; [including Covid-19 pandemic], you destroy those who speak falsely, a bloody and fraudulent man the LORD abhors" (Ps 5:5-7).

However, through physical and moral evils, we can see God at work. For example, of physical evil, Jesus was asked by his disciples about the man born blind. They asked him, "Rabbi, who sinned, this man or his parents, that he was born blind? Jesus answered, "Neither he nor his parents sinned; it is so that the works of God might be made visible through him" (Jn 9:2-3). Other examples, of moral evils, God turned Augustine of Hippo from being a sinful man to a saint, and he turned Nygudeng of Nuer from eating human faces into a prophet. In our theological reflection, we ought to know that nothing is impossible to God, even with the Covid-19 pandemic, he brings good out of it. God has a divine power to bring out good in physical and moral evils. Therefore, any principles he stipulates in the sacred Scripture are not for retribution or punishment, he gave the Israelites hygiene principles against the contaminative germs and taught the necessity to quarantine the sick (Cf. Lk 21:11). "He shall remain unclean as long as he has the disease" (Lev 13:46). However, God take cares of us when we are infected by contagious disease and other non-contagious diseases in our life. He loves us throughout our lives till the end. God neither uses physical or moral evil to punish us, he rather works in us in those situations to manifest his power of love in us.

The divine power of God to bring good out of both physical and moral evils can be seen through our experience in life. For example, during the winter season, we South Sudanese have a culture of burning grass, forests and everything that is dried. Our experience can testify that we see everything as dead as a consequence of fire. However, when the first rains begin, once again, we see millions of species germinating, beginning with grass the biggest population on earth. God brings good out of the moral evil we have committed by burning millions of species alive. For example, Dr. Anthony Fuaci, the Top Infectious Disease in America, once said, 'Covid-19 pandemic is like a wildfire with enormous capacity.' In our theological reflections, if God can bring good out of moral evil we have done by burning lower living species, are we not more valuable than those lower species? (Cf. Mt 6:24-34). Even though the Covid-19 pandemic has made our lives a laughingstock, God will bring good out of it.

We are told that the perfect creation of humankind was disfigured by human ambition on the eve of creation. The teaching of the Church calls it 'Original Sin.' Adam and Eve transgressed and consequently, mankind became fragile and liable to anything. (Cf. Gen 3:6-7). The consequence of original sin incurred condemnation upon Adam, Eve and the snake. (Gen 3:14-17). The last thing, that is, the Creation, the fall in proctology, reveals to us that as the consequence of the fall, that radical rebellious…"alienated man from God and takes away the dominion over nature which God conferred upon man in creation."[190] Modern scholars prefer to treat the account as a story through which the Hebrews enunciated their belief that fell from their primitive harmonious relationship with God. Therefore, L. McKenzie states that the present condition of man can be due only to his failure to meet the standards which God has set for him. However, it is argued that the question of the reality of the fall of man, which is theologically connected with

---

190   John L. McKenzie, *Dictionary of the Bible*, Tokyo, Simon & Schuster, 1965, p.273.

the reality of redemption, is distinct from the question of the historical character of Gen 2-3.)

In dealing with covid-19 pandemic, one cannot ignore the historical origin of sin in the Sacred Scriptures, which is the mirror of every situation in humanity. In this context, the mysteries of the ambivalence of human perfection and its fragility after the original sin can find a suitable explanation. Consequently, humanity ought not to focus on dominion over nature, but rather to make efforts to discover and to realize that nature itself wages a constant fight against human pseudo claim of dominion over it in a more complex, complicated style and a rigid manner.

11.5 Principle of Preferential Option for the Vulnerable

According to Pope Francis, "The storm exposes our vulnerability and uncovers those false and superfluous certainties around which we have constructed ranges from our daily schedules, our projects, our habits and priorities. It shows us how we are allowed to become dull and feeble due to the very things that nourish, sustain and strengthen our lives and our communities."[191] His Holiness Pope Francis asserts that we have realized that we are on the same boat, all, fragile and disoriented, but at the same time all of us are called to row together, each of us in need of comforting the other. It is further stated that the risk is that we may then be struck by an even worse virus, that of selfish indifference. Now, facing the pandemic, we have widely and vividly experienced our interconnectedness in vulnerability. However, much of humanity has responded to that vulnerability with resolve and solidarity.

In terms of the list of vulnerabilities during covid-19 pandemic, Pope Francis went on to say that the family album goes on to include:

---

191   Francis, *Life After the Pandemic,* Nairobi, Paulines Publications Africa, 2020, P.17.

doctors, nurses, supermarket employees, cleaners, caregivers, providers of transport, law and order forces, volunteers, priests, religious men and women, fathers, and mothers, grandparents and teachers, persons who work in nursing homes, or live in barracks and prison and so on. During covid-19 pandemic, humanity has shown compassion that never existed before. God's compassion, His loving care, and His generosity were exercised by those who were touched by the suffering of others. The principle of preferential option for the vulnerable was put into practice almost by all.

11.6 Eschatology and COVID-19 Pandemic

The COVID-19 pandemic ought to help Christians to reflect on proctology, the doctrine about the first things that is, (Creation, the fall). The doctrine about the first things (creation, the fall, neither does the fall decide for us the end nor does the present decide for the end (finality. Neither any one of us can determine the end nor can the Covid-19 pandemic determine the finality. However, only God alone will determine the end in the future through Christ. According to M. Schmaus, "The word *eschatology* means doctrine about the last events and final circumstances towards which the history of mankind and the life of each individual are directed."[192] It is believed that eschatology cannot be understood as an appendix to the other divisions of theology: it is fundamental to the whole of theology. Every theological tract has an eschatological character insofar as each is oriented to the last things. Consequently, proctology and eschatology are inseparably joined.

In our theological reflections, we do believe that the future is for the sake of Christ whom all things were created, and for whom everything in the past has happened. Everything depends on that end and serves it. Nothing happens for its own sake; everything presses forward

---

192   Michael Schmaus, *Justification and the Last Things*, p.149.

beyond itself. The Church believes that from the beginning, creation was ordered to the end. The COVID-19 pandemic cannot determine our destiny and movement towards the future preordained by God through Christ. Whatever happens such as the Covid-19 pandemic, will not distract the plan of God, because the consummation in Jesus Christ was willed from the beginning. The Church proclaims the whole of world history and salvation history as one inexorable movement into the future. By an external divine determination, this movement is dependent on its pre-ordained end. Consequently, the Church comforts and consoles all human beings to believe and have hope in God who is the master of the beginning and the end of history.

The Church's Magisterium argues that the theological doctrine of the oneness of the past, future history, and prophecy, serves as a corrective not only to an excessively narrow appraisal of the past as if it were the exclusive measure of value but also to a one-sided evaluation of the future-as if it could be shaped in any way desired, without reference to the past. This belief about this doctrine cannot be distorted by the Covid-19 pandemic. M. Schmaus asserts that the past on which the Christian faith rests on Christ reveals the steps into the future, a future which is already present in faith. The doctrine of eschatology states that the future is the meaning and goal of the past; the past is the light and the impetus to the future. It is stated the "golden age" lies not in the past but in the future, in the real sense, the absolute future predestined by God and only known to him alone.

How can we differ from the rest of mankind when we reflect on the COVID-19 pandemic or other types of catastrophic disasters? We ought to believe that our Christian eschatology is distinguished by its transcendental character from that of secular faith in progress which in modern times has become a dominant theme of the European outlook on history. It is pointed out that history, it is thought, is moving forward towards the realization of a society based on a human ideal of freedom and equality, an idea formed by pure reason and advanced by the technology and industry which are its product. This pseudo-assumption of mankind is challenged by the COVID-19 pandemic in the 21st century.

According to M. Shamus, what is overlooked by this evolutionary faith is that technological progress provides no guarantee, no norm for civilization as a whole, especially for morals, religion, freedom and justice. Mankind cannot and can never be a point of reference to himself, a human person ought to look to God as a point of reference otherwise, and mankind with all technological progress will be slapped in the face by the Covid-19 pandemic in the 21st century. The COVID-19 pandemic has reminded mankind to be aware of its vulnerability and fragility. Human beings are reminded by the Covid-19 pandemic not to be overconfident in themselves and their reason.

11.7 The Last Things about the Future of God's People

From a proctologic perspective, life has its beginning in creation. However, life does not end with the creation and the fall. There is yet a long journey which leads to the end (finality). We have said earlier that the past on which the Christian faith rests. Christ reveals the steps into the future, a future which is already present in faith. Based on the doctrine of eschatology, it will be unfortunate and premature for anyone to conclude somewhere before the end (finality) which is pre-predetermined and pre-ordained by God himself through Christ. In our efforts to discuss the Last Things concerning the future of God's people, we will briefly present the following elements such as the pilgrim Church (people of God); the second coming of Christ (Parousia); the resurrection of the dead and finally the judgment of the world.

11.7.1 The Pilgrim Church (People of God)

When God decided to liberate the Israelites, he promised to journey with them through Moses. A long journey of forty years in the desert before they arrived in the promised land which God says "So I have decided to lead you out of your affliction in Egypt into the land of the Canaanites; the Hittites, the Amorites; the Perizzites, the Girgashites, the Hivites and the Jubbusites, a land flowing with milk and honey" (Ex 3: 17). The decision taken by God to liberate Israel was provoked by Pharaoh who maliciously decided to terminate the lives of innocent infants of Israel. Pharaoh the king of Egypt and Herod were the first to legalize the death of innocent children. In the book of Exodus, we are told that the king of Egypt Pharaoh called Shiphrah and the other Puah "When you act as midwives for the Hebrew women look on the birth stool: if it is a boy, kill him, but if it is a girl, she may live" (Ex 1:16). Those moral evil acts carried out by Pharaoh and Herod were Covid-19 pandemic for the innocent children.

This journey of forty years in the desert, on the one hand, consisted of constant rebellion and the manifestation of an exhibition of radical hostility against God by the people of Israel and on the other hand, on the faithfulness to the covenant by God. It is stated that forty years, there were forty days were dedicated to spying and surveying the Promised Land. God decided to involve Israel in their liberation from slavery to freedom. Although the Israelites were constantly rebellious against God, nevertheless, their choice remains an example for those who believe in God. Consequently, God decided that only younger generations ought to enter the Promised Land (cf. Num 14:32-34).

In this communal journey, it was God who accompanied and protected Israel through the clouds as a guide for the people (Cf. Ex 40:43-38); and the provision of 'quail' and 'manna' in the desert as food for the journey (cf. Ex 16:4). In this journey, the people of Israel require anthropological approach to fulfill the various needs of spiritual; physical; psychological; emotional; social; cultural; political; and economic.

The serpent biting people of Israel in the desert (cf. Num 21:4-9). In this journey, with its ups and downs which consisted of constant grumbling demonstrated through exhibiting hostile behaviors, the making of a golden calf which was an act of apostasy; the covenant and legislation at Sinai (cf. Ex 19:4-6), we can still see progress. In all these, one could see the dimension of the evolution of this pilgrim church in the areas of setting social structures such as prophets, kings, elders, and priests, norms for cultic worship, legal norms, and morals to prepare and to guide this communal journey to the Promised Land. In those incidents of liberation, we could see the hands of God guiding the people of Israel and protecting them from evil harm. Consequently, God protects us from the COVID-19 pandemic as he did to the people of Israel in the desert, although sometimes, we tend to throw everything to God without acknowledging our faults in the world.

According to *Lumen Gentium*, "He, therefore, chose the race of Israel as a people unto Himself. With it, He set up a covenant. Step by step He taught and prepared this people, making them know its history both Himself and the degree of His will and making it holy unto Himself. All these things, however, were done by way of preparation and as a figure of that new and perfect covenant, which was to be ratified in Christ, and of that fuller revelation which was to be given through the Word of God Himself made flesh" (LG Ch 11: N0. 9).

In our current situation, specifically in the catastrophic situation of the COVID-19 pandemic in which many people have lost their lives, others are infected and many are psychologically depressed and traumatized, social gatherings are proclaimed nonexistent with the consequences of not celebrating the Holy Mass (the Eucharist, the real Manna), no way of the cross during the Lenten season, no celebration of funeral rites, in short, every spiritual exercise which involve social dimension is shunned. In our theological reflections as people who are on the journey to the Promised Land, can we still see God guiding the Church and guiding each of us? Do we feel abandoned by God or we do still see Him accompanying the Church as a whole? Are we tempted not to believe in him who is our Master and Guide?

We did mention earlier that the COVID-19 pandemic has affected all of us at all levels such as: physical; psychological; social; spiritual; emotional; cultural; political; and economic. Like the people of Israel who journeyed to the Promised Land guided by God, even today, in our catastrophic situation of covid-19 pandemic, God is still with us. He never abandoned us, because his eternal Word still echoes in our ears. The Psalmist was right when he says "If I forget you, Jerusalem, may my right hand forget. May my tongue stick to my palate if I do not remember you if I do not exalt Jerusalem beyond all my delights (Ps 137:5-6) Furthermore, the prophet Isaiah on his part consoles us with a powerful word from God the Father "Can a mother forget her infant, be without tenderness for the child of her womb?

Even should she forget, I will never forget you (Is 49:15). "Then he approached and said to them, "All power in heaven and on earth has been given to men. Go, therefore, and make disciples of all nations, baptizing them in the name of the Father, and of the Son and the Holy Spirit. Teaching them to observe all that I have commanded you. And behold, I am with you always, until the end of the age" Mt.28:18-20). With love, faith and hope, we ought to know that everything is in the hand of God and that God has the power to bring out good from evil such as the Covid-19 pandemic.

Our love, faith and hope require us to adapt ourselves to a new situation as we journey towards the future and to learn how to deal with new situations such as COVID-19 in the light of the gospel values and principles which are unchangeable and unchanged. According to *Lumen Gentium* "Destined to extend to all regions of the earth, the Church enters into human history. Though it transcends at once all times and all racial boundaries. Advancing through trials and tribulation…she ceaselessly renews herself through the action of the Holy Spirit, until, through the cross. She attains to that light which knows setting" (LG .9). The requirement for the renewal of life demands constant readiness to repentance, purification of heart, change of mind, change of heat (*metanoia*) through the help of the Holy Spirit, in the sacred sacraments of the Lord.

In dealing with the unprecedented catastrophic situation of the COVID-19 pandemic, we ought to know that we are not alone in this suffering. The Church in heaven is with us and consequently, those who are living as pilgrims on earth (militant Church); those who have died and are in need to be purification before entering heaven (purgatory)' those who have reached the eternal joys of the glorious Church. *Lumen Gentium* states that "At the present times some of the disciples are pilgrims on earth; other have died and are being purified; while still others are in glory, contemplating in full light, God himself, triune and one, as he is" (LG no. 49).

In our suffering during the COVID-19 pandemic, the saints in heaven constantly intercede for us as we also intercede for those in purgatory. The Church believes that all who belong to Christ, having his Spirit, form one Church and cleave together in Him. Therefore, the union of the pilgrim brethren with the brethren that have gone to sleep in the peace of Christ is not at least interrupted.

On the contrary, according to the perennial faith of the Church, it is strengthened through the exchanging of spiritual goods" (LG no. 49). Consequently, the relationship between the pilgrim Church and the Glorious Church in heaven is expressed at two levels: veneration of the saints and the invocation of the theme. In venerating them we honour the Lord because the Lord himself was the very reason for their life and the last cause of their heroic holiness. When the Church invokes the saints, she is aware of being united in a single "we" with those who are already in Christ. The Church believes that within the communion of saints, a special role belongs to the Blessed Virgin Mary.

11.7.2 The Second Coming of Christ (Parousia)

We believe in the doctrine about the second coming of Christ that nothing can interrupt it even the catastrophic Covid-19 pandemic. Even though our Sunday celebrations are interrupted by this unprecedented disease, yet, our belief about the second coming of Christ is another source of strength. We do believe that God can bring good out of evil specifically the Covid-19 pandemic that has taken a lot of lives. We journey as a community, aiming to arrive at the Promised Land (paradise) through the second coming of Christ.

In our every Sunday celebration, all the Catholic believers demonstrate their faith in the second coming of the Lord by singing or reciting the creed. The part of the creed contains one of the fundamental doctrines of our faith. According to M. Schmaus, "The final fulfilment of creation will mean the end of a long process. It will be reached not through an event but through a personal encounter, the "coming" of Christ."[193] It is stated that when we speak of the "second coming" of Christ, it is not a spatial event that is meant but a personal experience. Just as in his ascension from the earth Christ did not have any particular place belonging to him from which to take his leave, so he will not in his return to earth come from a particular place to the whole world.

Certain essential elements concerning the doctrine of the second coming of Christ are listed as follows: 1. The first coming of the eternal Logos involved his taking on a relationship of a special kind to a man, and through him to all mankind and the rest of creation as well. 2. In his resurrection from the dead this man experienced in his human nature the final consequence of the special relationship to the eternal Logos. The change wrought in the man Jesus through the resurrection was such that his life was cut off from all historical existence and was thereafter not directly perceptible within history.

---

193   Michael Schmaus, *Justification and the Last Things*, p.177.

3. The return of Christ will mean an actualizing of his glorified mode of existence whose effect will be that it can no longer be veiled: visible: his presence will be immediately visible so that no one can fail to see him. This presumes that the whole of mankind has transformed into a condition wherein it can recognize the glorified Christ. This transforming capacity belongs not to the love of creatures but only to God's love. Nevertheless, the transforming powering of human love gives us a likeness of the mystery which the creative force of God's love contains.

11.7.3 The Faith in the Second Coming of Christ

Our Liturgical celebration does not only profess the second coming of Christ by professing the creed only but all the sacraments specifically the Eucharistic prayers and their efficacies from the past because they are instituted by Christ, confer the grace for the present. St. Paul reminded the people of Corinthians "Every time you eat this bread and drink from this Cup you proclaim the Lord's death until he comes" (1 Cor 11:26). Some passages testify the second coming of Christ: "This Jesus who was taken from you into heaven, will come back in the same way that you saw him go to heaven" (Acts 1:11). The gospel of St. Mathew said, "The Son of man will appear in the sky: and all peoples of the earth will weep as they will see the Son of man coming on the clouds of heaven with power and great glory" (Mt. 24:30). "The Son of man is about to come in the glory of his Father with his angels, and then he will reward each one according to his deeds (Mt 16:27).

According to L. Penzo, from the theological point of view, the second coming of the Lord is a mystery. On one side, the risen and glorious Christ has assumed a way of existence which cannot be perceived by our ordinary senses. On the other side, it cannot be described as a change of place, as if he were a local passing from heaven to earth. It is asserted that "The theologians affirm that the second coming of the Lord consists in the manifestation to all men of the glory of his resurrection. But this manifestation can be perceived only if men receive a special capacity that enables them to see the glorious body of the risen Lord."[194] While waiting for the second coming of Christ, faith in him, hope and love for our salvation are prerequisites even during the Covid-19 pandemic. The recitation of the creed or singing it in our liturgical celebration, is itself a sign of victory over the Covid-19 pandemic. It means the proclamation of Christ as he was yesterday, as he is today and as he will be tomorrow. This is our faith that we proclaim in our Sunday liturgical celebrations and other solemnities to convey the message of hope even during the COVID-19 pandemic while waiting for Christ.

11.7.4 The Time of the Second Coming of Christ

The second coming of Christ which is eschatology is unquestionable. What seems not to be clear in the mind of Jesus Christ is the fixation on the time of his second coming. Jesus categorically refused to give a definite answer. "No one knows, however, when that day or hour will come; neither the angels in heaven nor the Son; only the Father knows" (Mk 13:32). The synoptic gospel seems to put the second coming of Christ to a remote and indefinite future. For example, Jesus sometimes compares the coming of the kingdom to the grain which matures very slowly in the field (cf. Mt 13:31) or like a mustard seed which takes a lot of time to grow into a big tree or like the yeast that puts to trail the woman's patience before fermenting the whole flour (cf. Mt 13:33).

"The Good News about the Kingdom will be preached through all the world for a witness to all mankind, and then the end will come" (Mt 24:14). Jesus said, "I assure you that whenever this gospel is preached all over the world, what she has done will be told in memory of her" (Mt 26:13). When he sent his disciples, he said, "I will be with you

---

194   Luigi Penzo, *The Last Things,* notes for the students of St. Paul's Major Seminary, Khartoum, 2002, P.8-9.

always, to the end of this age" (Mt 28:20). Some passages in the gospels present an attitude of sober and vigilant because his coming is compared to a thief coming to steal at night (cf. Mt 24:43), or like a master who chooses to return unexpectedly from a feast and is seriously disappointed if he finds that the coming of the Lord will take place in a way that is surprising and unexpected; thus the need of being constantly vigilant is required (Lk 12:35-36). Jesus' sermons about the "Parousia" (Mk Ch. 13, Mt ch. 24, and Lk ch. 17) seem to present and create difficulties because they present the coming of the Lord as a near and immediate event. Jesus himself asserts "In truth, I tell you, before this generation has passed away, all these things will have taken place" (Mt 24:34).

According to L. Penzo, the scholars explain the sermons on, the "Parousia" by affirming that the Lord was foretelling about two different future events, namely, the destruction of Jerusalem and the end of the world. The Evangelists grasped the difference between the two events but reported the words of the Lord without minding their distinction. It is argued that if we keep in mind this distinction, we perceive without difficulty the words referring to the destruction of Jerusalem and the words referring to the end of the world. The destruction of Jerusalem was an event, which was different from the end of the world, although, there is a deep connection between the two. The temple which perished and the walls of the city that fell to pieces symbolize the ruin of all the earthly things that are destined to dissolve at the second coming of the Lord.

Such uncertainty about the time of the second coming of Christ, once made St. Paul think that the "Parousia" would be imminent and would find him alive. For example, he said, "We can tell you this from the Lord's teaching that we who are still alive for the Lord's coming will not have any advantage over those who have fallen asleep" (1 Thess 4:15). "Now I am going to tell you: we are not all going to fall asleep, but we are all going to be changed instantly, in the twinkling of an eye, when the last trumpet sounds" (1 Cor 15:51). (This had led to erroneous conclusive belief that the "Parousia" was going to be imminent, and so it was useless to marry or to work or attend any earthly affair. Consequently, this led St. Paul to correct this erroneous conclusive belief in the second letter. Finally, St. Paul realized that the Parousia would not find him alive as he assumed to be. Consequently, it will require the conversion of both the Jewish and the Gentiles. Even with the COVID-19 pandemic, Christ is asking each of us to be patient and to trust in him.

In the year 2000, we had an unfortunate situation certain denominations in Uganda decided to make an erroneous conclusion about the second coming of Christ. For example, during the celebration of 2000, they decided to burn themselves in their church. It is clear that during the Covid-19 pandemic, due to depression, and the erroneous conclusion that the world is coming to an end, some people might have a tendency to commit suicide and some may become hopeless.

11.7.5 The Concept of Anti-Christ (Serpent)

Since we are dealing with concepts of culture of life and culture of death, we make ourselves familiar with the term 'serpent.' According to L. McKenzie, there are at least 33 species of serpent in Palestine, several of them venomous, and allusions to the serpent are common in the Bible. 1. A serpent is a symbolic figure, the serpent is an important figure in the religions of the ancient Near East and the Old Testament and New Testament. By definition, "The serpent is a demonic figure in many regions of the world, and it is such in the mythology of Mesopotamia, Persia, Egypt, Greece, and Rome."[195]

L. McKenzie states that as a demonic figure, it may be beneficent or

---

195   John L. McKenzie, *Dictionary of the Bible*, New York, Simon & Schuster, 1995, P.789.

maleficent. Furthermore, the serpent is a divine or demonic symbol on Mesopotamian boundary stones and is included among the gods who are invoked to bring imprecations on the trespasser of the boundary. Its symbolism as a divine figure or a divine emblem is obscure; however, its association with the deities of fertility is ever assured. According to L. McKenzie, as a symbol of fertility, the serpent becomes a figure of life and health as in the modern caduceus, the emblem of medicine, which is derived from the emblem of the Greek healing god Asclepius/Asclepius (Salvation).

On the other hand, the serpent is also a cosmic figure, identified with a monster of chaos which is conquered by the creative deity. As such, it is the very emblem of the power of evil and darkness. This serpentine character of the monster of chaos is explicit in the mythological text of Ugarit. It is argued that the symbolism of the serpent is not therefore uniform and must be identified by the context in which the symbol appears. It is said that the symbolism of the ancient Near East must recall the symbolic value of the serpent in the bible. As a celestial demonic figure, the emissary of Yahweh, the serpent is noticed under SHERAPH.

The serpent as a cosmic figure appears in some OT allusions: Yahweh smites the fleeing serpent, the twisted serpent, and the dragon in the sea (Jb 26:13; Is 27:1). The adversary of the creative deity appears in the mythological texts of Ugarit described in the identical words which are used in Is 27:1. Am 9:3 alludes to the serpent on the floor of the sea, the cosmic serpent. More obscure and much more discussed in the symbolism of the serpent in Gn 3. The identification of the serpent with Satan occurs only in late Jewish literature, from there it passed to the New Testament (WS 2:24, 2 Co 11:3). Serpent here is just one of God's creatures but hostile to him and human beings. Consequently, the Covid-19 pandemic can be considered as the serpent or Lucifer trying to destroy human life. It has brought chaos to the world and even darkness to human life.

11.7.6 The Sacred Scripture on the Signs of Anti-Christ

According to St. Peter, "God's measure of time is different from man; for God, a thousand years are like a day. God is withholding his judgment, waiting patiently for sinners to repent" (2 Pt 3:1-14). "The Good News about the Kingdom will be proclaimed through all the world for a witness to all mankind, and then the end will come" (Mt 24:14). Consequently, this will require the conversion of all nations. Christ speaks often of the "adversary", "the tempter", "the accuser", and "The prince of this world", who spares no effort to destroy the Saints of God. St. John the Evangelist in his letters speaks of the "Antichrist" (1 Jn 20: 18; 22; 4:3). "About the coming of Our Lord Jesus Christ, brothers… never let anyone deceive you in any way. It cannot happen until the Great Revolt has taken place and has appeared the wicked One, the lost One, the Enemy who raises himself above every so-called God" (2 Thess 2:1-3). "A great rebellion or apostasy" (2 Thess 2:3).

Consequently, the disciples will be seduced by his false doctrines and will abandon Christ and his Gospel. Other false prophets will also appear, working together with the wicked Ones, and seduce the Christians by presenting themselves as "the saviours of the World." The number of the apostates will be great. 2. "He will come with the power of Satan and perform all kinds of false miracles and wonders, and use every kind of wicked deceit on those who will perish…The result is that all who have not believed the truth but have taken pleasure in sin will be condemned" (2 Thess 2:11-12. 3. He will declare himself "God", and will find many who are ready to accept him and to adore him as their god. "He will oppose every so-called god or object of worship and will put himself above them all. He will even go in and sit down in God's temple and claim to be God" (2 Thess 2:4)

4. The wickedness is already at work on earth, but in a secret and hidden way; on the contrary, when the wicked one appears, he will succeed in spreading such an antichristian spirit, that the faith will

almost disappear from the earth. And this seems to confirm the words of the Lord. "Will the Son of man find faith on earth when he comes?" (Lk 18:8). 5. However, "When the Lord Jesus comes, he will kill him with the breath from his mouth and destroy him with his dazzling presence" (2 Thess 2:8).

The travail or chaos of the universe: In announcing his second coming, the Lord foretells the manifestation of abnormal radical hostile activities on earth. "You will hear of wars and rumours of wars...Nations will fight against nations, and kingdom against kingdom, and there will be famines and earthquakes in various places. All this is only the beginning of the birth pangs" (Mt 24:3-8). Even the powers of heaven will take part in the travail, and the universe will fall into general chaos: "immediately after this distress of those days the sun will be darkened, the moon will not give its light, the stars will fall from the sky and the powers of the heaven will be shaken' (Mt 24:28-30). Nothing in human history has brought darkness to human lives more than the Covid-19 pandemic. Consequently, the Covid-19 pandemic can be compared to both World I and World II which we shall present below.

11.8 The Signs of Anti-Christ in the Course of History

The Scriptural citations above reveal something very important to us. The fighting between good and evil takes place at different levels and on many fronts. Now we are experiencing the COVID-19 pandemic that has led to the loss of many lives. We saw many signs of anti-Christ in the course of human history such as World War I, which was fought between 1914 and 1918, with..." an estimated 16 million soldiers and civilians dead and countless other physically and psychologically wounded persons."[196] World War II was initiated by Adolf Hitler

---

196   Cf. J. Tab Charoa, *The Dramatic Clash Between the Culture of life and Culture of Death*, p.24.

between 1939 and 1945, and it claimed many lives ..."40,000,000-50,000,000 deaths incurred...make it the bloodiest conflict as well as the largest war in history."[197] The attack on the World Trade Center which led to the death of more than 3,000 people and the Rwanda genocide led to the death of 500,000-800,000 people in a hundred days. These, without adding the ongoing wars between nations, civil wars and other natural disasters, are true signs of anti-Christ. The fighting between good and evil, truth and lie, justice and injustice. However, with these signs of Anti-Christ, nobody is allowed to make erroneous conclusions about the end of the Word. Below are some signs of anti-Christ in our contemporary society.

1. The signs of Anti-Christ at the ecological level: We have a good reason why our theological reflection should not focus only on the Covid-19 pandemic. It ought to include the following signs of anti-Christ at the ecological level. 1. The indiscriminate application of advances in science and technology whose applications of these discoveries in the fields of industry and agriculture have produced harmful long-term effects. 2. The gradual depletion of the ozone layer which is related to the "greenhouse effect" has now reached a crisis as a consequence of industrial growth, massive urban concentrations and vastly increased energy needs. 3. The Industrial wastes. 4. The burning of fossil fuels. 5. Unrestricted deforestation. 6. The use of certain types of herbicides. 7. The Coolants and propellants. All these, contribute to the harm of the atmosphere and environment. It is stated that the resulting meteorological and atmospheric changes range from damage to health to the possible future submission of low-lying lands.

2. The signs of Anti-Christ at the technological level: 1. Technological intervention has made a lot of progress, however; it applies various methods and procedures in the critical area of life and family such as: 2. Research on human embryos. 3 It uses stem cells for therapeutic

---

197   Ibid. P. 23.

purposes. 4. Other areas of experimental medicine. 5. Euthanasia (false mercy, incurable illness). 6 Abortion. 7 Contraception. 8. Eugenic. 9. Biological material. 10. Heterogonous artificial fertilization. 11. Homologous artificial fertilization, 12. Human cloning. I3. LGBT rights such as: Lesbian; Gays, homosexual and transsexual (sexual re-assignment. 14. Sterilization.

3. *The signs of Anti-Christ at the Legal Level*: The request for legalization is as follows: 1. Abortion to be passed by the majority of the members of parliament in some countries .2. Legalization of both lesbian and homosexual. 3. Legalization of sexual reassignment. 4. *The signs of Anti-Christ at Various theoretical levels*: 1. Promethean mentality. 2. Ethical relativism (subjectivism. 3. Proportionalists. 4. Radical views on pluralistic society. 5. Relative deprivation. 6. Instinctive theory of violence. 7. Egoistic theory of violence. 8. Calculative theory of violence. 9. Frustration reduction theory of violence. 10. Cultural conditioning theory of violence. 11. Violence and social change.

T. Hobbes has identified three essential causes of quarrels such as 12. Competition. 13. Diffidence (mistrust). 14. Glory. I6. Consequence of original sin and various types of sins. Child molestation. 17. Religious ideologies such as extremism and terrorism. 18. Individualism that includes requests for absolute freedom, absolute autonomy, and absolute right without regard to eternal truth, love and moral law 19. Indifferentism. 20. Atheism.21. Demographic explosion (population explosion). 22. Poverty. 23. Human trafficking. 24. Racism. 5. *The signs of Anti-Christ at the natural level*: 1. Earthquake. 2. Volcanos. 3. Floods. 4. Drought. 5. Tsunami. 6. Hurricanes. 6. Tornados. 8. Various kinds of diseases which include the Covid-19 pandemic. 7. Various viruses and epidemics.

11.10 Signs of Antic-Christ in Slavery and in Racism

The practices of racism and slavery have something to do with a superiority complex. Some human beings consider themselves as superior to the rest. Consequently, they subjected the inferior races to total dehumanization such as racial discrimination and slavery. For example, black people suffered so much as a consequence of such a doctrine of superiority that is upheld and believed by those classes of human beings. No wonder, even a false justification in the book of Gen 9: 18-27 was claimed by Western Christians. This was based on naïve narration of Noah's cursing of Ham. Christian tradition understood the text as if black people were cursed by God as a consequence of the sin of their father Ham. Consequently, even the colour of their skin was associated with the curse. According to B. Bujo, the analysis of this text, which was already pioneered by the Fathers of the Church Origen and Ambrose of Milan, can be followed up to the First Vatican Council.

Unfortunately, in "1873 the Congregation of Indulgences published even a prayer for the conversion of Ham's offspring in Central Africa, approved with a 300-day indulgence by Pope Pius IX. Part of this prayer reads: Let prayer for the most miserable Ethiopian peoples in Central Africa, who form a tenth of humanity, so that God almighty may take away from their hearts the curse of Ham and give them the blessings of Jesus Christ, our God and Lord."[198] This wrong interpretation of the book of Gen 9:18-27 was the legitimization of the exercise of the sign of antic Christ upon the black people by the missionaries that have left dark traces in the evangelization. According to B. Bujo, Consequently, the slave trade in Africa cannot be properly understood without this theological legitimization. Therefore, racial discrimination and slavery

---

198   Bénzêt Bujo, *The Ethical Dimension of the Community, the African Model and the Dialogue Between North and South*, Paulines Publications Africa, Nairobi, 1997, p. 135.

as signs of Antic-Christ, deprived the black population of its dignity because many were brutally tortured and killed.

However, later on, in the course of history, many theologians were embarrassed about the wrong interpretation of the text of Gen 9:18-27. B. Bujo states, let us *pars pro toto* remember the island of Goree in Senegal, when in February 1992 Pope John Paull II asked for forgiveness for the inhuman slave trade. This brutal act of the sign of antic Christ is not sufficiently addressed, "Only at the threshold of the third millennium has John Paul II seen a parallel between this inhuman act and the crimes of the Nazi regime."[199]

In the United States of America, an act of brutal massacre was inflicted upon the Negros in Tulsa Race Riot (or the 1921 TULSA RACE massacre the attack on Greenwood). The 1921 Attack on Greenwood was one of the most significant events in Tulsa's history. Following World War, I, Tulsa was recognized nationally for its affluent African-American community known as the Greenwood District. This thriving business district and surrounding residential area was referred to as "Black Wall Street." In June 1921, a series of events nearly destroyed the entire Greenwood area.

May 31-June 1, 1921, in the morning of May 30, 1921, a young black man named Dick Rowland was riding in the elevator in the Drexel Building at Third and Main with a white woman named Sarah Page. The details of what followed vary from person to person. Accounts of an incident circulated among the city's white community during the day and became more exaggerated with each telling.

Tulsa police arrested Rowland the following day and began an investigation. An inflammatory report in the May 31 edition of the Tulsa Tribune spurred a confrontation between black and white armed mobs around the courthouse where the sheriff and his men had barricaded the

---

199   Cf. Běnzět Bujo, *The Ethical Dimension of the Community*, p.177.

top floor to protect Rowland. Shots were fired and the outnumbered African Americans began retreating to the Greenwood District.

In the early morning hours of June 1, 1921, Greenwood was looted and burned by white rioters. Governor Robertson declared martial law, and National Guard troops arrived in Tulsa. Guardsmen assisted firemen in putting out fires, took African Americans out of the hands of vigilantes and imprisoned all black Tulsans not already interned. Over 6,000 people were held at the Convention Hall and the Fairgrounds, some for as long as eight days.

Twenty-four hours after the violence erupted, it ceased. In the wake of the violence, 35 city blocks lay in charred ruins, more than 800 people were treated for injuries and contemporary reports of deaths began at 36. Historians now believe as many as 300 people may have died.

In the 21st century, in the United States of America, another ugly brutal act of killing George Floyd took place. This brutal act took place on May 25, 2020, George Floyd, a 46-year-old black man, was murdered in Minneapolis, Minnesota, while being arrested on suspicion of using a counterfeit $20 bill. During the arrest, Derek Chauvin, a white police officer with the Minneapolis Police Department, knelt on Floyd's neck for over nine minutes after he was handcuffed and lying face down. Consequently, Floyd died as a result of the physical force exerted upon him by Chauvin. This ugly act reactivated the memory of the sign of Antic-Christ and consequently, prompted an outrage around the globe.

11.11 Signs of Anti-Christ in Human Trafficking

Pope Francis addressed participants in a Vatican conference that examined the implementation of the Pastoral Orientations on Human Trafficking. According to Robin Gomes, Pope Francis on Thursday **condemned trafficking** in human beings as one of the most dramatic manifestations of the "commercialization of the other", a crime against humanity that disfigures both the victims as well as those who carry it out."[200] An economy without human trafficking is an economy with market rules that promote justice, not exclusive special interests. Human trafficking finds fertile ground in the approach of neo-liberal capitalism, in the deregulation of markets aimed at maximizing without ethical limits, without social limits, without environmental limits.

In a video message for the International Day of Prayer and Reflection against Trafficking in Persons, Pope Francis calls for an economy of care, courage, and the promotion of justice aimed at building a society that puts the human person at the centre. By Vatican News staff writer: Pope Francis on Monday, sent a video message on the occasion of the 7th International Day of Prayer and Reflection against Trafficking in Persons. Pope Francis said, "I address all of you who work against human trafficking and who are spiritually united today on this World Day of Prayer, which also has a specific intention: 'An Economy without Human Trafficking',"[201]

Recalling that 8 February is the liturgical memorial of St. Josephine Bakhita-a slave girl who became a saint and a universal symbol of the Church's commitment against Slavery-Pope Francis also extended his message to "all people of goodwill who pray, engage, study and reflect on the fight against human trafficking," especially to those who, like St. Bakhita, "have experienced the tragedy of trafficking in their own lives." *8 February: International Day of Prayer Against Human Trafficking 07/02/2021*. Pope Francis, highlighting the significance of World Day, said that it helps us to "remember this tragedy and encourages us not to stop praying and fighting together" as reflection and awareness should

---

200   https://www.vaticannews.va/en/pope/news/2019-04/pope-francis... retrievedas from 29/08/2021.

201   https://www.Vaticannnews. Va/en/pope/news/2021-02/pope-Francis-human trafficking-world-day-prayer.htm. retrieved as from 29/08/2021.

always be accompanied by concrete gestures that open paths to social emancipation. Furthermore, the Pope stressed, "is for every enslaved person to return to being a free agent of his or her own life and to take an active part in the construction of the common good."

Further, Pope Francis emphasized the need to pray to support victims of trafficking and those who accompany the process of integration and social rehabilitation, adding also, that we need to pray that "we may learn to approach with humanity and courage those who have been marked by so much pain and despair, keeping hope alive. "Prayer enables us to be beacons, capable of discerning and making choices oriented towards good," said the Pope. "Prayer touches the heart and impels us to concrete actions, to innovative courageous actions, able to take risks, trusting in the power of God."

In this regard, the Pope expressed joy in noting that several moments of prayer organized for the occasion this year have an interreligious character, including one held in Asia. The International Committee of the World Day, coordinated by Talitha Kum (the network of consecrated life against trafficking in persons of the International Union of Superiors General, as well as other partners, organized an online Marathon of Prayer from 10 am to 5 pm CET as part of the activities to mark the occasion. They hope, through this 7th International Day of Prayer and Reflection against Trafficking in Persons, to invite all "to multiply and promote new economic experiences that oppose all forms of exploitation."

St. Bakhita

Speaking further on St. Bakhita, Pope Francis explained that her liturgical memorial is a strong reminder of the dimensions of faith and prayer because "her witness always resonates, alive and relevant" and it is a call to "place trafficked persons, their families, their communities at the centre." Saint Bakhita reminds us that they are the protagonists of this day and that we are all at their service," said Pope Francis. Below, Pope Francis prioritizes three essential areas of ethics of economy.

1. An economy of care, 21 November 2020. An economy without human trafficking is an "economy of care." Care, he explained, is "taking care of people and nature, offering products and services for the growth of the common good." An economy of care is also one that "cares for work, creating employment opportunities that do not exploit workers through degrading working conditions and gruelling hours."

At the same time, continued Pope Francis said, that an economy of care means an economy of solidarity, working for a solidity that is combined with solidarity. He added that solidarity, when well administered, gives rise to a more secure and sound social construction. However, the Pope notes that in the wake of the ongoing COVID-19 pandemic, which has exacerbated conditions of labour exploitation, the loss of jobs has adversely affected many victims of trafficking who are in the process of rehabilitation and social reintegration.

"At a time when everything seems to disintegrate and lose consistency, it is good for us to appeal to the 'solidity' both of the consciousness that we are responsible for the fragility of others as we strive to build a common future," he said.

2. An economy that promotes justice: Another characteristic of an economy without human trafficking is one with "market rules that promote justice and not exclusive special interests," Pope Francis said. Trafficking in persons, he explained, "Finds fertile ground in the approach of neo-liberal capitalism and the deregulation of markets aimed at maximizing without ethical limits, without social limits and environmental limits."

If we follow this logic, the Pope warned, "There is only the calculation of advantages and disadvantages": choices will be made not based on ethical criteria but by pandering to dominant interests, often cloaked by a humanitarian or ecological veneer. They will not be made by considering people, as people would be just one of the numbers to be exploited.

3. A courageous economy: Also central to the creation of an economy without human trafficking is courage—not in the sense of recklessness or risking operations in search of risky gains, but rather, "the courage of patient construction," of planning that does not only consider short term gain, but also medium- and long-term fruits, and, above all, people. It is also the courage "to combine legitimate profit with the promotion of employment and decent working conditions."

Pope Francis further emphasized the need for courage to strengthen an economy in a long-lasting, solid way, especially in the face of severe crises, such as the current one, which leads to the proliferation of trafficking in persons. Concluding his message, Pope Francis invited the faithful to pray, invoking the intercession of Saint Bakhita, "for every person who is a victim of trafficking at this moment.

One may as to why should we include the signs of Antic-Christ in the course of the history of the COVID-19 pandemic. We do this to avoid fragmentation of knowledge. In life, it seems whenever we touch one thread, we automatically touch all the threads. It will be unfortunate to focus only on the COVID-19 pandemic as if its impact on human life is irrelevance to the rest of other unfortunate catastrophic disasters that happened before it. However, to have a holistic approach to issues that affect our lives requires an inclusive perspective, rather than a myopic outlook of them.

Consequently, our lives consist of the past, present and future. Therefore, those unfortunate catastrophic disasters which happened in the past, are in some way, relevant to the presence of the unfortunate catastrophic disaster of the COVID-19 pandemic in the 21st century. In faith, we ought to understand them as signs of Antic-Christ whether they happened in the past, present or in the future. Jesus presents us with a holistic view in the Gospel of Mathew as he says, "You will hear of wars and rumours of wars…Nations will fight against nations, and kingdom against kingdom, and there will be famines and earthquakes in various places. All this is only the beginning of the birth pangs" (Mt 24:3-8).

11.12 Death and Resurrection

In dealing with the original sin, physical death is the consequence of a natural process affecting the entire material organism, as it happens to plants and animals. In the past, the theologians believed that man would have lived forever if he had not sinned (gift of immortality). But such a view is now abandoned by everybody; the punishment of God (death) is to be understood not in a physical, but in a religious meaning.

Death is now considered as a consequence of sin in the tragic way as it is experienced by man; as the catastrophic disaster, as the loss of everything and as the last failure. Moreover, it is accompanied by the pain of agony, with feelings of fear and desperation. All these things are rightly considered as the result of God's punishment for the sin committed by the first parents. "You will return to the ground as you were taken from it, for dust you are and to dust you will return" (Gn 3:19)

In our liturgical Creed, we the believers of Christ sing the hymn of the resurrection. When "we say we look for the resurrection of the dead, and the life of the world to come." The doctrine of the resurrection of the dead is fundamental to Christian belief and in the history of salvation realized in Christ's resurrection. This doctrine is demonstrated in the teaching of the Church and fundamentally expressed in the liturgical celebration.

Death is described as a cession of biological and physical activities of the human body represented by (corps). Death in this sense, means an act of giving up all rights that are patterned to basic needs of human life such as eating; drinking; breathing; walking; talking; laughing; coughing; sneezing; sleeping; sitting; and standing; etc. Death is described as a cession of feelings such as sensations, emotional; psychological; physical; social interaction; and sociological etc. How many people have died during the Covid-19 pandemic? The number is so great and the death toll is increasing every day worldwide.

The COVID-19 pandemic has reminded us that our biological and physical lives are fragile and vulnerable, but for those who believe in God, death is the beginning of a new life in Christ. Christ himself has revealed such marvelous mysteries after his resurrection. Even Jesus does not use the word "death" when he conveys the message of the resurrection, he rather uses the word "sleep." Therefore, for our brothers; and sisters; relatives; parents; friends and other people from different statuses in society, if they died in Christ, they will rise with him in the resurrection.

11.13 The Significance of the Problem of Resurrection

The Unbelievers: Christian doctrine of the resurrection is fundamentally linked with the resurrection of Jesus Christ. It ought to be pointed out that for those who do not believe in Jesus Christ, resurrection seems to be stupidity and absurdity. 1. For example, the Jewish set of Sadducees who considered themselves liberal thinkers often ridiculed the Pharisees who believed in the doctrine of the resurrection of the dead. Jesus sometimes intervened to defend the Pharisees and corrected the materialistic interpretation. "When the dead rise to life, they will be like the angels in heaven" (Mt 22:30). 2. Another example was the failure of St. Paul at Athens when he spoke about the resurrection of Christ.

When he stood in the Areopagues the cradle of Greek culture of civilization, he praised them for their religiosity, and the Athenians paid attention to him for a while seriously. As St. Paul preached about the risen Lord from the dead by the power of God, they considered it as non-sense and absurd and consequently, they could no longer take him seriously, they burst into laughter and sent him away (cf. Acts 17:32). 3. This significance of the problem of the doctrine of the resurrection includes other traditional believers who do not yet believe in Jesus Christ and his resurrection thus, this also includes atheists.

5. *The believers*: According to M. Schmaus, "so closely bound

together are Christ's resurrection and that of the Christina, it must be said that if the Christian will not rise from the dead, then Christ is not risen." But then mankind is not saved. Salvation means union with the risen Lord and through him, peace with God and between all men and this is meant not merely in a spiritual sense but in a real and corporal sense."[202] It is unfortunate that in our contemporary society today, some do not believe in God (atheists). During this Covid-19 pandemic that does not distinguish between a believer and non-believer, many of them might have died. However, it will depend on God to judge them based on their moral lives.

11.14 The Sacred Scriptures on Resurrection

1. The Old Testament on the resurrection: The Old Testament presents a Jewish materialistic mentality about the resurrection. The Jews were preoccupied with material advantages and associated this concept of material with fidelity. We heard several times in the sacred Scripture that the Lord promises and assures blessings which consist of material provisions to the people of Israel. For example, "Yahweh will love you and bless you, so that you will increase in number and have many children; he will bless your fields so that you will have corn, wine, and olive oil; and he will bless you by giving you many cattle and sheep. No people in the world will be as richly blessed as you (Dt 7:13-14).

The contact between the Greeks and the Jewish people had allowed the Israelites to believe in immortality as is expressed in the book of Wisdom. "The upright will live forever; their recompense is with the Lord, and the Most-High takes care of them. So they will receive the glorious crown and the diadem of beauty from the Lord's hand" (Wis 5:15-16). According to L. Penzo, the faith in the resurrection developed mainly from the experience that the just are frequently persecuted and

---

202   Michael Schmaus, *Justification and the Last Things*, p.188.

made to suffer here on earth, whilst, on the contrary, the wicked prosper and enjoy life, and seem blessed by God.

The belief that absolute justice is impossible to find among humans, then it is clear that God will be the one to reward innocent and punish wicked ones in this process of preparation. The book of Prophet Daniel put it right by stating "Many of those who have already died will live again; some will enjoy eternal life, and some will suffer eternal disgrace. The wise leaders will shine with all the brightness of the sky" (Dan 12:2-3). The book of Maccabees says "Do not fear this executioner, but prove yourself worthy of your brothers and accept death, so that I may receive you back with them on the day of mercy" (Mac 7:29.)

2. *The gospels: on the resurrection*: The gospel of John states "I know that my brother will rise to live on the last day" (Jn 11:24). Jesus did not only teach about the doctrine of the resurrection but he became an example for the resurrection. He exercised the power of the resurrection in the cases of the daughter of Jairus (cf. Mk 5:21); and the son of the widow of Naim (cf. Lk 7:11-17; his personal friend Lazarus (cf. Jn Ch.11). The prophetic predictions: the Son of man must die and rise on the third day (cf. Mk 8:31); "the sign of Jonah, that is, will be for three days and three nights in the bosom of the earth (cf. Mt 12:40); destroy this temple and I will rebuild it in three days…Now he was speaking of the temple of his body" (Jn 2:19). According to L. Penzo, "This announcement of his resurrection from the dead remained unintelligible for the twelve…and for enemies, who placed guards around his tomb."[203]

The doctrine of the resurrection is linked fundamentally to the belief in Jesus Christ and to the eating and drinking of his body and blood. "I am the resurrection and the life. Whoever believes in me will live, even though he dies and whoever lives and believes in me will never die" (Jn 11:25. "Whoever eats my flesh and drinks my blood has eternal life, and I will raise him to life on the last day" (Jn 6:54).

---

203   Luigi Penzo, *The Last Things,* Notes for the Students, p.16.

3. *Saint Paul on resurrection:* St. Paul's doctrine on the resurrection is very explicit. Paul realized that some faithful who came from Hellenist backgrounds gave a pure spiritual meaning to the resurrection of the dead that is, they understood it as the spiritual renewal and resurrection that takes place in baptism. In support of this belief, they quoted even the words of Paul: "The resurrection of the dead happened" (2 Tim 2:18). In response to this, Paul said "Now if Christ is proclaimed as raised from the dead, how can some of you be saying that there is no resurrection of the dead?" (Cf. 1 Cor 15:12). St. Paul justified the reason why the resurrection is real, not simply symbolic or spiritual is because Christ rose really and not symbolically from the dead, and the faithful are destined to share fully in the divine mysteries of Christ's life. He truly rose from the dead, and we shall truly rise like him; he truly ascended into heaven; one day we shall truly ascend like him. According to Paul, "Christ has been raised from the dead as the first fruit of all who have fallen asleep" (1 Cor 15:21). He reaffirmed "If there is no resurrection of the dead, then Christ cannot be raised either; and if Christ has not been raised, then our preaching is without substance, and so is our faith" (1 Cor 15:13-14).

Paul compared the earthly life with the future one: According to him, "What is sown is perishable, but what is raised is imperishable; what is sown is corruptible, but what is raised is glorious; what is sown is weak, but what is raised is powerful; what is a natural body, and what is raised is a spiritual body" (1 Cor 15:32). Contrary to the materialistic conception of the resurrection, Paul responded "They will be like angels of God" (Mt 22: 20). Being provoked by this doctrine about the resurrection, Paul enthusiastically, said "death, where is your victory? Death, where is your sting? Thanks be to God, for giving us the victory through Jesus Christ our Lord" (1 Cor 15: 35).

St. Paul was able to give a theological explanation about the continuity of existence between our earthly and glorious life by using the comparison of the seed and the tree: "Someone may say: How are dead people raised and what sort of body do they have when they come? How foolish! What you sow must die before is given new life; and what you sow is not the body is to be, but only a bare grain of wheat or some other kind…" (1 Cor 15:35). To answer the question raised to those who do not share the salvation brought by Christ, although Paul was not interested to answer that question nevertheless, he said "As all die in Adam, so in Christ all will be brought to life" (1 Cor 15:22).

This answer of Paul agreed with the doctrine of Jesus about the resurrection when he said "The hour is coming when the dead will leave their graves at the sound of his voice: those who did good will come forth to life, and those who did evil come forth to judgment" (Jn 5:28). This proclamation of the resurrection of the dead including our brothers and sisters who died during Covid-19 pandemic. Jesus is the final judge of the living and the dead. He will judge with love and mercy. He will judge us not according to our merits but on his merit.

11.15 The Church's Magisterium on Liturgy and Resurrection

The Creed of the Apostles says "I believe…the resurrection of the body and the life every lasting." The Nicaeno-Constaninopolitan Creed: "We look for the resurrection of the dead, and the life of the world to come." According to L Penzo, the faith of the Church is confirmed by the Acts of the Martyrs, by the veneration which the Church has always surrounded the bodies of the dead people. The Christian cemeteries are all the beautiful monuments that are built inside them and are a vivid witness to this faith of the resurrection. The liturgy of the dead has been celebrated by the Church in the old centuries up to this present Christian generation. The various prayers and the musical compositions that are used for the celebrations are wonderfully blended with artistic worship and faith.

The preface of the Roman Canon: "In him, who rose from the dead, our hope for resurrection dawned. The sadness of death gives way to the bright promise of immortality. Lord, for your faithful people life is changed, not ended. When the body of our earthly dwelling lies in death we gain an everlasting dwelling place in heaven."[204] During the COVID-19 pandemic, we mourned our dear ones, we prayed for them, and we celebrated masses for the purification of their souls in purgatory. For example, some religious and laity offered mass intention to priests to pray for their dear ones The Church in heaven prayed for them and the militate Church prayed for them too. All these spiritual activities testify to our belief in the resurrection of the dead through the resurrection of Christ.

11.16 Theological Problems about the Resurrection

1. The resurrection as a radical transformation of the human person: According to M. Schmaus, the affirmation of the awakening of the resurrection implies the reanimation of the one who was dead. But the word reanimation (or resuscitation) does not convey the full meaning, for between death and resurrection man lives, in an intermediate state. Thus the resurrection can only signify a transformation from one mode of existence into another. M. Schmaus states "How this takes place is a mystery."[205] Since it is outside the sphere of our experience. However, our experience has made us familiar with how our human body from a chemistry and biological point of view gradually diminishes. For example, the constant change in the human body is so pervasive that the physical components of an old man's body do not contain the slightest trace of the physical material that constituted that same person's body at age five.

The theologians affirm that the resurrection is like a "transformation", similar to the one that takes place in the seed that has to die

---

204 Cf. Luigi Penzo, *The Last Things*, Notes for the Students, p.18.
205 Michael Schmaus, *Justification and the Last Things*, p.192.

under the earth and undergo radical change to become a plant (Cf. 1 Cor 15:35). They further assert that this transformation is an exclusive work of God and not the result of a human capacity; it is "God's power" (Mt 22:20); it is a fruit of Christ's victory: Thank God then, for giving us the victory through Jesus Christ" (1Cor 15:57). Lastly, this transformation affects the whole person; the body that passes from mortality to immortality, and the soul that enters into a new way of existence as a result of its unity with an immortal body.

2. The qualities of the transformed human person: against the argument of the Sadducees in favour of no resurrection and the materialistic concept of the Pharisees about the doctrine of the resurrection, the Lord Jesus asserts that men "will not marry because they will be like the angels of God" (Mt 22:20). St. Paul on his part states that the transformed bodies will be endowed with "immortality, incorruptibility and glory (1 Cor 15:24). As a consequence, God will wipe away all tears from their eyes; there will be no more death, and no more mourning or sadness or pain: the world of the past has gone" (Rev. 21:5).

3. The identity between the earthly and the risen body: Christ assured his disciples about his own body "See my hands and my feet, that it is I" (Lk 24:39). Based on this assertion, the Church's Magisterium always teaches that men will rise from the dead with their own body: in him all men will rise again with their bodies which they now bear; but Christ will change our lowly body to his glorious body. The Church emphasizes the existence between the glorified body and the sacrament of the Eucharist which is called "the seed of immortality."

In answering the problem of the identity between the earthly and its risen body, the theologians follow two different opinions. 1. Some affirm that the body identity requires in the risen body the presence of some material element that belonged to the previous earthly body. 2. The majority believe that this presence is not needed and the identity is given by the soul as it is "the form of the body." As a matter of fact, during our earthly life the material elements of our body change completely every seven years, and our identity is not at all destroyed; we remain the same person.

The soul is the vital principle which informs the matter transforming it into a human person. Thus, the identity of the risen body with the earthly person is assured if the selfsame soul is represented in a body whose matter it animates (cf. M. Schmaus p. 195). Our brothers and sisters in Christ, who died during the Covid-19 pandemic, will experience bodily glorification like Christ. Christ will glorify them and accept them in his kingdom based on his love for the all salvation of humanity.

11.17 The Judgment of the World

At his eschatological coming, Christ will 'judge the word' both at the universal and final judgment which will conclude the human history. 1. *Importance of the final judgment:* at present, we are aware that the whole world is historically moving towards its final and limitless future. However, it is not clear and we do not know what role persons or groups are playing in the drama of human history, and how they are carrying it out. Moreover, we are also aware many things have gone in the wrong direction which we consider "negative" (sin) in the course of human life may appear 'positive and beneficial" in the end; whereas many that seem favourable will be seen as hindering our progress. Nevertheless, only Christ's judgment will explain and pass an objective judgment on persons and events.

2. *Purpose of judgment:* the judgment that Christ will execute, will have twofold purposes at his second coming. 2.1. first, to reveal, in front of the whole, the good actions of the just people, and the bad actions of the evil ones; the judgment will be "universal" not only regarding the persons but also regarding their deeds in the course of their lives concerning gospel's virtues and values. 2. To degree the corresponding eternal destiny of each person; either reward or punishment. For those who have sought God, it will be a fulfilment, for those who have hated him, it will be a condemnation.

3. Expectation of the judgment: for the early Christian the expectation of the second coming of the Lord and waiting for it "with great hope." According to them, the judgment was mainly the joyful encounter with the Lord, the saviour and the friend, and the beginning of eternal salvation in the happiness of his companion. For example, in the Middle Ages, however, the idea of Christ as the coming judge, who would examine man's life in every detail started to exert a much stronger influence; the joy and confidence of the early Christians were replaced by anxiety, fear and trembling before the day of the Lord.

4. The message of the Scripture: The Apostles' Creed is sung and recited by the Church; "He will come again to judge the living and the dead. The Church proclaims her faith in the final judgment, especially in the liturgical celebrations. This faith finds its root in the message of the sacred Scripture.

4.1. The Old Testament: The Sacred Scripture states God's judgment at the beginning of mankind. For example, our first parents, Adam and Eve were expelled by God as a consequence of their sins. The prophets proclaim this imminent judgment in public disasters such as wars, the end of the empires, earthquakes etc., and implying symbols of the final judgment. Sometimes, they describe those symbols as the day of the Lord in which "God will gather the wheat into his barn; he will burn the chaff in a fire that never goes out" (Mt 3:12).

4.2 The New Testament: the idea of the Old Testament reached a climax in Christ: "He is set for the fall and the resurrection of many (L2:24). According to L. Penzo, whoever opens himself to Christ, and through him turns to the Father is freed from his sin and exempted from condemnation: Whoever rejects Christ and persists in his stubbornness and his refusal, is already judged. Jesus Christ asserts that he will be the future judge of mankind. "The Father has given the Son the right to judge because he is the Son of man. Do not be surprised that this time is coming when all the dead will hear his voice and come out of their graves; those who have done good will rise and live, and those who have done evil will rise and be condemned" (Jn 5:28). However, sometimes, the sacred Scripture presents the God as the supreme Judge "God will reward every person according to what he has done" (Rom 2:6). The apparent contradiction is resolved by the fact God accomplished his work through Christ, and that Christ does nothing but the will of the Father.

According to M. Schmaus, it is God, therefore, who speaks the last word on man's actions and destiny, but he speaks through Christ. In that hour, then, it is Christ who speaks, and this divine word is decisive. Before it all must be silent. "During their earthly lives men can utter many empty and hostile words against him and he remains silent, but in that hour of judgment he alone will speak and the whole creation must listen."[206] The time of final judgment will surely come though it only remains unknown to men but known to God. "There is no difference in the Lord's sight between one day and a thousand years; to him, the two are the same. The Lord is not slow to do what he has promised, as some think. Instead, he is patient with you, because he does not want anyone to be destroyed, but wants all to turn away from their sins" (2 Pt. 3:9). The criteria of the final judgment will be love and mercy upon human beings including our brothers and sisters who died during Covid-19 pandemic.

11.17.1 The Nature of the Final Judgment

1. *The judge:* without doubt, the Lord will be the judge. This will take place at the second coming of him when he will reveal himself as the Son of God, the risen and the King of all creation. In that specific supreme hour all men, both friends and enemies, will at last recognize that he is the climax of human history, that he is the alpha and omega, the beginning and the end, and that all beings have been created by

---

206   Michael Schmaus, *Justification and the Last Things*, p.202.

him and for him and that he holds all things together. The separation of the wicked from the goodwill eliminate forever the evil from the world, and that will be the starting of a new community ruled by love.

2. *The truth of the judgment:* according to theologians, the judgment consists of a flash of illumination wherein everyone can see in an instant the whole course of human history and the part that every individual has played in it in the course of his life. At the same time, he is enabled to judge in truth what he sees, that is according to the light which he receives from God. The enlightenment arising from God's truth is so powerful that no one can resist it.

Nothing remains obscure; everything comes into a clear knowledge, through the divine light. St. Paul asserts "I am not all concerned about being judged by you, or by any human standards; I don't even pass judgment on myself. My conscience is clear, but that does not prove that I am innocent. The Lord is the one who passes judgment on me" (1 Cor 4:4). The book of Revelation says "All people living on earth will worship the beast, except those whose names were written before the creation of the world in the book of the living, which belongs to the lamb that was killed. (Rev. 13:8).

3. *The norm of the judgment:* according to which men will be judged, is love, that love which has appeared in the life of Jesus Christ. Thus, the law by which a man will be judged as a living person by Jesus Christ is his life, his Gospel, his love for men and his commitment to the salvation of the world. Each will be judged according to his likeness or conformity to Jesus Christ. According to M. Schmaus, "This means that the life of every man and the significance of every action and every institution is appraised according to the service it has rendered to fellow human beings" (M. Schmaus 202). According to the Gospel of St. Mathew, "I tell you, whenever you did this for one of the least important of these brothers of mine, you did it for me" (Mt 25:40).

4. *The subject of the judgment:* the general judgment will consider to the public all that has been thought, done, and undertaken in the course

of history from the beginning to its end, manifesting everything as good or evil and showing its significance for world history. It is stated that the countless particular judgments that have taken place before will only be confirmed; with the difference that in that particular judgment, the stress was on the responsibility of the individual, whereas in the general judgment, the emphasis will be on the influence that the individual life had within history and society.

"The judgment of the world will make public the struggle, defects, and victories, the rebellion and submission of the individual in world history. Everyone will be able to see, concerning himself and everyone else, that the state that Christ assigned to him was the right one. The divine justice will be manifested before the whole world in its infinite perfection. Hence, man's wounded senses of justice, never perfectly satisfied during the course of history, can look forward with hope to the coming judgment" (M. Schmaus p. 203).

An important element of the judgment will be also the revealing of our inner intentions; namely, whether our activity was the fruit of an altruistic motivation or the fruit of a hidden self-interest. Since, too, repented in the past will be made public, however, they will no longer be the occasion for shame and confusion, but will only administer to the glory of God since they will serve to reveal that he can bring good out of man's rejections. "There is nothing that can be hidden from God; everything in all creation is exposed and lies open before his eyes. And it is to him that we must all give an account of ourselves" [207] Lasting things concerning the future of individuals such as death; immortality; particular judgment; purgatory; hell and heaven will not be discussed in this theological reflection.

---

207   Luigi Penzo, *The Last Things, Notes for the students of St. Pauls' Major Seminary*, p. 24.

Conclusion

Chapter Eleven has discussed thoroughly the reason and purpose of theological reflections on the COVID-19 pandemic; the fragility of human perfection; the principle of preferential option for the vulnerable; and eschatology. It has also presented doctrine of the last things concerning the future of God's people such as the Pilgrim Church (people of God); the second coming of Christ (Parousia); the faith in the second coming of Christ; the time of the second coming of Christ; the concept of anti-Christ (Serpent); the Sacred Scripture on the signs of anti-Christ and the Signs of anti-Christ in the course of our lives.

The chapter has treated and has dealt with death and resurrection; the significance of the problem; the Sacred Scriptures on resurrection; the Church's Magisterium & and liturgy on resurrection; theological problems about the resurrection; the judgment of the world, and, the nature of the final judgment. Finally, the chapter has recommended to every human person to take care of himself in terms of health.

Chapter Twelve:
Recommendation

Introduction

Chapter twelev recommends ethics of power and implementing key emerging points by the South Sudan government. It will also discuss the importance of dialogue as a task which requires favourable conditions. Such favourable conditions also demand listening for the parties to learn and arrive at real and fruitful dialogue. Dialogue requires readiness to unlearn and it also demands openness, and mutual respect which involves respect for different opinions. In dealing with an issue at hand, dialogue demands two measures that is, to judge our opponents and also to judge ourselves severely. Fruitful dialogue is for action while putting in mind the difficulties of its implementation. The chapter also presents special moral concerns both for South Sudanese politicians and the citizens of South Sudan. It will recommend presuppositions of ethics to be practiced by all.

12. Ethics of Power

Any exercise of power requires the execution of the ethics of power. Therefore, these recommendations ought to be considered by those who exercise power over others. 1. The capacity to produce intended effects upon the outer world, be it human or non-human is an essential part of human nature. 2. Power should not be a means to something else. 3. The end (or purpose) if achieved, should help to satisfy the desires of the others too. 4. The success should not be for oneself but satisfaction for others too. 5. The means must be proportionate to the achieved end. It is asserted that the bad effects of the means you use must not outweigh the good end to be achieved.[208] Because of the presence of criminals and other anti-social ambitions in society using force is ethically inevitable and necessary. Where force is unavoidable, therefore, it should be exerted by the constituted authority with the will of the community as stipulated in the criminal law. The environment and circumstances of each person will contribute a lot to the young ones in society. The opportunity and skill contribute a lot to the community.

12.1 Dialogue and Negotiation as Culture of Life

It ought to be pointed out that returning evil for evil brings more burden to life. Whether it at personal and interpersonal, in the family, in the society, in the political system, and the religious matters produces, more evil. For example, Old Testament precepts which say 'an eye for an eye and a tooth for a tooth' became heavy in their applications. However, the Jewish people emphasize that any part of the human body cannot be substituted with material things. However, such precepts were recommended as a warning for any further damage to be done to the human person more than the part that has been damaged.

---

208 Augustine Mugarura, *Impulse to Power According to Russell*, p.85.

In our continent, an attempt to teach a tough lesson to an opponent or opposition in areas of political wrangling over power sometimes fails. This approach is not genuine, it requires a substitute for the exploration of other positive options. Therefore, many attempts were made to solve political problems through dialogue and negotiation. This seems to be the best way to solve political crises and civil wars in each country. Humans are endowed with intellectual capacity and understanding. Therefore, when there arises a political crisis and civil war in the country, the best way for politicians and political leaders to resolve problems ought to be through dialogue and negotiation which must require compromise and honesty from the disputed parties. African political leaders when faced with political crises ought to avoid this proverb which says "Favours, shoot first and asks questions later, and lack of coolness can easily lead people to judge first and ask about the facts afterwards."[209]

Often, our conceptual analysis of the terms we use to resolve the problem is superficial. Therefore, all the terms we use ought to be known thoroughly without ambiguity. Merriam Webster's Collegiate Dictionary has offered descriptions of the meaning of the word 'dialogue.' 1. Etymologically, the root meaning of the word dialogue means to converse. 2. A written composition in which two or more characters represented are conversing. 3. A conversion between two or more persons; also a similar exchange between a person and something else. 4. "An exchange of ideas and opinions… a discussion between representatives of parties to a conflict that is aimed at resolution…"[210] 5. The conversational element of literary or dramatic compositions. 6. A musical composition for two or more parts suggestive of a conversation.

Merriam-Webster's Collegiate Dictionary defines the term

---

209   Cf. J. Tab Charoa, *Beyond the Fourth Classical Cardinal Virtues: The Basic Principles of Social Justice & their Relevance to our contemporary society,* Kampala: James Holy Blest Co, 2018, p.75

210   Merriam Webster's Collegiate Dictionary Eleventh Edition, p.344

negotiation as "the action or process of negotiating or being negotiated…often used in the plural."²¹¹ It is also described as the verb to negotiate from it Latin root *negotiates,* which means to carry on business, and *negotium* means business. To confer with another to arrive at the settlement of some matter. This dictionary offers a lot of descriptions of negotiation such as 1. To deal with (some matter or affair that requires ability for its successful handling. 2. To arrange for or bring about through conference, discussion, and compromise a treaty). 3. To transfer (as a bill of exchange) to another by delivery or endorsement. 4. "To convert into cash or the equivalent value-check. 5. To successfully travel along or over."²¹²

With such richness of these two terms, one cannot wonder why we always resort to them for solving political crises in our continent and elsewhere in the world. We should highly value both dialogue and negotiation as cultures of life. This is precisely because they both contribute to the promotion of life rather than the destruction of it. For instance, the long brutal civil war between Sudan and South Sudan was finally settled through dialogue and negotiation which ended with the signing of the Comprehensive Peace Agreement in 2005, and the bold decision taken recently by the Prime Minister of Ethiopia Abiy Ahmed to resolve the disputed area between Eritrea and Ethiopia in 2018. This incident demonstrates the dialogue and the negotiation speak stronger than ballet and with no destruction of human life.

12.2 South Sudan Four Days Reports on National Dialogue

When the National Dialogue Steering Committee commenced the debate on what are the root causes of the problems that the country, they discovered these factors: 1. power struggle among politicians. 2.

---

211   Merriam Webster's Collegiate Dictionary Eleventh Edition, p.830
212   Ibid

Objectives of the South Sudan National Dialogue. 3. Stakeholders. 4. Diversity, misunderstanding of ethnicity, tribes. 5. governance system, issues/demarcation of areas such as Abei, Kefiy Kenji and Hulfra Al Nihas and reconciliation among communities- Wunlit, South Sudan dialogue. These above-mentioned issues are considered by the National Dialogue steering committee as the objectives of National Dialogue. According to the South Sudan Catholic bishop's conference, "Dialogue must be at the service of the common good of all."[213]

12.2.1 Summary of the Proceedings Issues in the Debate

Monday, 29th, May 2017, time: 9:30-13:30, venue: Juba-Freedom Hall. The National Dialogue Steering Committee has identified key issues repeated in the debate in such a manner they have listed as the basis for conflict identification. Therefore, the National Dialogue Steering Committee has presented a summary of the proceeding of the first day of highly emerging key points such as 1. The need to respect the rule of law. 2. "Institutional reforms/transformation (Civil services, security sector, judiciary)"[214] 3. Land reforms. 4. Addressing corruption. 5. Inclusive governance. 6. Election preparedness. 7. Demobilization and disarmament. 8. The need to define the system of governance to be adopted (Constitutions). 9 National healing and reconciliation. 10. The need to build a national identity.

12.2.2 The Second Day Key Emerging Points

Tuesday, 30th May 2017, time: 9:30-13, venue: Juba-Freedom Hall. 1. Divisions within the SPLAM starting from 2nd convention. 2.

---

213   Sudan Catholic Bishops' Conference, *letters to the Church of Sudan of Sudan*, Khartoum: Secretariat, 1982-200, p. 120.

214   South Sudan National Dialogue Steering Committee, Document No. 2, Activities Report, p. 16-17.

Constitution: first, there is a need to draft the permanent constitution delayed for over ten years. 3. Good governance: accountability and transparency, delivery of services, reviving the policies on agriculture, vocational school etc. 4. Security sector reform: discipline in the army, pension of army. 5. Revisit the national force set during the liberation period before independence. 6. Relations between a particular tribe or ethnic group and the state. 7. Rule of law and abuse of the justice system. 8. Representation of persons with disabilities. 9. Communal problems, farmers and cattle keepers. 10. Inclusion of Dr Riek Machar and other armed groups, the displaced persons, and the refugees. 11. Relations between SPLM and SPLA as the Army. 12. Need to change the name of the Army from SPLA.

12.2.3 The Third Day Key Emerging Points

Wednesday, 31st May 2017, time: 9:30-13-30, venue: Juba-Freedom Hall. The Deputy Co-chair, Hon Gabriel Youk Dok was called to order the meeting with the Deputy Rapporteur, Amb. Dr. Francis Mading Deng clarified the discussions the National Dialogue Steering Committee is holding when some members still felt confused regarding the ongoing debate. M. Deng "…then went to summarize the emerging points in previous discussions of the day two."[215] 1. Create a conducive environment for dialogue: through a follow-up on the decree of the President on the release of the political detainees by visiting: the 1:1 National Scrutiny detention facility. 1:2. Military intelligence prison in Bilpam; 1:3. National prison. To this, the report of the national dialogue steering committees confirms that "to ascertain from the lists in these institutions the number of those released."[216]

---

215   South Sudan National Dialogue Steering Committee, Document No. 2, Activities Report, p. 18-19.

216   Sudan Catholics Bishops' Conference, letters to the Church of the Sudan, p. 120.

2. The budget from the national dialogue should be made public for the citizens to know. 3. Rule of law: Execution of sentences from the judiciary to avoid chaos and confusion. 4. Too many army Generals without qualifications as such result in a leadership struggle. 5. Role of parliament as an oversight body. 6. Separation of powers between the National government and the State government. 7. Land grabbing. 8. Protection of women and children. 9. Acknowledgement and reward to women for their role in the struggle for independence. 10. Army killing unarmed civilians (women and children). 11. Federalism. 12. Consultations to involve Riek, Lam, Olony, Thomas Cirilo, Bakasoro, Wau group and others. 13. Comprehensive security strategy: there is confusion in the role of policy, National security and Army. 14. The Council of Elders is formed of the educated elite, influential politicians with little connections to the grassroots. 15. Internal division within the SPLA. 16. Need for reconciliation and forgiveness.

12.2.4 Fourth Day Key Emerging Points

Thursday, 1ˢᵗ, June 2017, time: 9: 30-13-30, Juba-Freedom Hall. According to the Sudan Catholic Bishops' Conference, "Dialogue aims at removing suspicion, division, prejudices and confrontation."[217] Therefore, the following key emerging points are in line with what was said by the Sudan Catholic Bishops' Conference. 1. Inter-ethnic conflict 1:1. Dialogue between the Nuer and Dinka to be supported by other ethnic groups. 1:2. The need to build confidence and inter-ethnic relations. 2. Food insecurity. 2:1. Tractors are without plough. 3. National Army. 3:1 Lack of proper training of the SPLA after the CPA 2005. 3:2. The Army is staying in the civil residential area instead of barracks. 4. Corruption. 5. Women (rape, defiled, displaced, killing and early

---

217   South Sudan National Dialogue Steering Committee, Document No. 2, Activities Report, p.19.

marriages). 6. Priority of education and health. 7. Execution of the rule of law. 8. Cattle rustling. 9. No implementation of the peace agreement (ARCSS). 10. Appointment of unqualified personnel to high positions in the government. 11.

The question of independent management of the funds of the National Dialogue steering committee. 12. The need to include the armed groups. 13. The question of Constitutional Review. 14. Building a national identity. 15. The problem of economic crisis. 15:1. Devaluation of the South Sudanese Pound. 15:2. Alternative sources of revenue. 15:3. Development of the private sector. 15:4. Foreigners running the business in the country. 16. Identification of the stakeholders according to the concepts Note. 16:1. Criteria of selection of the members. 16:2. Development of a questionnaire. 17. "Setting up committees"[218] 18. Ideological paralysis after 2005 (within the ruling party). 19. The system of governance after 2005. 20. The problem of power struggle. 21. The land issues. 21:1 taking of ancestral lands. 21:2. Land grabbing. 21:3. Fighting over land. According to the Sudan Catholic Bishops' Conference, "In dialogue, it is not enough to search for objectivity, for it is unattended subjective and felt the pain that generates quarrels and discontent."[219]

12.3 Identification of Stakeholders and Criteria for Selection

The National Dialogue Steering Committee has reported that "At the end of the debate, it was agreed that dialogue process will always involve everyone to have sustainable future to a nascent country emerging out of the long history of the liberation struggle."[220] The National Dialogue

---

218   Sudan Catholic Bishops' Conference, Letters to the Church of Sudan, p. 119.

219   Sudan Catholic Bishops' Conference, Letter to the Church of Sudan, p.119.

220   South Sudan National Dialogue Steering Committee, Document No. 2, Activities Report, p. 20.

Steering Committee argues that the identified stakeholders listed below with others later to be found by specific sub-committees based on their presence on the ground with the people. It is asserted there are unique issues that have to be tracked by stakeholders while affirming that the sub-committees too, prioritize with their stakeholders during the consultations. The above-mentioned committee concludes that "this is what inclusively and transparency mean in the process of National Dialogue."[221]

12.3.1 Stakeholders in the Country

The National Dialogue Steering Committee has listed these categories of groups as stakeholders in the country. 1. The National Executive. 2. National Assembly, the council of the states and State Legislative Assemblies. 3. State and Local government. 4. The Judiciary. 5. People with special needs. 6. Profession associations. 7. Business communities. 8. Political parties. 9. The faith-based institutions. 10. Traditional leadership. 11. Women. 12. Youth. 13. Civil society leaders, 14. Military and security services. 15. IDPs. 16. Armed groups including Aguelek.

Opposition leaders and armed groups outside the country: 1. SPLA-OI (Dr Riek Machar's loyalists). 2. Fds. 3. NDM (Dr. Lam Akol). 4. National Salvation Front (Gen. Thomas Cirilo). 5. Federal Democratic Party (Changson Chang) (6) People's Democratic Movement PDM (Dr. Dario Hkim Moi). 7. Bakasoro Group. 8. All the other armed groups whose leadership are not identified. 9. Refugees. The Sudan Catholic Bishops' Conference acknowledges that dialogue must be persevering because it is a difficult exercise. It asserts that "one reason is that it is an exercise in which all parties should emerge as winners."[222]

---

221 Ibid.

222 Sudan Catholic Bishops' Conference, Letters to the Church of Sudan, P. 120.

These "key emerging points" were the products of Four Day meetings as follows that is, first day, date: Monday, 29th May 2017, time: 9:30-13:30 venue: Freedom Hall; second day date: Tuesday, 30th May 2017, time: 9: 30-13:30, venue: Freedom Hall; third-day date: Wednesday,30th May 2017, time: 9:30-13:13:30, venue: freedom hall; and the Fourth-day date: Thursday, 1 June 2017, time: 9:30-13:30, venue: freedom hall.

12.4 The Benefits of Dialogue and Negotiation

For South Sudanese Politicians and all the Citizens If one has eyes to see, if one has ears to hear, if one has faith to believe, if one has a heart to listen, if one has a mind and intellect to perceive, he/she would not doubt that the reports of the National Dialogue Steering Committee on Four Days' Meetings identified various " Key Emerging Points" ought to be for bettering this young nation with indispensable implementations. I do consider these key emerging points raised by South Sudanese people through the National Dialogue Steering Committee as mirrors for our young nation and as signposts for a new journey of the culture of life.

The South Sudanese citizens and especially the politician's stakeholders to make sure what has been said by us, ought to be implemented to the letter. We must consider those key emerging points, as prime factors for the culture of life in our young nation. These key emerging points require serious observation and wisdom for their implementation such that our words can match our actions. The faithful implementations will speak stronger than losing innocent lives. Therefore, let the results of the National Dialogue summarized in those key emerging points and the results of the high level of political negotiation never contradict us but complement each other for bettering this young nation.

12.5 The Sudan Catholic Bishops' Conference on Dialogue

The above-mentioned conference argues that the basic legitimate reason for dialogue as the culture of life depends on the fact that we all aspire for peace and peaceful resolutions to our conflicts. It is believed that with such reasonable conviction, we can recognize our capacity and the need to eradicate not only war but also everything that leads to war. We ought to be affirmed that we all have a desire for an atmosphere of peace which is sustainable and will guarantee our search for well-being particularly when faced with consequences of war such as displacement of many people, refugees, hunger, economic crisis, dehumanization, looting of properties of others, rape, indiscriminate killing, and unknown-gunmen, we feel that such evil acts threaten the life of everyone in our nations. It confirms that in such a situation, to create a conducive atmosphere for peace as the culture of life, we are inspired and must take the right means for dialogue so peace and well-being become our reality. It ought to be pointed out that "The most effective means is to adopt an attitude of dialogue that is, patient introduction of mechanisms and phase of dialogue wherever peace is threatened or already compromised, in families, in society ... between tribes, religious and ethnic groups."[223] It means that each of us should seize the many opportunities at his/her disposal to break down the barriers of selfishness, aggression and lack of understanding, by carrying on dialogue, every day in the family, the village, and the neighbourhood. Therefore, world political leaders are recommended to embrace all the dimensions of dialogue above, mentioned above to avoid any evil act which can threaten human life. Martin Luther King Jr concurs with this idea in his assertion that "The result of nonviolence is redemption

---

223   Sudan Catholic Bishops' Conference, *Letters to the Church of Sudan*, Khartoum, SCBC Secretariat, 1982-2002, p. 108-109.

and reconciliation.[224]

It was to be recommended that if dialogue is a task for all, then no one must be excluded because such exclusion exists even if it is not declared, when freedom of speech and expression is curtailed or denied; when legitimate complaints are systematically ridiculed or ignored; when no room is allowed for differences and dissensions; when the climate of suspicion, fear and hostility pervades society if normal relationships and communication between people become impossible; and when people feel they are not accepted or respected. Such situations in human community or human society can be symptoms of a culture of death. Dialogue as the culture of life, is everyone because it deals with the common good and peace. Common good and peace can never be constructed by some without others.

12.5.1 Favourable and Unfavourable Conditions for Dialogue

Dialogue should take place between two or more persons, groups or parties. We resort to dialogue when people feel the need to re-establish greater unity, mutual understanding, peace and cooperation between them, or wish to defuse tension and conflict. Some state that the parties in conflict should be open and establish suitable channels of communication, discussion, and exchange of ideas because of identifying areas of conflicts and disagreement and their underlying causes. Both parties ought to search for factors of common concern for all the parties and the common action to take to reduce tension and restore good understanding. However, dialogue is not restricted to talk and discussions, party dialogue partners achieve the same end by adopting attitudes and ways of behaviour that express mutual respect and acceptance to them, and cooperation and collaboration in common endeavours. Dr. King

---

224   Fundamental tenets of Dr. King's philosophy of nonviolence describes in his first book, *Stride toward Freedom*, www.thethingcenter.org/king-philiosohy, retrieved as from 22/08/2018.

Jr, as discussed in chapter five on principles of culture of life states that "It is essential to inform others, including your opponents about your issue."[225] Some argue that this minimizes misunderstandings and gains you sympathy support.

12.5.2 Fruitful Dialogue

Real and fruitful dialogue requires that the parties concerned ought to mutually listen to one another. The prerequisite and the purpose for listening are for the parties to come to know and understand one another's point of view. The technique in listening is not only to listen to words but to the person who speaking. It ought to be pointed out that the person who speaks, brings through the dialogue many factors such as background, their problems, their experiences, their feelings, and their history of pain they have gone through. True listening demands that the parties put themselves into each other's shoes and try to understand not only what is said, but also why it is said, and why it is said that way."[226]

It is required that dialogue partners should listen to learn, and even invite their opponents to tell them frankly what annoys them and what created their differences. It is believed that true dialogue can therefore take place only if all the parties are sincerely and honestly eager to learn together and to search earnestly for truth and unity. It is asserted that dialogue will fail if any of the parties' claims to know the whole truth and so dictates to the others. This was affirmed by Mahatma Gandhi when he said "We each have a piece of the truth and the un-truth."[227]

---

225 Based on Martin Luther King jr's "Letter from Birmingham Jail" in *Why We can't wait*, Penguin books, 1963, www.thekingcenter.org/king-philosophy, retrieved as from 22/08/2018.

226 Sudan Catholic Bishops' Conference, *Letter to the Church of the Sudan*, p. 109.

227 Gandhi's nonviolence principle, www.cpt.org/files/Pw-Principles-Gandhi, retrieved as from 22/08/2018.

In this viewpoint in dialogue, all the participants are partners. It ought to be pointed out that both parties meet on Level Ground, not from above-similarly, dialogue will fail if the participants begin with the pre-established decision to concede nothing and to dictate or impose their opinions. Such attitudes can be a culture of death not a culture of life and every person who would like to engage should shun them. It must be clarified that "Such a situation prevails also where participations refuse by a claim to be-themselves and only the measure of truth, justice and right."[228]

12.5.3 Readiness to Unlearn and Demands for Openness

Through dialogue, in search of common truth and for peace, it ought to be emphasized that each of us realizes that we have been relating to one another based on many wrong and unfounded generalizations and assumptions. Through dialogue, we often come to discover the honesty, the kindness, the wisdom hidden in the others. This dimension of discovering the truth from others, helps us to discover our limitations, hidden motivations, and the inadequacy of our procedures in tackling several issues. "In this way dialogue helps us to unlearn, to wash away the old, to replace it with new that has come out because we exchanged ideas with the others."[229] This is what Christians call "conversion" which sometimes involves a complete "turn about" in our opinions, ideas, programs, and vision of reality and conversion is the divine culture of life.

Willingness and readiness to consider and recognize the real problems as expressed by the other partners, requires consideration of the differences that exist, and the specific nature of the other party's viewpoint. This entails the uniqueness of the other party, who thinks and

---

228   Sudan Catholic Bishops' Conference, *Letter to the Church of the Sudan*, p. 110.
229   Ibid.

acts differently from us. We ought to believe that openness which is the culture of life, makes us eager to discover more, to understand the position of the other party; and to look better at the causes, environment, motives, and mentalities at play under discussion. Some say "To be completely open, we must be aware of prejudice, prejudgment, and suspicions we bring into dialogue, and at the same time, to allow them to be challenged by what we received from the other party."[230] In this way, we ought to know that everyone should realize that our vision of reality, any reality, is always partial. Dialogue can become the culture of life only if we put together the pieces supplied by the parties to obtain a complete vision. According to Mahatma Gandhi, "We reaffirm our unity with others when they transform "us" versus transform" thinking and doing."[231]

12.5.4 Mutual Respect of Differences in Dialogue

In dialogue, respect for each other views requires unconditional respect for the other such as his opinions and his behaviour. It is believed that it is only through unconditional respect for others that we can discover and understand our diversity, and appreciate their point of view, respect their legitimate hopes, aspiration, even if they seem "strange" to us. Such respect for others should include respect for rights and communities to which they belong. The purpose and main goal of dialogue as the culture of life is to seek the common good. Some state that "One of the aims of dialogue is the search for the common good of all and the inalienable rights of every human being."[232] Consequently, such unconditional respect will be deemed absent if we start our dialogue with prejudice, suspicions, and an air of superiority.

---

230   Sudan Catholic Bishops' Conference, *Letter to the Church of the Sudan*, p. 110.

231   Gandhi's nonviolence principle, www.cpt.org/files/PW-Principle-Gandhi, retrieved as from 22/08/2018.

232   Sudan Catholic Bishops' Conference, *Letter to the Church of the Sudan*, p. 110.

The characteristic of suspicion is that it makes us doubtful about the goodwill of others. For example, prejudice, particularly if their negatives compel us to judge them as bad and consequently, make us judge whatever they do as bad. With prejudice, we conclude that others are incapable of offering anything good. Mahatma Gandhi challenges us by stating "We are called to celebrate both our differences and our fundamental unity with others.[233]" It ought to be concluded that their reflections indicate that only a genuine respect for the other can enable us to give him or her free a and impartial hearing. For world political leaders, taking dialogue as the culture of life, ought to allow them to verify all various forms of prejudices related to political issues and respect for another party.

As we have mentioned earlier dialogue requires respect for our differences, because it is differences which cause friction and misunderstanding. Those frictions and misunderstandings caused by our differences ought to be carefully handled and treated respectfully, otherwise, they cannot be smoothed out or rendered least harmful to the common good of all. Some say that dialogue as the culture of life, should bring humans into contact with one another as members of the human family with all the richness of their various cultures and histories. It ought to be pointed out that diversity is to be a source of blessing, and peace rather than a source of discord, hatred, and enmity.

12.5.5 Severe Judgment upon Ourselves and Our Opponents

The good measure of the virtue of dialogue will not frankly and humbly acknowledge past and present failings and errors for those in power, partial abuse of authority, but also will generally urge a more charitable judgment of the stranger or opponent while requiring from us

---

233 Gandhi's nonviolence principles, www.cpt.org/files/PW-Principles-Gandhi, retrieved as from 22/08/2018.

severe judgment. It ought to be believed that each of us has his or her limitations; only an honest acknowledgement of them can pave how to open dialogue and a real search for light and truth. According to the principle of nonviolence of M. Gandhi "Human beings are more than the evil they sometimes commit."[234]

Dialogue for peace and common good, ought to aim at eradicating divisions and confrontation. By its characteristics, dialogue persists and perseveres to defend the fragile treasure of truth still lingering between opposing parties. It strives to promote solidarity and cooperation among people. Some state that dialogue should search for the common good for all the parties, vital to their existence and required by the common concern because it is what is true, right, and just. As a principle, it ought to emphasize that dialogue partners should seek first what unites them before confronting divisive problems. Otherwise, that peace can never be constructed by some without others, in a unilateral way. It is believed that the welfare of a people can never be accomplished in opposition to the welfare of other people. Some further argue that just one person can never be able to destroy another. Some further state that such a conviction will help the participants to realize there are rights of persons and communities to respect, destructive procedures, are dangerous for all, to be avoided, and put aside. In dialogue, the parties should not emphasize theories, procedures, or doctrines which, here and now, these present circumstances help nobody.

It is required that dialogue partners must be authentic selves, to avoid any form of pretension or personification of others. The focus of the dialogue should be on the issue under discussion. In this sense, it is believed that true dialogue demands us to present our true identity precisely because dialogue is for mutual knowledge and understanding; for learning and unlearning; and for what is right and true. It argues

---

234   Gandhi's nonviolence principles, www.cpt.org/files/PW-Principles-Gandhi, retrieved as from 22/08/2018.

that we have however to remember that our real identity excludes our identity in solidarity with others: the community, society, and group we belong to make up our identity. We must never forget that in situations of tension and misunderstanding, we are part of the problem. Some argue "If we put on masks and pretend to be what we are not, we distort the problem and derail the dialogue completely. Given the sheep skin we wear, deceive people to come out unarmed only to find themselves confronted by a ferocious wolf."[235] It ought to be emphasized that in dialogue we need not reinforce their suspicions and prejudices. According to Dr. King Jr, "Daily checks affirm your faith in the philosophy and methods of nonviolence. Therefore, eliminate hidden motives and prepare yourself to accept suffering, if necessary in your work for justice."[236]

12.5.6 Dialogue for an Action and Its Difficulties

A true dialogue should not remain at the level of theory, discussions and exchange of ideas but into concrete reality of the *status quo* otherwise; it will be a waste of energy and entertainment. Dialogue should aim at targeting some concrete program of the common action. The Church's Magisterium confirms that "This is simply because tensions, quarrels, war do not happen only at the level of words: sooner or later the hard words will turn into blows and other undesirable acts."[237] It concludes that only action will undo action.

Everybody must remember that dialogue as the culture of life is difficult. The nature of true dialogue exposes us to discover some concedes some reasonable proposition and this annoys us sometimes.

---

235   Sudan Catholic Bishops' Conference, *Letter to the Church of the Sudan*, p. 111.
236   Gandhi's nonviolence principles, www.cpt.org/files/PW-Principles-Gandhi, retrieved as from 22/08/2018.
237   Sudan Catholic Bishops' Conference, *Letter to the Church of the Sudan*, p. 112.

To rationalize our position, we try to reject or furnish it with conditions that make it impossible or delay it for good. In the atmosphere of dialogue, sometimes, we feel insecure. This aggravates the levels of tension through the inevitable search by every means and by all sides to ensure military superiority, even to gain the upper hand through acts of naked terrorism. Dialogue demands clear-headedness, firmness, and perseverance. The obstacles which can make dialogue difficult are fear, suspicion, distrust, and uncertainty, and unless we can dispel those obstacles, we can achieve constructive dialogue.

It is recommended that every person who engages in dialogue, should begin with firm will and determination to discover and hold on to the truth, to focus on what is for the common good for all, to what unites the different parties in the dialogue, and to what is just true and right. The Church encourages the dialoguing parties they must be resolute in their wish to adhere solely to peaceful means. It is further highlighted that dialogue is an activity for men and women of goodwill, asserting that the persons in dialogue should not allow themselves to be discouraged by real and apparent failure. Rather, they should consent to begin again ceaselessly to propose true dialogue by removing obstacles and by eliminating the defects of dialogue...and to travel to the end of this single road which leads to peace, with all its demands and conditions. Some say that to give up dialogue is to lose faith in man, the human. "We must continue to preserve enough confidence in man, in his capacity of being reasonable, in his senses of what is good, of justice, of fairness, in his possibility of brotherly love and hope ..."[238] F. Copleston concurs with T. Hobbes by defining a law of nature as 'the dictate of right reason,'[239] which should help us to resolve our problems. This is the dialogue, the culture of life which

---

238   Sudan Catholic Bishops' Conference, *Letter to the Church of the Sudan*, p. 112.
239   Cf. Frederick Copleston, *A history of philosophy*, Volume V: Modern Philosophy, p. 34.

we most need for our world political leaders and for our daily lives to resolve our minor conflicts and misunderstandings.

12.6 For Geologists

We ought to clarify that Mother Nature is constantly providing various means of culture of life but also at the same time, waging a culture of death on many fronts. In confronting Mother Nature, we ought to know about nature as our weapon. According to Aristotle, knowledge is power and good knowledge from different fields of specialization allows one to acquire the right information about certain moral issues than the rest. Geologists who deal with the study of the earth should be more knowledgeable than other people, especially ordinary people. Besides, scientific knowledge is very precise and the scientific community of geologists should assume their moral responsibility for issues that are related to earthquakes and volcanos which always claim the lives of many people.

Unfortunately sometimes when earthquakes do occur; sometimes there is no serious warning and no right information to people from the scientific community of geologists. Everyone would presume that geologists should monitor the abnormal activities of the earth caused by earthquakes. Therefore, geologists should assume their moral duty to make sure that the right information is received and serious warning is given to the people of that region before the culture of death happens. For example, sometimes back in Italy, some members of the scientific community of geologists were charged because they did not give a warning and the right information to the people in the area where the earthquake took place.

It will be unfortunate if geologists remain silent when they have all the scientific tools for analyzing the abnormal activities of the earth initiated by earthquakes to inflict violence upon people. It ought to be recommended strongly that the scientific community of geologists in this specific area of specialization should protect the lives of people. Other scientists also should keep on warning and informing world political leaders for the protection of the ecological system. Humanity should stop such activities which look as if we are leaving the world today. The earth belongs to the past, present and the future. No human person has a moral authority to determine its end.

12.7 For Meteorologists

The same moral duty is also expected from meteorologists those who are specialized in weather. We have seen many places in the world affected by various kinds of violence such as tsunamis, hurricanes, tornados, floods, and droughts. Where are the meteorologists? Are they there only to pass information or to urge governments and communities to be ready for any eventuality? Can they not move from the level of passing information to moral duty with various governments and different communities in the world? Our knowledge today needs to be more beneficial to our fellow humans than ever before. Announcing evil without its prevention may not help. We may not overcome all evils inflicted upon us by natural disasters but at least we may do some natural disasters if serious warnings and the right information are received before.

God was very clear when he said to the prophet Ezekiel, "Son of man, I have appointed you a sentinel for the house of Israel. When you hear a word from my mouth, you shall warn them for me. If I say to the wicked, you shall surely die if you do not warn them or speak out to dissuade the wicked from their evil conduct to save their lives they shall die for their sin, but I will hold you responsible for their blood. However, if you warn the wicked and they still do not turn from their wickedness and evil conduct, they shall die for their sin, but you shall save your life" (Ezek 3: 17-19). Sentinel means a person always on the lookout to warn the people of impending danger. Prophet Ezekiel is commissioned to pass on to the people the word of God about individual accountability likewise, both geologists and meteorologists are expected to do the same about any warning from the culture of death.

12.8 For Physicians and Nurses

In a dramatic clash between the culture of life and the culture of death, the position of the Catholic Church in defence of human life in areas of abortion, euthanasia, suicide, and other illicit therapeutic methods, the doctrine remains unchanged and unchangeable. Pope Paul VI states "I declare that direct abortion, that is, abortion will as an end or as a means, always constitutes a grave moral disorder, since it is the deliberate killing of an innocent human being. This doctrine is based upon the natural law and the written Word of God, is transmitted by the Church's Tradition and is taught by the ordinary and universal Magisterium."[240]

Furthermore, Pope John Paul II on his part confirms that by the authority which Christ conferred upon Peter and his Successors, and in communion with the Bishops of the Catholic Successors, "I confirm that the direct and voluntary killing of innocent human beings is always gravely immoral. This doctrine is based upon that unwritten law which man, in the light of reason, finds in his own heart" (Cf. Rom 2:14-15).

According to the doctrine of the Catholic Church, euthanasia the so-called false mercy, or "assisted suicide" means to cooperate in, and at times to be the actual perpetrator of an injustice which can never be exercised, even if it is requested. In a remarkably relevant passage, Saint Augustine writes "It is never licit to kill another even if he should wish it, indeed if he request it because, hanging between life and death, he begs for help in freeing the soul struggling against the bounds of the body and longing to be released; nor is it licit even when a sick person

---

[240] Cf. John Paul II, Encyclical letter: *Evangelium Vitae*, no. 62.

is no longer able to live.[241] The Church's Magisterium asserts that euthanasia is a grave violation of the law of God since it is the deliberate and morally unacceptable killing of a human person.

The response to various techniques of artificial reproduction, various legal systems and theories which contribute to the culture of death, requires fundamental steps towards this culture of transformation consists of. 1. Forming consciences within the comparable, alienable, and inviolable worth of every human life. In this fundamental step, it is very important to re-establish the essential union between life and freedom. These are indispensable and inseparable goods otherwise, if one is violated, the other is violated too. 2. The formation of conscience, is a prerequisite to discovering the link between freedom and truth.

According to the Church's Magisterium, the least grave and disturbing is the fact conscience itself is darkened by such widespread conditioning, and is finding it increasingly difficult to distinguish between good and evil in what concerns the basic value of human life. Some further state that when freedom is detached from objective truth, it becomes impossible to establish personal rights on a firm rational basis; and the ground is laid for society to be at the mercy of the unrestrained individuals or the oppressive totalitarianism of public authority.

Based on this doctrine, a human person must know that life is a gift which requires a moral duty towards it. Only when the human person acknowledges this valuable gift of life and freedom as gifts from God, then a human person exercise this life in full freedom while respecting and knowing his/her limits. The Church argues that where God is denied and people live as though He did not exist, or his commandments are not considered, the dignity of the human person and the inviolability of human life also is rejected or compromised.

It ought to be pointed out that this situation, with its lights and shadows, ought to make us all fully aware that we are facing an enormous

---

241   Cf. No. 66.

and dramatic clash between good and evil, death and life, and the "culture of death and "culture of life" (*Evangelium Vitae* no.28). It is ought to be strongly recommended to all the members of the Church, the people of life and for life by saying, I make this most urgent appeal, that together we may offer this world of ours new signs of hope, and work to ensure that justice and solidarity will increase and that a new culture of human life will be affirmed, for building an authentic civilization of truth and love (*Evangelium Vitae* no. 6).

The Church argues that very closely related to the formation of conscience is education. Education means helping people to know the truth which leads to respect for life and trains them in the right interpersonal relationship. The a need for education about the value of life from its very origins otherwise, it is an illusion to think that we can build a true culture of human life if we do not help young to accept and experience sexuality and love and the whole of life according to their true meaning and their close interconnections. Such education should involve cultural and social values. The Church believes that in today's cultural and social context, in which science and the practice of medicine risk losing sight of their inherent ethical dimension, healthcare professionals can be strongly tempted at times to become manipulators of life or even agents of death.

In support of this doctrine for human life, the Congregation for the Doctrine of the Faith argues "Such fertilization entrusts the life and identity of the embryo into the power of doctors and biologists and establishes the domination of technology over the origin and destiny of the human person. Such a relationship of domination is in itself contrary to the dignity and equality that must be common to parents and children.[242] The principle for the respect of human life confirms that no biologist or doctor can reasonably claim, by his scientific

---

242   Congregation for the Doctrines of Faith, Instruction Donum Vitae, on respect for human life at its origins and for the dignity of procreation (22 February 1987): AAS 80 (1988), no.70-102.

competence, to be able to decide on people's origin and destiny. Here the role of education in the formation of conscience should aim at embracing sound moral norms which reject anything contrary to the promotion and protection of human life.

12.9 Presuppositions of Ethics for Everyone

According to A. Furthermore, every science has to begin somewhere and therefore starts by laying down certain presuppositions. Presuppositions are described as truths not proved by the science in question but presupposed by it. By descriptions, the term 'proposition' denotes: 1. Something offered for consideration or acceptance or proposal. 2. The point to be discussed or maintained in the argument is stated in sentence form near the outset. 3. An expression in language or signs of something that can be believed, doubted, or denied or either true or false. 4. Some of an indicated kind to be dealt with.[243]

Presuppositions are statements borrowed from another science whose province it is to investigate and establish them. Because of metaphysics, something which would have been an endless and circular process is brought to an end. Metaphysics alone rests on deeper foundations; as the science of first principles, it takes on itself testing and proving the fundamental postulates and general presuppositions of all other sciences. Thus, it assumes a unique position in the hierarchy of knowledge.

Ethics could be studied anywhere in philosophy but it leans heavily on its presuppositions, to establish even its most preliminary considerations. It is customary to make ethics the last branch of philosophy to be studied. If ethics is grounded on the bedrock of metaphysics, three philosophical truths stand out as of primary importance to any sound system of ethics. Fagothey highlights them below:

It ought to be recommended that we all consider the three elements

---

243   Merriam Webster's Collegiate Dictionary, P. 997.

of presuppositions of ethics to be the "x-rays' of human freedom. If human freedom is to be exercised based on the search for absolute truth, love, justice, and equality, therefore, it ought to find its meaning in those three elements of presuppositions of ethics otherwise. Therefore, those elements of presuppositions of ethics are discussed below.

1. The freedom of the will.[244] Unless the human will is free, a man cannot choose between rights and wrong, he is not responsible for what he does, and cannot direct the course of his life. It ought to be pointed out that all acts of a man are equally right if they are his only possible acts; no acts can be wrong if they cannot be avoided. Determinism leaves no meaning to the sought. Freedom of the will should be manifested in all spheres of human life and various fields of specialization. The freedom to choose should not contradict the absolute truth; it must contribute to what is excellent, and noble for human life otherwise, contrary to this is the destruction of human life. Like King Solomon, wisdom is needed in exercising the freedom of choice.

2. The immortality of the soul. Unless the human soul outlives the present life, there is no sufficient motive for doing right and avoiding wrong since we see that virtue often goes unrewarded and vice-punished in this world. Why be good, especially when it is hard if it makes no difference eventually? The belief in what is good requires a certain attitude in life. Doing what is excellent and noble can become important in our lives and because of that, some people do sacrifice their own lives for others. Therefore, technological intervention in human life requires both the true exercise of the freedom of the will and the belief in the immortality of the soul. It ought to be emphasized that such ethics is the priority of ethics over technology, and the primacy of the human person over things and the superiority of spirit over mat matter

3. The existence of God. Unless God exists, there is no highest good. God is not only man's Creator, the Source from which he comes,

---

[244] Austin Fagothey, *Right and Reason*, p. 26.

but also man's Last End, the Goal of all his striving. Without God as the Absolute Lawgiver and Supreme Judge, there could be no moral law prescribing what we ought to do, and therefore no ought and no ethics. The Church's Magisterium points out that the eclipse of God will involve the eclipse of man and this is very dangerous in human life. With absolute assertion, the disappearance of the image of God in our horizon will also involve the disappearance of the image and likeness of man to God, and therefore, the darkness will be great in human reason.

To summarize the presuppositions (three truths or propositions) will be very misleading but it is enough for us to have pointed out how indispensable these propositions are to any study of ethics worthy of the name. These presuppositions are due to the influence of E. Kant these three truths have been singled out as having special reference to ethics. We take them as established in metaphysics and as presuppositions to ethics; E. Kant takes them as incapable of proof by pure reason in metaphysics and as corollaries of practical reason in ethics.

The premises are formulated: "We say that because God exists and the will is free and the soul is immortal, therefore there must be a moral law; he says that because we have direct intuition of the moral law, therefore we must admit that God exists and the will is free and the soul is immortal."[245] A. Fagothey points out that we agree with his vigorous assertion of the moral law and its essential connection with these three truths; we disagree with the logical sequence in which E. Kant places them, and with his method of deducing metaphysics from ethics instead of ethics from metaphysics.

Some other philosophical schools which have no use for these three propositions, whether taken as preambles or as corollaries to ethics, must give the study of ethics quite a different meaning. For example, psychology merely takes ethics as a comparative investigation of actual human customs; a history of the schools of ethical thought (history

---

245   Austin Fagothey, *Right and Reason*, p.26.

of philosophy), or a set of practical maxims on how to make life more enjoyable (applied psychology), or an endeavour to fit man more comfortably into his human environment (applied sociology). It is concluded that as useful as such studies may be, they are not ethics in the strict sense.

12.10 The Loser or Winner Between the Two Cultures

To discover the correct answer which says who the loser is or the winner in this dramatic clash between the culture of life and the culture of death, would require serious assessments and evaluations. The war between the culture of life and the culture of death is taking place on many fronts and at various levels of moral issues. At least, we ought to identify four essential categories which contribute to the culture of death in human lives.

1. Technological intervention: it has made a lot of progress however; it applies various methods and procedures in the critical area of life and family such as (1.1) research on human embryos. 1.2 It uses stem cells for therapeutic purposes. 1.3. Other areas of experimental medicine. 1.3. Euthanasia (false mercy, incurable illness). 1.4. Abortion. 1.5. Contraception. 1.6) eugenic. 1.7. Biological material. 1.8. Heterogonous artificial fertilization. 1.9. Homologous artificial fertilization, 1.10. Human cloning. I.I I. Lesbian; Gays, homosexual and transsexual (sexual re-assignment (LGHT). 1.12. Sterilization.

2. Legal justification: Request for legalization of the following such as: 2.1. Abortion to be passed by the majority of the members of parliament in some countries. 2.2. Legalization of both lesbian and homosexual, (2.3); legalization of sexual re-assignment.

3. Various theories: 3.1. Promethean mentality. 3.2. Utilitarianism (teleological or consequential. 3.3. Ethical relativism. 3.4. Proportionalists. 3.5. Radical views on pluralistic society. 3.6. Relative deprivation. 3.7. Instinctive theory of violence. 3.8. Egoistic theory of

violence. 3.9. Calculative theory of violence. 3.10. Frustration reduction theory of violence. 3.11. Cultural conditioning theory of violence. 3.12. Violence and social change. T. Hobbes on three essential causes of quarrel such as 3.13. Competition. 3.14. Diffidence (mistrust). 3.15. Glory. (3. I 7. Consequence of original sin and various types of sins. Child molestation. 3.18. Religious ideologies such as extremism and terrorism. 3.19. Individualism includes requests for absolute freedom, absolute autonomy, and absolute right without regard to eternal truth, love and moral law 3.20. Indifferentism. 3.2 I. Atheism. 3.22. Demographic explosion (population explosion).

4. Natural calamities such as 4.1. Earthquake. 4.2. Volcanos. 4.3. Floods. 4.4. Drought. 4.5. Tsunami. 4.6. Hurricanes. 4.6. Tornados. 4.8. Various kinds of diseases.

Those four essential categories which contribute to violating human dignity are fitting in the language of Pope John Paul II. He said, 'We are facing an enormous and dramatic clash between good and evil, death and life, "the "culture of death and "the "culture of life. Here, everyone should understand that the dramatic clash is between good and evil, death and life, and the culture of life and culture of life. It ought to be admitted that in these moral issues, the clash is enormous and dramatic.

At least, in the first three categories such as: 1. Technological intervention into critical areas of life and family. 2. Legal justification based on false rights; and various theories which perpetuate violence against human life. Without hesitation and reservation, we can conclude that humankind has declared war against himself/herself. S. Freud might be true when he said; that masses would destroy each other except for their fear of divine retribution or civil restrain. But here and now, the dilemma is that even with divine law and civil law, mankind asks civil authority to legalize his/her death or to terminate the life of others. In this enormous and dramatic clash between good and evil, death and life, the culture of life and culture of death, the causalities are high on the side of the culture of life.

Papal responses: the papal teaching office throughout history has never given up her position in defence of human dignity. According to Pope Paul VI, the doctrine of the principle of the respect of human dignity remains unchanged and unchangeable. Pope Leo XIII in response to the condition of workers confirms ..."conscious of our apostolic office admonishes us to treat the entire question thoroughly, so that the principles may stand out in clear light, and the conflict may thereby be brought to end as required by truth and equity" (*Rerun Novarum* no.3). He added that "Moreover, since the safeguarding of religious and of all things within the jurisdiction of the Church is primarily our stewardship, "silence on our part" might be regarded as failure in our duty" (*Rerun Novarum no.*24).

In an issue related to abortion, Pope Paul VI said, "I declare that direct abortion, that is, abortion willed as an end or as a means, always constitutes a grave moral disorder, since it is the deliberate killing of an innocent human being. This doctrine is based upon the natural law and the written Word of God, is transmitted by the Church's Tradition and taught by the ordinary and universal Magisterium" (*cf. Evangelium Vitae* no. 62). The Magisterium bases her conviction on three theological virtues that are, faith, hope and love. Pope John Paul II states that the certainty of future immortality and hope in the resurrection which sheds new light on the mystery of suffering and death, and fill the believer with extraordinary capacity to trust fully in the plan of God" (*Evangelium Vitae* no.67). The teaching of the Magisterium for the respect of human dignity confirms that human life should be respected from the conception till natural death and no human has a moral power to terminate the life of others.

According to Pope John Paul II, "In our present social context, marked by a dramatic struggle between "the culture of life and the culture of death" there is a need to develop a deep critical sense, capable of discerning true value and authentic needs" (*Evangelium Vitae* no.95). The Church acknowledges that human dignity is abused and violated by various methods. However, the Church proclaims the Gospel of life to all humanity. It announces that Christ has won the victory over death and therefore, death is the beginning of new life. The Church will keep on teaching the doctrine of respect for human life which is unchanged and unchangeable.

However, the "Promethean mentality" of our contemporary society can be compared to a man with paralyzed limbs who does not respect the command of the will. Aristotle states that:

> For exactly a paralyzed limb when we intend to move them to the right turn on the contrary to the left, so is it with the soul; the impulses of incontinent people move in contrary directions. But while in the body we see that which moves astray, in the soul we do not. However, we must none lest suppose that in the soul too there is something contrary to the rational principle, resisting and opposing it. ... At any rate in the continent man it obeys the rational principle ... in the temperate and brave man, it is still more obedient, 208 for in him it speaks on all matters with the same voice as the rational principle.[246]

The separation of human life from law and justice can be a dangerous adventure, and worse if human asks for that separation. According to Aristotle, "For man, when perfected, is the best of animals, but, when separated from law and justice, he is the worst of all; since armed injustice is the more dangerous, and he is equipped at birth with the arms of intelligence and with moral qualities which he may use for the worst ends."[247] It is further asserted that wherefore, if he has not virtue, he

---

246   Aristotle, Book. 1: Ch), Nicomachean Ethics, 1102b, 15-25.
247   www.goodreads.com/quotes/109939-for-manwhen-perfected-is-the-best-of-animals-but, retrieved as form 13/10/2018.

is the most unholy and the most savage of animals, and the most full of lust and gluttony. In his own opinion, justice is the bond of men in states, and the administration of justice, which is the determination of what is just, is the principle of order in political society. Jesus echoes the same call for man's perfection as Aristotle did he when says, "Therefore you shall be perfect, just as your Father in heaven is perfect" (Mt 5: 48). In response to various methods and procedures which violate the dignity of the human person, Pope John Paul II states these issues must be cross check by Christian "x-ray," "that is, in the priority of ethics over technology, in the primacy of person over things, and the superiority of spirit over matter."[248]

The position of the Catholic Church is very clear on the principle of respect for human dignity specifically on deontological theory. The argument in favour of deontology states "All beings are equipped with their qualities and faculties, which enable them to perform the tasks proper to them and in the case of living beings to provide for their existence. An analysis of these qualities and faculties and the laws according to which they function permits conclusions to the correct treatment and use of beings, including the treatment and use of man's being, organs, and functions.[249] The principle of deontology concludes that from there corresponding moral obligations result, because the correct appropriate use of being and the respect for their nature is not left to the free discretion of men, but are moral duties.

Conclusion

The chapter recommended the ethics of power and its priorities, dialogue and negotiation as a culture of life. The chapter also presented

---

248 Cf. J. Tab Charoa, Ecology, *Principle of Stewardship of Creation: the Basic Principle of the Social Teaching of Church, its relevance to the African context*, Juba: Universal Printer Company Ltd, 2018, p.44.

249 Karl H. Peschke, Christian Ethics, p. 161-162.

nigger as a danger to life. It has presented the four-day reports by the national dialogue and it has identified the stakeholders and Criteria for selection. It recommended the implementation of key emerging points.

The chapter has discussed broadly the importance of dialogue as a task which requires favourable conditions. It has emphasized that such favourable conditions also demanded listening for the parties to learn and to arrive at real and fruitful dialogue. The chapter pointed out that dialogue requires readiness to unlearn and it also demonstrated that it demands openness and, mutual respect which involves respect for different opinions exchanged by the parties. It argued that in dealing with an issue at hand, dialogue demanded two measures that is, to judge our opponents and also to judge ourselves severely. The chapter has clarified that fruitful dialogue is for action while keeping in mind the difficulties of its implementation. It also has presented special moral concerns both for South Sudanese politicians and the citizens of South Sudan as a whole. It gave ethical recommendations for geologists, meteorologists, physicians and nurses. The chapter also recommended strong presuppositions of ethics to be observed by everyone. Finally, the chapter declared Christ as the winner of the culture of life.

Bibliography

1. Magisterial Documents

The African Bible, Nairobi, Publication Africa, 1999.

The Catechism of the Catholic Church, Citta del Vaticano, Liberia Editrice, Vaticana, 1994.

Congregation for the Doctrine of Faith, Instruction *Donum Vitae*, on respect for Human life at its _____, origin and for the dignity of procreation (22 February 1978): AAS 80 (1988) 70-102.

Congregation for Divine Worship and the Discipline of the Sacraments, *Degree* on the Mass in

Time of Pandemic, 30, March 2020.

Vatican Council II, Lumen Gentium, Paulines Publications Africa, 2013.

2. Papal Encyclical Letters

Benedict XVI Post-Synodal Apostolic Exhortation, *Africae Munus*, Nairobi, publication African, _____, 2011.

John Paul II, Encyclical Letter: *Evangelium Vitae*, March 25 1995, 82: AAS. 87, (1995)

_____, Encyclical Letter: *Veritatis Splendor*, The Splendour of the Truth, n. 34-35, in AAS _____, 85(1133-1228).

_____, Encyclical Letter: *Redemptor Huminis*, The Redeemer of man, no. 16.

_____, Encyclical Letter, Fides et Ratio, Nairobi, Paulines Publications Africa, 1998.

3. Local Document

Sudan Catholic Bishops' Conference: *Letters to the Church of the Sudan*, Khartoum: Secretariat, _____, 1982-2000.

4. Books

Adler, Mortimer J. (ed.), *Great Books of the Western World: Saint Augustine, the Confessions, the* _____, *City of God on the Christian Doctrine*, Chicago, Encyclopaedia Britannica, inc., 1961.

Akol, Deny, D.A. Rauy, *the Policies of Two Sudans: The South and the North, 1821-1969*, Motala-_____, Sweden, Motala Grafiska, 1994.

Antonio, Luigi Clerici (ed.), a Reader in Early Patristic Writings, Nairobi, Paulines Publication _____, Africa, 2014.

Béneëzet Bujo, *The Ethical Dimension of Community, The African Model and the Dialogue between North and South*, Nairobi, Paulines Publications Africa, 1997.

Cencini, Amedeo, *To Live Reconciled, Psychological Aspects*, Bologna, St. Paul Publications, _____, 1988.

Charoa, J. Tab, *Beyond the Four Classical Cardinal Virtues: The Basic Principles of Social Justice* _____, *& Their Relevance to our Contemporary Society*, Juba: Universal Printers Company _____, Limited, 2018.

_____, *Ethics of Human Sexuality: A Call for Chastity in Christian Family*, Nairobi: CUEA Press, _____, 2017.

_____, *The Key Principles of the Catholic Social Teaching Their Relevance to the African World View*, Nairobi, CUEA Press, 2019.

Copleston, Fredrick, *a History of Philosophy*, New York, Doubleday, 1959.

Glenn, Paul, *A Tour of the Summa of St. Thomas Aquinas*, (Qq. 57-80), Bangalore, Theological _____, Publication in India, 2007.

Khandelwal K. N. *Shakespeare's Othello*, Narian, Educational Publishers, Agra-3

Lamoureux, Patricia and Paul J. Wadell, *the Christina Moral life: Faithful Discipleship for a* _____, *Global Society*, Bangalore, Theological Publications in India, 2011.

Lennox C. John, *Where is God in a Coronavirus World?* United Kingdom, the Good Book Company, 2020.

Idris, Amir H. *Sudan's Civil War: Slavery, Race and Formational Identities*, Lewiston, The Edwin _____, Mellen Press, 2001.

Faupel, J. F., *African Holocaust: The Story of the Uganda Martyrs*, Nairobi, Paulines Publication _____, Africa, 1984.

Friesen, Duane K., *Christian Peacekeeping & International Conflict: A Realistt Pacifist* _____, _____, *Perspective*, Pennsylvania, Herald Press, 1971.

Machiavelli, Niccolo, *the Prince and the Discourse*, New York, the Modern Library, 1950.

Mathias, Koffissan Adossi, *Conflict Resolution and Transformation: A Participation Approach* _____, *for Youth*, Nairobi, Paulines Publication Africa, 2009.

McBride, Richard, *Introduction to Aristotle*, New York, Random House, Inc., 1947.

Mbiti, John S. Introduction to African Religion, Second Edition, Kampala, East Africa Educational Publisher, 1991.

Mokhtar, G. (ed.), *General History of Africa: II Ancient Civilization of Africa*, Nairobi, UNESCO, _____, 1990.

Mugarura, Augustine, *Impulse to Power According to Russell: A Critique Leading to a Principle* _____, *of Integral Development*, Uganda, Fort, 1993.

Okoth, Assa, *A History of Africa,* Vol. II: African Nationalism and the De-colonialisation Process, _____, Nairobi: East African Educational Publishers, 2006.

Pazhayampallil, Thomas, (ed.), *Pastoral Guide: Fundamental Moral Theology and Virtues,* Vol.

Bangalore, Theological Publication in India, 2009.

Penzo, Luigi, *The Last Things,* Notes for the Students of St. Paul's Major Seminary, Unpublished Work, Khartoum, 2002.

Peschke, Karl H., *Christian Ethics: Moral Theology in the light of the Vatican II,* Vol. 1, General _____, Moral Theology, Alcester, C. Good Life Neale Ltd, 1986.

Schmaus, Michael, *Justification and the Last Things,* London, Sheed and ward Inc., 1977.

Van, Meine Noordwijk, *Ecology Textbook for the Sudan,* Khartoum, Khartoum University Press, _____, 1984.

5. National Dialogue Steering Committee

South Sudan National Dialogue Steering Committee, Document Number 2, Activities Report, _____, Juba, 2018.

6. Dictionary/ Encyclopedia/ Commentary

Brown, Raymond E. (ed.), *the New Jerome Biblical Commentary,* London, Prentice-Hall, Inc., _____, 1990.

Childress, James F. and John Macquarrie (ed.), *a New Dictionary of Christian Ethics,* SCM Press, _____, 1986.

Hunter, Rodney J. (ed.), *Dictionary of Pastoral Care and Counseling,* Expanded Edition,

_____, Abingdon Press, 2005.

Komonchak, Joseph A. Mary Collins and Dermot A. Lane (ed.), *the New Dictionary of Theology,* _____, New York, Gill and Macmillan, 1987.

Macquarie, John (ed.), *Dictionary of Christian Ethics*, Philadelphia, the Westminster Press, 1967.

Mclean, Iain and Alistair McMillan, (ed.), *Oxford Concise Dictionary of Politics*, New York, _____, Oxford University Press, 2003.

McKenzie, John L. (ed.) *Dictionary of the Bible*, Milwaukee, the Bruce Publishing Company, _____,1996.

Merriam Webster's Collegiate Dictionary, Eleventh Edition, Massachusetts, Merriam-Webster's, _____, incorporated, 2003.

Merriam Webster's Collegiate Dictionary, Eleventh Edition, Massachusetts, Merriam-Webster's, _____, incorporated, 2000.

Pietro Palazzini, (ed.), *Dictionary of Moral Theology*, the Newman Press, 1962.

Sinclair B. and Ferguson (ed.), *New Dictionary of Theology*, Downer Grove, Inter-Varsity Press, _____, 1988.

Stockle, Bernhard (ed.), *Concise Dictionary of Christian Ethics*, London, Burn & Oats, 1979.

Webster's New Encyclopedia Dictionary, Cologne, Könemann, 1993.

7. Article/Journal

Anthony, Michael Abril *"Lamentation 5:25 within the Development of Thomas Aquinas's* _____, Theology of the Grace of Conversion" *International Journal of Systematic Theology*, _____, Volume 16, Number 3, July 2014.

Aquinas, St. Thomas *Summa Theological: First Complete American Edition*, Vol. 3. Benziger _____, Brothers, Inc., (1948), p. 3493.

Brotherton, Joshua R. "The Integrity of Nature in the Grace-Freedom Dynamic: Lonergan's _____, Critique of Banezian Thomism" *Catholic University of America, Theological Studies*, _____, Vol., 75, (3) (2014), p 537-563.

Cowan, Steven, *"Does 1 Corinthians 10:13 imply Libertarian freedom? A reply to Paul Himes"* _____, JETS 55/4(2012), p 793-800.

Gründel, J. "Sins, Seven deadly" *In the Concise Dictionary of Christian Ethics*, Bernhard Stoeckle _____,(ed.) London, Burn & Oates, 1979, (229-236), p. 229.

Highfield, Ron, "The Freedom to say *"NO"? Karl Rahner's Doctrine of Sin*" Pepperdine _____, University, California, Theological Studies 55 (1995) 485-505.

Lodber, Peter, "*Grace and Reconciliation as Gift: A Journal of Theology*" volume 54, number 3, _____, September (2014), 235-248.

Faulkner, U. Harold, "World War II" *in the Catholic Encyclopedia for School and Home*, New York, McGraw-Hill Book Company, (1965) p. 534-536.

Miller, D. Earl (ed.), "Violence" *in the Dictionary of Pastoral Care and Counseling*, Nashville, _____, Abingdon Press, (2005), p. 1303-1305.

Ormerod, Neil "*The Grace-Nature Distinction and the Construction of a Systematic theology*" _____, Australian Catholic University, Theological; Studies, Vol. 75 (3) (2014), p. 515-517,

Schepers, M>B. (ed.) "Violence" *in the New Catholic Encyclopedia*, New York, McGraw-Hill _____, Book Company, (1967), p. 690.

8. Internet Sources

www.britannica.com/event.Haiti-earthquak-of-2010, retrieved as from 19/07/2018.

www.iwm.org.uk/histroy/5-things-you-need-to-know-about-the-first... retrieved as from 24/07/2018.

www.britannica.com/event/world-War-II, retrieved as from 25/07/2018.

Pope ends visit with frank talk, "State Journal-Register, Springfield, Illinois (August 16, 1993): en-wikipedia.org/Culture-of-life, retrieved as from 02/08/2018.

Bush Woos Catholic on abortion Nominee, Echoes Pope's 'Culture of life' retrieved as from _____, 22/03/2021.

Phrase, "Boston Globe (October 9, 2000): en-wikipedia.org/Culture of life, retrieved as from _____, 02/08/2018.

www.thekingcenter.or/king-philosophy, retrieved as of 01/08/3018 Where Do We Go from Here: Chaos or Community? By Dr. Martin Luther King, Boston, Beacon Press, 1967.

Based on Martin Luther King, Jr.'s *"Letter from Birmingham Jail"* in Why We Can't Wait, Penguin Books, 1963, www.thekingcenter.org/king-philosophy, retrieved as of 01/08/2018.

Sydney Alternative Media-independent, community, nonprofit, trustworthy,, _____,Gandhi's10principlesofnonviolence,www.sydneyalternativemedia.com/id73,html, _____,retrieved as from 02/08/2018.

www.ciam-int.info/article-E_POPU_504_0401--- retrieved as of 02/07/2018.

www.bbc.com/news/world-africa-26875506, retrieved as from 26/07/2018.

https:// www.goodrx. Com/blog/what-does-covid-19-mean-who-named-it, retrieved as of 13/04/2020.

https:www.bbc.com/news/world-us-canada-52264860, retrieved as from 16/04/2020.

www.statehouse.go.ug/media/news/2020/03/25/presidents-address-covid-19-new-guidelines, retrieved as of April 13, 2020.

https://time.com/5815838/south -sudan-africa-coronavirus-covid-19/ retrieved as from 15/04/2020.

https:www.aa.com.tr/end/Africa/coronavirus-south-sudan-bans-socail gatherings/17/68378, retrieved as from 13/04/2020.

https:/www/hsph/edu/covid-19/articles/coronavirus-facts-vs-myths.html, retrieved as of April 13, 2020.

Index

Abdulmenam 152
Abei 239
Abel 28-29
Abingdon 47, 63, 83, 272, 274
Abiy 238
Abril 83, 273
Adam 3-6, 11, 14, 16-8, 20-2, 24, 26, 59-60, 185, 195, 226, 230
Addams xxi
Adler, Mortimer J. 95, 270
Adolf 38-39, 41, 54-5, 211
Adossi 121-122, 271
Advent xxv, xxx, 151, 179
Africa xvi, xxi, xxi, xxv, xxx, xxx, xxx, 38, 40, 94, 113-5, 118-120, 123, 125-6, 135, 145, 155, 162, 171-2, 196, 214, 269-272
Africae 114, 269
African xiv, xvi, xxi, xxx, xxx, 59, 112, 115, 118, 120, 122-6, 133, 155, 170, 172, 186, 214, 216, 237, 266, 269-272
Africans 113, 124
Aguelek 243
Ahmed 238
Akim 179
Akol, Deny 124, 270
Albanian 39
Albert xxi
Albright 148
Alcester 61, 272
Alicia 150
Alistair 74, 273
Allergy 130, 176
Allis 55
Almighty xiv, 151
Alphonse 178, 180
Amb 240
Ambrose 118, 214
Ambrozio 118

Amedeo 12, 18, 270
Amen 151
America xxv, xxi, xxx, 43, 83, 86, 130-2, 135, 137, 142, 145, 155, 162, 168-9, 172, 195, 215-6, 273
American xxi, xxi, xxi, 39-44, 85-6, 96, 98, 111, 133, 167, 273
Americans 93, 97, 137, 173, 216
Americas 172
Ameyu xii
Amin 126
Amir 124, 271
Amorites 95
Anaxagoras 33
Andrea xv
Andrew 140, 169
Angelique 170
Anne xiv
Anthony 83, 130, 136, 165-7, 170, 176, 195, 273
Antibodies 165
Antoni 94-95
Antonine 128
Antonio, Luigi Clerici 169, 270
Aquinas 3, 11-2, 59-61, 66, 69, 71, 82-3, 271, 273
Arab 124, 169
Arabs 120, 124
Archdiocese xii, 151, 177, 179
Archduke 37
Areopagues 222
Aristotelian 33, 35, 45, 110
Aristotle 3, 34-5, 41, 110, 254, 265-6, 271
Armand 136
Aron 42
Arrupe xix
Asclepius 2, 209
Asia 135, 146, 172, 218
Asian 128
Assa 126, 272
Assyrian 65
Astarte 10
Athenians 222
Athens 222
Augustine xx, xxi, 83, 95, 117-8, 126, 179, 194, 236, 256, 270-1
Austin 260-261
Australia 135
Australian 83, 274
Austrian 37
Authority 31-32, 44, 144
Auxiliary 177
Aviation 44
Axis 40, 55
Babylonian 116
Bahri xiv, xxv
Bakasoro 241, 243
Bakhita 113, 217-8, 220
Banda 126
Banezian 83, 273
Bangalore 12, 271-2
Bangladesh 146

Beijing 132
Belgium 39
Benagaino 102
Benedict 114, 117, 269
Benjamin 148
Benziger 59, 273
Berlin 41, 43
Bernhard 67, 75-6, 78, 273-4
Beta 130
Biden 169
Binaisa 126
Biotech 168, 173
Birmingham 107, 109, 247, 275
Biyongo 126
Blest 237
Bokassa 126
Boko 120
Bologna 12, 270
Bonaventure xxx
Books xix, xxi, 95, 270, 275
Boris 147, 150, 170
Bosco xiv
Bosnia 37
Boston 43-44, 97, 105-6, 275
Britannica 270
Britanninca 95
British 5, 35, 39-41, 87, 134, 136, 140, 147, 150, 164
Broadly 154
Brotherton 83, 273
Bruce 83, 273
Bujo xxx, 214-5, 270

Bulgaria 37, 39
Butigan 121
Cain 28-29
Calculative 55, 213, 263
California 66, 274
Campaigners 102
Capital 71
Cardinal xii, 35, 93, 100, 237, 270
Castration 117
Catechism 66-68, 269
Catholicism 60
Cavendish 36
Celsius 158
Cencini, Amedeo 12, 17-8, 270
Centrality 184
Ch 201, 207, 224
Chapman 60
Charis 82
Charles 117, 147, 173
Charoa, J. Tab xiv, xvi, xx, xxi, xxi, xxv, xxv, xxx, xxx, 2, 4, 6, 8, 10, 12, 14, 16, 18, 20, 22, 24, 26, 28, 30, 34-6, 38, 40, 42, 44, 46, 48, 50, 52, 54, 56, 60, 62, 64, 66, 68, 70, 72, 74, 76, 78, 80, 82, 86, 88, 90, 92, 94, 96, 98, 100, 102, 104, 106, 108, 110, 112, 114, 116, 118, 120, 122, 124, 128, 130, 132-4, 136, 138, 140, 142, 144, 146, 148, 150, 152, 154, 156, 158, 162, 164, 166,

168, 170, 172, 174, 176, 178, 180, 182, 184, 186, 188, 190, 192, 194, 196, 198, 200, 202, 204, 206, 208, 210-2, 214, 216, 218, 220, 222, 224, 226, 228, 230, 232, 236-8, 240, 242, 244, 246, 248, 250, 252, 254, 256, 258, 260, 262, 264, 266, 270, 272, 274
Chastity 270
Chauvin 216
Chester 40
Chicago 270
Children 157
Childress, James F. 60, 66, 272
China xxv, 40, 129-130, 132-5, 137, 145, 162-3, 166, 169, 175-6
Chinese 129-130, 132-4, 137, 166-7, 169
Chop xiv, xxv
Chris 162
Christ xii, xxi, xxi, xxv, 16, 20, 30-1, 82, 84, 86, 88-93, 96, 118, 151, 179, 182-5, 197-9, 201, 203-8, 210-2, 214-5, 221-2, 224-234, 256, 265, 267
Christian xix, xx, xxi, xxi, xxx, 21, 47, 55, 60-8, 75-6, 78, 81, 83, 87, 90, 94-5, 102, 184, 189, 192, 198-9, 214, 221-3, 226, 230, 266, 270-4
Christianity 62, 123, 125

Christians 4, 25, 28, 82, 87, 184, 188, 192-3, 197, 210, 214, 230, 248
Christina 223, 271
Christity 102
Christmas xxx
Christopher 179-180
Churchill xxv, xxx, 42
Cirilo 241
Citta 269
Clerici 270
Coetzee 170
Collins 82, 272
Colonizers 124
Colorado xxx, 85, 93, 111
Com 129, 275
Congo 119-120, 126
Conspiracy 173
Contraception 213, 262
Coolants 212
Cooperation 126
Copleston, Fredrick 35-36, 253, 271
Cor 27, 188, 205, 208, 225-6, 228, 232
Corinthians 80, 205, 273
Cormac 100
Coronavirus 128-129, 131, 141-2, 147, 150, 155, 160, 163, 167, 172, 176-7, 271
Costa 146
Coventry 168

Covid 170
Cowan, Steven 79-80, 273
Creation xiv, 184, 191, 195
Cuomo 140, 169
Cup 205
Cyprian 121
Daniel 224
Dario 243
Dashboard 176
Decalogue 88
Decolonialsation 126
Delhi 76
Demobilization 239
Democritus 33
Deng 124, 240
Denmark 39
Denver xxx, 85, 93, 111
Depo 102
Derek 216
Dermot 82, 272
Derna 152
Desdemona 5
Deuteronomy 94
Devonshire 36
Dick 215
Didache xxx, 94-5
Diem 113
Dinka 241
Discipleship 64, 271
Dogmatic xvi
Dok 240
Donum 258, 269

Dorian 136
Doubleday 36, 271
Douglas 40
Downer 273
Drexel 215
Drug 168-169
Dt 26, 91
Duane 47, 271
Dulles 44
Durban 126
Earl 47, 50-1, 54-5, 57, 274
Early 94-95, 171, 270
East 1-2, 9-10, 38, 43, 126, 155, 162, 172, 208-9, 271-2
Eastern xxx, 15, 38, 43, 118
Ebola 167
Ecology 53, 266, 272
Economic 126
Eden 6, 14
Editrice 269
Eduactional 126
Edwin 124, 271
Egypt 2, 116, 123-4, 200, 208
Egyptian 120, 124
Egyptians 124
Einstein xxi
Elijah 26
Elizabeth 140
Elohistic 191
Emeritus 114
England 124, 128, 134, 162
English 36, 82, 168

Envangelium 97
Envy 28
Eph 82
Equatorial 126
Eschatology 197
Estella 13
Ethic 60, 81
Ethics 62-63, 65-7, 75-6, 78, 87, 90, 102, 138, 236, 259, 265-6, 270, 272-4
Etymologically 3, 81, 237
Eucharist 151, 201, 228
Eucharistic 205
Eugenic 101, 213
Eurasia 128
Europe 37-38, 42-3, 113, 135, 137, 146, 150, 172
European xxi, 35, 38, 198
Euthanasia 101, 213, 262
Evangelist 210
Evangeliu xxx
Evangelium xvi, xxi, 81, 99-100, 102, 104, 256, 264, 269
Evangelization xxi
Eve 3-6, 11-2, 14, 16-7, 20-2, 59-60, 185, 195, 230
Everybody 147, 252
Evil 4, 104-6, 112, 193
Exhortation 114, 269
Exodus 200
Ezekiel 255
Facemasks 165

Fagothey 259-261
Fareed 148
Fauci 130-131, 136, 165-7, 170, 176-7
Faulkner, U. Harold 38-41, 274
Faupel, J. F. 117-118, 271
Fds 243
Federalism 241
Ferdinand 37
Ferguson 82, 273
Fides xxx, 270
Flinging 9
Floyd 216
Foffissan 122
Formational 124, 271
France 36-37, 39-41, 162
Francis xxi, xxv, xxv, xxx, 140, 148-9, 151-2, 191, 196, 216-220, 240
Franz 37
Frederick 253
Fredrick 36, 271
French 116, 120
Freud 55, 263
Friesen, Duane K. 47, 271
Frustration 56, 213, 263
Fuaci 195
Gabriel 240
Gadarene 31
Gadarenes 31
Gaddafi 120
Gal 71, 82

Galatians 71
Galen 128
Galileans 22
Galilee 23
Gandhi 85-88, 92-3, 109-110, 247, 249-252
Gaudium xxi
Gays 213, 262
Genesis xvi, 18, 80, 95, 185, 191, 194
Genital 167
Genocide 120
Gentium 201-203, 269
Geoffrey 60
George 45, 97, 216
German 39, 54
Germans 40-41
Germany 37-42, 145
Gil 82
Gill 272
Girard xvi, xxi, xxi
Girgashites 200
Glenn, Paul 12, 66, 271
Gn 2, 4, 10, 16, 209
God xii, xiv, xv, xvi, xxi, xxi, xxv, xxv, xxx, xxx, 3-6, 10-8, 21-32, 60-4, 66-71, 78-81, 83-4, 86-8, 90-6, 101, 106-7, 128-9, 151, 183, 185-195, 197-204, 210, 214, 218, 221-5, 228-233, 255-7, 260-1, 264, 270-1
Godfrey 126

Gomes 216
Goodlife 61
Goree 215
Grafiska 124, 270
Greece 2, 208
Greek xxi, 2-3, 33-4, 52, 65, 74, 81, 84, 209, 222
Greeks 66, 223
Greenwood 215-216
Gregory 71
Guardsmen 216
Guido xii, xiv, xvi, xxv
Habyarimana 121
Hahn 169
Haiti 19, 116
Haitian 19
Ham 214
Hammurabi 116
Haram 120
Harbor 39
Harold 39, 41, 274
Harvard 141, 165
Hatred 23
Havana xxv
Health xxv, 128-130, 132, 134, 137-9, 141-2, 146, 152, 159, 163, 165, 169, 172, 177, 191
Hellenist 225
Hellenistic 64
Hepatitis 191
Herbert 36
Herod 200

Heterogonous 213, 262
Hezekiah 65
Highfield, Ron 66, 274
Highfields 67
Hiller 39
Himes 79
Hints xvi
Hippo 83, 95, 194
Hirohito 42, 133
Hiroshima 41-42, 55, 133
Hispaniola 19
Hitler 38-41, 54-5, 211
Hittites 200
Hivites 200
Hkim 243
Hobbes 33, 35-7, 45, 54, 213, 253, 263
Holiness xxv, xxx, 140, 149, 191, 196
Holland 51
Holocaust 100
Hominis 28
Homologous 213, 262
Hon 240
Hong 128, 134
Hopkins 163, 176
Hosni 120
Howard 136, 140
Hriues 80
Hubei 129-130, 135, 163
Hughes 39-41
Hulfra 239

Humanae 78, 100-1
Humanity xxv, 78, 118, 148, 187, 255
Huminis 270
Hungary 39
Hunter, Rodney J. 63-64, 83, 272
Hutu 121-122
Hutus 121
Iain 74, 273
Ibid xxi, 27, 36, 38, 40, 42, 44, 48, 51, 56, 58, 61, 70, 73, 78, 83, 87, 91, 107, 114, 119, 121, 125-6, 212, 238, 243, 248
Idi 126
Idris, Amir H. 124, 271
Illinois 93, 274
Illiteracy 104
Imperialism 106
Inculturation xix, xx
Indian 19
Indifferentism 213, 263
Indigenous 123
Individualism 213, 263
Indonesia 146
Inexpertly 178
Infectious 130, 176, 195
Influenza 158
Iniquity 4
Insofar 72
Instantly 178, 180, 188
Intolerant 29
Inyani 13

Isaiah xxi, 30, 99, 202
Iscariot 7-9, 20-1
Ishater 10
Ishmaelite 29
Islam 123-125
Israel 25, 27, 65, 94, 102, 147, 152, 172, 200-2, 223, 255
Israelites 194, 200, 223
Italian 41
Italy 36, 39-41, 145, 149, 162-3, 254
Jackie 127, 154, 156, 160
Jackson 177
Jail 107
Jairus 224
Jake 173
James xxi, xxv, xxv, 13, 60, 66, 118, 178-180, 237, 272
Jan 133-134
Jane xxi
Japan 39-41, 55, 134, 162, 166
Japanese 41-42, 133
Jephthah 65
Jerome 23, 26, 91, 272
Jerusalem 22, 80, 202, 207
Jesuits xix
Jesus xx, xxi, xxi, 1, 7-8, 16, 20-8, 31-2, 80-1, 86-93, 95-6, 108, 117, 151, 179, 188-9, 191-4, 198, 204-7, 210-1, 214, 220, 222, 224-6, 228, 230, 232, 266

Jewish 2, 78, 86, 208-9, 222-3, 236
Jews 55, 188, 223
Jn 80, 83, 210, 224
Job 7, 21, 30, 150, 190
Joe 169
John xii, xiv, xv, xvi, xxv, xxx, xxx, xxx, 2-3, 9-10, 14, 16, 23, 28, 60, 66, 78-81, 83, 85-7, 92-3, 96-104, 111, 128-9, 155, 195, 208, 210, 215, 224, 256, 263-4, 266, 269, 271-3
Johns 163, 176
Johnson 150, 170
Johnsons xxi, 177, 180
Jonah 23-24, 224
Jos 95
Joseph 29, 82, 272
Josephine 13, 113, 217
Joshua 83, 95, 273
Juan 13
Juba xii, 133, 151, 177, 179, 272
Jubbusites 200
Judas 7-9, 21
Julius 125
Justinian 128
Juvenal 121
Kabakamwanga 118
Kampala 155, 271
Kamuzu 126
Kant 261
Karl 61-63, 65-6, 87, 90, 266, 272, 274

Keenan 168
Kefiy 239
Kenji 239
Kenya 120
Kenyi 13
Kg 65
Khandelwal K. N. 5, 12, 99, 271
Khartoum xiv, xxv, 53, 206, 245, 272
Khmer 100
Kibuba 118
Kibuka 118
Kiir 145-147
Kingian 104
Kingly 116
Kiragu xiv
Kizito 118, 179
Koffissan 271
Komonchak, Joseph A. 82, 272
Kong 128, 134
Korea 134
Kum 218
Lam 241, 243
Lamentation 83
Lamoureux, Patricia 64, 68, 271
Lastly 228
Latin 3, 47, 82, 91, 238
Law 23, 93
Lawgiver 261
Lawrence 177-178
Lazarus 224
Lechwe 54

Legalization 213, 262
Lennox C. John 128-129, 271
Lenten xxv, xxx, 201
Leo 264
Leopold 125
Lev 91
Lewiston 271
Liberation 80
Liberia 126, 269
Libya 120
Lightening xxi
Lisa 173
Liturgical 205
Liturgist xxv
Liturgy xix, 226
Lk 194, 207, 224
Lockdown 141
Lodber, Peter 274
Lodberg 84
Lodu 13
Logos 204
Loku 177-178
London 23, 185, 272-4
Lonut xii
Lucifer xvi, xxx, 1, 5-9, 11, 19-22, 24-7, 30, 32, 209
Luigi 94-95, 206, 224, 227, 233, 270, 272
Luke 22, 26, 87, 92-3, 192
Lumen 201-203, 269
Luther xvi, xxi, 83, 85-6, 92-3, 104-7, 109-111, 245, 247, 275

Luxembourg 39
Lwanga 117
Maccabees 224
Machar 145, 147, 240
Macia 126
Macmillan 82, 272
Macquarie 81, 273
Macquarrie 60, 66, 272
Madeleine 148
Mading 240
Magisterial 269
Magisterium xxx, 69, 93-4, 99-100, 114, 182, 198, 226, 228, 234, 252, 256-7, 261, 264
Mahatma xvi, 85-8, 92-3, 109-111, 247, 249-250
Mahdism 124
Mahdists 124
Mahdiya 124
Majesty 140
Malawi 126
Maldives 146
Malmesbury 36
Malnutrition 104
Manchukuo 39
Mandela 125
Manhatta 44
Manichaean 64
Manicharism xx
Mankind 199
Margaret 168
Maria 191

Marshall 135
Martinelli 190-191
Mary 15, 82, 191, 203, 272
Maryknol xxi
Maryknoll xix
Massachusetts 7, 29, 273
Mathew 8, 26, 87-8, 90-1, 117, 192, 205, 220, 232
Mathias, Koffissan Adossi 122, 271
Matthew 26, 31
Mbiti, John S. 118, 154-5, 271
Mckenzie 83
Mclean, Iain 74, 273
Meine 53, 272
Melinda 165, 173
Mellen 124, 271
Mercy 179
Merriam 7, 29, 51-2, 237-8, 259, 273
Mesopotamia 2, 208
Mesopotamian 2, 209
Messiah 26
Metaphors 3
Metaphysics 259
Meteorologists 255
Michael xxv, 1, 13, 30, 32, 83, 140, 185, 197, 204, 223, 227, 231, 272-3
Michigan 162, 169
Microsoft 173
Midianite 29

Midrash 26
Mifepristone 97
Milan 214
Military 150, 240, 243
Milwaukee 83, 273
Minneapolis 216
Minnesota 216
Minster 150
Missouri 162
Miti 118
Mobuto 126
Modena xxi, 167-8, 177
Mokhtar, G. 123, 271
Monday 146, 169, 217, 239, 244
Moralists 69, 73
Mori 102
Morocco 152
Mortimer 95, 270
Moscow 40
Moses 23, 26, 200
Motala 124
Msgr xii
Mss 172
Muall xii
Muammar 120
Mubarak 120
Mugarura, Augustine 114, 116-8, 126, 236, 271
Mukherjee 136
Munus 114, 269
Museveni 143
Nagasaki 41-42, 133

Naim 224
Nairobi xxv, xxx, xxx, 186, 196, 214, 269-271
Namirembe 117
Namugongo 117-118
Nanking 39
Narain 5
Narian 271
Nashville 83, 274
Nationalism 126, 272
Nazi 100, 215
Nazis 54
Neale 61, 272
Negros 86, 105, 215
Neil 83, 274
Nelson 125
Netanyahu 148
Netherlands 39
Newark 44
Newman 67, 273
Nguema 126
Niccolo 117, 271
Nicomachean 265
Nigeria 120
Nihas 239
Nile 54, 124
Niminee 100
Nimitz 40
Nineveh 24
Nkrumah 125
Noah 19
Nobel xxi

Nobody 141, 184
Nonaggression 40
Nonviolence 85, 107, 109
Noordwijik 53
Noordwijk 53, 272
Nordic 39
Nov 170
Novarum 264
Ntaryamiria 121
Nu xxv
Nuer 194, 241
Num 200-201
Nunciatur xii
Nyerere 125
Nygudeng 194
Oates 67, 274
Oats 273
Octave 151
Okoth, Assa 126, 272
Oliana xii, xiv, xvi, xxv
Olony 241
Omicron 169, 171-2
Orbis xix, xxi
Origen 214
Ormerod 83, 274
Othello 5, 12, 99, 271
Oval 45
Oxford 74, 167, 273
Pacific 40
Pacifist 47, 271
Palazzini 67, 69-72, 82, 273
Palestine 1, 135, 152, 208

Pantocrator 89
Papal 115, 264, 269
Parousia 208
Paschal xvi, xxi
Pastoral 47, 50-1, 54-5, 57, 63-4, 69, 83, 216, 272, 274
Patel 136
Patricia 64, 68, 271
Patrick 164
Patristic 270
Paul xii, xiv, xvi, xix, xxx, xxx, xxx, 5, 9, 12, 14, 28, 34, 64, 66, 68, 78-81, 85-7, 93, 96-104, 111, 187-8, 205, 207-8, 215, 222, 225-6, 228, 232, 256, 263-4, 266, 269-271, 273
Paula 93
Paulines xxi, xxv, xxx, xxx, 94, 118, 122, 196, 214, 269-271
Paulist xxi
Paull 215
Pazhayampallil, Thomas 69, 272
Peacekeeping 271
Peacemaking 47
Pedersen 3, 65
Pedro xix
Pelagian 64
Pennsylvania 44, 271
Penzo, Luigi 205-207, 223-4, 226-7, 230, 233, 272
Pepperdine 66, 274
Perizzites 200

Persia 2, 208
Peschke, Karl H. 61-66, 87, 90, 266, 272
Peter 84, 95, 210, 256, 274
Pew 173
Pfizer xxi, 167-9, 172-3, 177
Pharisees 23-24, 86, 222, 228
Pharmacy 173
Philadelphia 81, 273
Philippines 39, 41
Philosophicum xv
Pietro 67, 69-72, 82, 273
Pilate 22
Pio 177-178
Pius 214
Plato 33
Pneumonia 138
Pol 100
Poland 39-40, 54-5
Polities 124
Poni 13
Presidency 98
Prevention 128, 169
Priti 136
Prof xii, xiv, xvi, xxv, 165
Promethean 101, 213, 262
Proportionalists 103, 213, 262
Protestants 96, 115-7
Provence 135
Ps 4, 150, 190
Psalmist 190, 194, 202
Pt 210, 231

Puah 200
Pythagoras 33
Qates 75-76, 78
Qumran 26
Racism 105, 213-4
Rafiki xxv
Raher 66
Rajaf 177
Rapporteur 240
Rationalization 17
Rauy 124, 270
Raymond 23, 26, 91, 272
Rea 120
Redeemer 28, 270
Redemptor 28, 270
Regardless 178
Reihok xv
Remdesivir 167
Reporters 134
Respiratory 138
Resurrection 221-223, 226-7
Riak 145
Rica 146
Richard 34, 59-60, 136, 148, 271
Riek 240-241, 243
Robertson 216
Rodney 63-64, 272
Rodny 83
Rom 83, 256
Roman 123-124, 226
Romania 39
Romans 5

Rome xii, 2, 123, 208
Ron 66, 274
Rowland 215-216
Russell 115, 118, 126, 236
Russia 37, 39-40, 152
Russian 38, 120, 169
Rwanda xvi, 112, 120, 122, 212
Rwandan 121, 126
Rwandans 121
Rwiza 125
Sacraments 150-151, 269
Sadducees 222, 228
Sako 126
Salva 145-147
Salvation 223, 243
Samaritan xxv
Samaritans xxi
Samuel xv
Santa 7
Santo 177-178
Sao 135
Sarah 215
Sarajevo 37
Satan xvi, xxi, 2, 10, 26, 30, 183, 209-210
Sayan 102
Schepers, M. B. 48-49, 274
Schiavo 98
Schmaus, Michael xxv, 184-5, 197-8, 204, 222-3, 227, 229, 231-3, 272
Schuster 2, 195, 208

Scriptural 211
Sears 51
Sebuta 118
Secretariat xii, 239, 245, 270
Segregation 86
Senegal 215
Senghor 125
Serbia 37
Serbian 37
Serpent 1, 3, 5-6, 209
Sese 126
Sexual 101
Shaba 120
Shakespeare 5
Shamus 199
Shankswville 44
Shattock 165
Sheed 185, 272
Shiphrah 200
Shortness 138
Shots 216
Sicily 41
Siddhartha 136
Siloam 22
Simon 2, 7, 95, 118, 195, 208
Sinai 201
Sinclair B. 82, 273
Singapore 166
Sinophma 169
Slavery 124, 214, 271
Slendor 78
Slovakia 39

Slpendor 79
Slum 104
Smith 39-41
Sneghor 125
Sociological 46
Socrates 108
Solemnities 151
Solomon 24, 135, 260
Somalia 120
Somewhere 192
Soul 33
Soumya 171-172, 177
Southeast 37-38
Southerners 124
Soviet 39-40, 42-3
Spain 162-163
Spes xxi
Spillover 132
Spirituality xxi
Splender 78
Springfield 93, 274
Sr xiv, 190-1
Stakeholders 239, 242-3
Stalin 43
Stalingrad 40
Stapleton xxx, 85, 93, 111
Stephen xii, 169
Sterilization 102, 213, 262
Steven 80, 273
Stewardship xiv, 266
Stockle, Bernhard 75-78, 273
Stoeckle 67, 274

Stokcle 76
Strejac xii
Suakin 113
Sudan xii, xiv, xxv, xxv, 53, 113, 120, 124, 127, 142, 144-6, 151, 154, 160, 191, 235, 238-243, 245, 247-9, 252-3, 267, 270, 272
Sudanese xvi, 124, 127, 144-5, 152, 195, 235, 242, 244, 267
Summa 12, 59, 61, 66, 71, 271, 273
Sunday 38, 140-1, 170, 179, 204, 206
Sundays 151
Suspension 146-147
Suzan 13
Swaminathan 171-172, 177
Sweden 270
Sydney 109-110, 173-5, 275
Tab xiv, xvi, xx, xxi, xxi, xxv, xxv, xxv, xxx, xxx, 2, 4, 6, 8, 10, 12, 14, 16, 18, 20, 22, 24, 26, 28, 30, 34-6, 38, 40, 42, 44, 46, 48, 50, 52, 54, 56, 60, 62, 64, 66, 68, 70, 72, 74, 76, 78, 80, 82, 86, 88, 90, 92, 94, 96, 98, 100, 102, 104, 106, 108, 110, 112, 114, 116, 118, 120, 122, 124, 128, 130, 132-4, 136, 138, 140, 142, 144, 146, 148, 150, 152, 154, 156, 158, 162, 164, 166, 168, 170, 172, 174, 176, 178, 180, 182,

184, 186, 188, 190, 192, 194, 196, 198, 200, 202, 204, 206, 208, 210-2, 214, 216, 218, 220, 222, 224, 226, 228, 230, 232, 236-8, 240, 242, 244, 246, 248, 250, 252, 254, 256, 258, 260, 262, 264, 266, 270, 272, 274

Tadeo xiv

Taiwan 134

Talitha 218

Tangibility 50

Tanzania 113, 125

Tapper 173

Tatha xx

Tenth 29

Terri 98

Terrorism 106

Texas 97

Thailand 134

Thaloka xiv, xxv

Theologica 61, 71

Theologicum xiv, xv

Thess 207, 210-1

Thirdly 69

Thucydides 36

Thursday 216, 241, 244

Tim 188, 225

Timaeus 33

Tokyo 195

Tome 135

Tomorrow 89

Transferal 135

Travelers 146

Tribune 215

Tripathi 76

Tulsa 215-216

Tulsans 216

Tum 150

Tumwesigire xiv

Tur xiv, xxv

Tutsi 121-122

Tutti xxv

Tutu 121-122

Twin 44

Uganda xxv, 117-8, 121, 124, 126, 142-4, 208, 271

Ugandan 143

Ugarit 2, 209

Ukraine 152

Unemployment 104

Unity 125

Unrestricted 212

Unvaccinated 170

Urban 125

Vaccination 177

Vallance 164

Vanuatu 135

Vatican xii, xxi, 61, 82, 214, 216-7, 269, 272

Vaticana 269

Vaticano 269

Verdugo 136

Veritable 98

Veritastis 78

Veritatis 78-79, 269
Vice 66, 97
Vietnam 47
Violence xxi, 31, 35, 46, 48, 50-1, 53-8, 98, 122, 213, 263
Violent 106
Vitae xvi, xxi, 81, 97, 99-102, 104, 256, 258, 264, 269
Vitaeae xxx
Wadell 64, 68, 271
Wajaras xiv
Washington 44, 132, 134
Watchdog 172
Wau 113, 241
Wenliang 130
West 19, 43, 95, 168
Westminster 81-82, 273
Westport 35
Whitty 162
William 168
Willy xx
Wisdom 24, 223
Women 12, 14, 241, 243
Woos 97-98, 274
Woro 13
Wuhan xxv, 129-132, 134-6, 156, 163, 176
Wunlit 239
Yahweh 2, 4, 209
Yahwist 16
Yahwistic 191
Yalta 43

Youk 240
Yoweri 143
Yuggusuk 177
Zakaria 148
Zanzibar 113
Zealand 146
Zubier 113

www.ingramcontent.com/pod-product-compliance
Lightning Source LLC
Chambersburg PA
CBHW031233290426
44109CB00012B/277